celluloid *jukebox*

stereo

celluloid *jukebox*

popular music
and the movies since the 50s

edited by **Jonathan Romney**
and **Adrian Wootton**

BRITISH FILM INSTITUTE

bfi

BFI PUBLISHING

First published in 1995 by the
British Film Institute
21 Stephen Street
London W1P 1PL

The British Film Institute exists to promote
appreciation, enjoyment, protection and development
of the moving image culture in and throughout
the whole of the United Kingdom.
Its activities include the National Film and Television Archive;
the National Film Theatre; the Museum of the Moving Image;
the London Film Festival; the production and distribution
of film and video; funding and support for regional activities;
Library and Information Services; Stills, Posters and Designs; Research,
Publishing and Education; and the monthly
Sight and Sound magazine.

British Library Cataloguing-in-Publication Data.
A catalogue record for this book is available from the British Library.

ISBN   0–85170–506–5
         0–85170–507–3 pbk

Back-cover photos: Elvis Presley in *Jailhouse Rock*, Robert De Niro in
Mean Streets, Sid Vicious in *The Great Rock 'n' Roll Swindle*
(photo: Tiberi June, 1978), Angela Bassett in *Tina: What's Love Got to Do
With It?*, Quentin Tarantino, Spike Lee.

Design by Tom Partridge
Typeset by D R Bungay Associates, Berkshire
Printed in Great Britain by The Trinity Press, Worcester

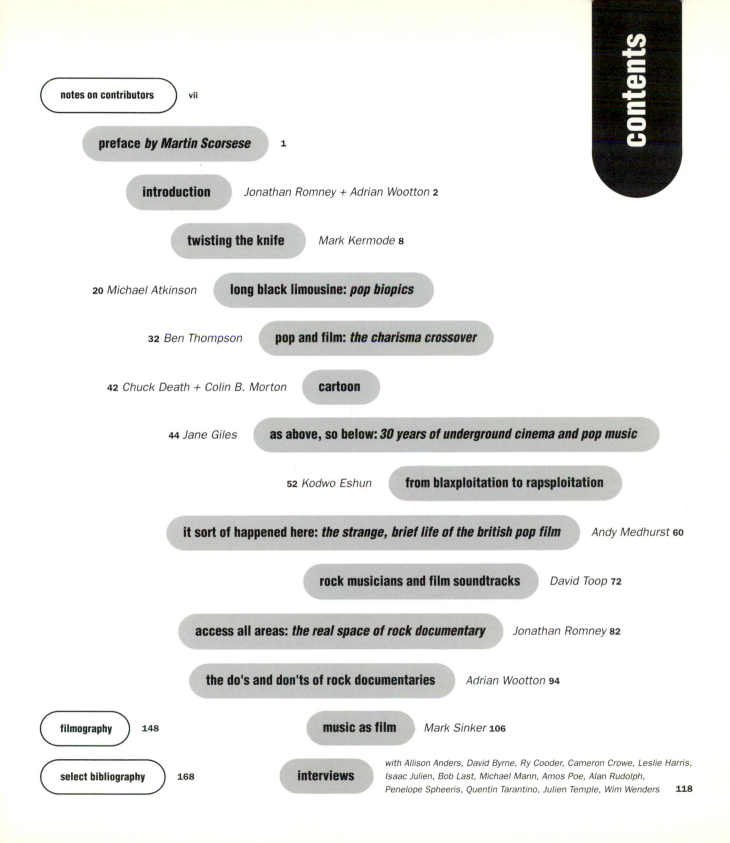

contents

ACKNOWLEDGMENTS

The editors would like to thank Jane Shaw, Sue Bobbermein, Roma Gibson, Ed Buscombe, Charlotte Housden, Liese Spencer, the *Guardian, The Wire,* Candice Hanson, Michael Mann, Martin Scorsese, Victoria Lucai, Margaret Bodde, Mark Cosgrove, Paul Taylor, Mark Adams, Tise Vahimagi, Eric Liknaitsky, staff at the BFI Library, Colin MacCabe, Wim Wenders, Laura Connelly, Mark Timlin, John Mount, Sarah Caplin, Lisa Stewart, Folk Roots, Rebecca Morton, Gavin Martin, Mark Espiner, Markku Salmi, Film and Video Umbrella, NFT Technical Services Department, BFI Computer Unit, BFI Stills, Posters and Designs, Yvonne Salmon, all our interviewees and the film and record companies who helped us out.

Photographs from the following films are courtesy of the production company/ies given in brackets:

American Grafitti (Universal/Lucasfilm), *Apocalypse Now* (Omni Zoetrope), *Backbeat* (Rank/Polygram/Scala/Channel 4 Films/Royal), *"Beat" Girl* (Renown), *Big Time* (Island), *Black Caesar* (American International Pictures), *Blade Runner* (Warner/Ladd), *The Bodyguard* (Warner/Tig/Kasdan Pictures), *Boyz N The Hood* (Columbia Pictures Industries, Inc.), *The Buddy Holly Story* (Columbia Pictures Industries, Inc.), *Buster* (Vestron/The Movie Group), *Car Wash* (Universal), *Catch Us If You Can* (Anglo Amalgamated/Bruton), *Clash* (Promundi), *The Coal Miner's Daughter* (Universal), *Cotton Comes to Harlem* (Formosa/UA), *Cocksucker Blues* (Rolling Stones Presentation), *Deep Cover* (First Independent), *Depeche Mode 101* (Mute Films), *Dick Tracy* (Touchstone/Silver Screen), *The Doors* (Touchstone Pictures), *Do The Right Thing* (Universal City Studios, Inc.), *Don't Look Back* (Leacock Pennebaker, Inc.), *Easy Rider* (Columbia), *Elvis on Tour* (MGM, Inc.), *Elvis - That's the Way It Is* (MGM), *Every Day's a Holiday* (Paramount), *Expresso Bongo* (BL/Britannia), *Fear of a Black Hat* (Oakwood), *Flame* (Republic), *Ghosts of the Civil Dead* (Electric/Correctional Services Film Productions), *GI Blues* (Paramount/Hal B Wallis), *Gimme Shelter* (Cinema 5), *The Girl Can't Help It* (Twentieth Century-Fox), *The Golden Disc* (Butcher's Film Productions), *The Graduate* (UA/Embassy), *Grease* (Paramount), *Great Balls of Fire* (Orion Pictures Corporation), *The Great Rock 'n' Roll Swindle* (Boyd's Co. and Virgin Film Ltd), *Hail! Hail! Rock n' Roll* (Delilah Films), *The Harder They Come* (New World Pictures Inc.), *Head* (Raybert Productions Inc. T.M. of Screen Gems Inc.), *Help* (United Artists), *The Hours and Times* (ICA/Antarctic Pictures), *The Hot Spot* (Orion Pictures Corporation), *I'm Gonna Git you Sucka* (United Artists Pictures Inc.), *In Bed with Madonna* (Rank Distribution), *It Couldn't Happen Here* (Picture Music International), *It's Great to be Young* (AB-Pathe), *Jailhouse Rock* (MGM), *Johnny Suede* (Artificial Eye/Vega/Baltharzar/Starr/Arena), *Jubilee* (Whaley-Main/Megalovision), *The Keep* (Paramount), *The Krays* (Rank/Parkfield), *La Bamba* (Columbia Pictures Industries Inc.), *Lady Sings the Blues* (Paramount/Motown/Weston/Furie), *The Last Emperor* (Columbia/Yanco Films/Tao Films/Recorded Picture Co.), *The Last Waltz* (United Artists), *Lisztomania* (Warner Bros. Inc.), *Magical Mystery Tour* (Apple Films), *Mean Streets* (Taplin-Perry-Scorsese), *Merry Christmas, Mr Lawrence* (Recorded Picture Co.), *Mi Vida Loca* (Cineville), *The Music Machine* (Norfolk International Films), *New Jack City* (Warner Bros. Inc.), *One Plus One* (Cupid/New Line), *Paris, Texas* (Road Movies/Argos), *Pat Garrett and Billy the Kid* (MGM Inc.), *Performance* (Warner Bros. Inc.), *Pink Flamingos* (Saliva Films), *Psych-Out* (American International Pictures), *Purple Rain* (Water Productions Inc. and Warner Bros. Inc.), *Quadrophenia* (Polytel), *Reservoir Dogs* (Rank/Manifesto), *Rock n' Roll High School* (New World), *Rock Around the Clock* (Channel Four), *Rude Boy* (Buzzy Enterprises), *Saturday Night Fever* (Paramount/Robert Stigwood), *Scarface* (Universal City Studios Inc.), *Shaft* (MGM/Shaft Productions), *Sid and Nancy* (Zenith), *Singles* (Warner Bros. Inc.), *Stop Making Sense* (Talking Heads Films), *Super Fly* (Warner Bros. Inc.), *Sympathy for the Devil* (New Line Cinema), *Thirty Two Short Films About Glenn Gould* (Telefilm Canada), *This is Spinal Tap* (Mainline/Polymer Records), *Tina: What's Love Got to Do With It?* (Buena Vista/Touchstone), *The Tommy Steele Story* (Insignia Films), *Tommy* (Hemdale), *Trespass* (Universal City Studios), *True Stories* (Warner Bros. Inc.), *Two Lane Blacktop* (Universal Pictures), *U2: Rattle and Hum* (Principle Management Ltd), *The Wanderers* (PSO/Polyc.), *What a Crazy World* (Capricorn/Ab Pathe), *Woodstock* (Warner/Wadleigh-Morris), *Young Soul Rebels* (BFI/Film Four/Sankofa/La Sept/Kinowelt/Iberoamericana), *Zabriskie Point* (MGM).

MICHAEL ATKINSON is a Contributing Editor at *Movieline*, and a regular contributor to *Sight and Sound*, *Film Comment*, *The Village Voice*, *Details*, *The Modern Review*, *City Paper* and others; he is also a widely published poet, and his work has appeared in *The Best American Poetry 1993* (Macmillan).

CHUCK DEATH and **COLIN B. MORTON** are both known as composers and musicians, having met in the aftermath of the Gwent punk explosion when there was no jobs and everything was covered in coal dust. Their cartoons have appeared regularly in *NME* and *L.A. Weekly*. An anthology, *Great Pop Things*, was published by Penguin in 1992; a second one, *They Tried to Change the World*, is to be published in 1995 in the US.

KODWO ESHUN has worked in film, television, radio and print as a researcher and scriptwriter. He is Music Editor of *The Modern Review* and a regular contributor to *The Wire*. *Escape Velocity*, his book on black electronic music and science, will be published in 1995.

JANE GILES is a freelance film programmer and writer, and is the author of *Un Chant d'Amour: The Cinema of Jean Genet* (BFI).

MARK KERMODE is a freelance film journalist contributing to *Sight and Sound* and *Q* magazine. He broadcasts on BBC Radio One.

ANDY MEDHURST is Lecturer in Media Studies at the University of Sussex, and writes for *Sight and Sound* and the *Observer*; he is currently writing a book on British film and television comedy.

MARK SINKER is a former editor of *The Wire* who has written on music in various publications; he is currently working on a critical history of music and technology, to be published by Quartet.

BEN THOMPSON writes for the *Independent on Sunday*, *Sight and Sound* and *Mojo*.

DAVID TOOP is a musician and music critic. The first record he ever owned was a film theme. His book *The Rap Attack* was first published in 1984 and updated in 1991. He has recently written a history of ambient and environmental music, to be published by Serpent's Tail.

the editors

JONATHAN ROMNEY is deputy film critic of the *Guardian* and film reviewer for *New Statesman and Society*. Formerly deputy editor of *Sight and Sound*, he has written on rock and world music for *New Musical Express* and *City Limits*, and contributes to *The Wire*.

ADRIAN WOOTTON is the Head of the British Film Institute on the South Bank, responsible for the National Film Theatre, Museum of the Moving Image and the London Film Festival. He is also Director of Shots in the Dark, Nottingham's International Crime & Mystery Festival. He has written a variety of articles on rock'n'roll and the movies for, among others, the *Monthly Film Bulletin*, *Film Dope* and *New Musical Express*.

The subject of popular music in motion pictures has been largely neglected in film studies – which is surprising, given its overwhelming importance. This book is a welcome guide to previously uncharted territory.

Popular music has the potential to give movies a forceful, dynamic edge. It doesn't have to serve simply as mood music or be an unimaginative device for establishing a time period. A striking early example of this is *The Public Enemy* (1931), where William Wellman uses popular tunes in the background played out against the chilling violence on screen, creating a sense of bitter irony and authenticity.

When I was young, popular music formed the soundtrack of my life – rock 'n' roll and Neapolitan love songs would rise from the jukeboxes in the little bars of my old neighbourhood, New York's Lower East Side, day and night. And so it was only natural that it would become such an important part of my work as a director, beginning with my first student films. Music has always been a key source of inspiration for me – it has the power to bring entire sequences to life.

Since the advent of sound, motion pictures and popular music have enjoyed an intimate relationship. I am delighted that this book has been produced. To my knowledge, this is the first comprehensive look at this subject, and I hope it will not only provide an accompaniment to the National Film Theatre programme and touring season but will stand on its own as a valuable document.

September 1994

Martin Scorsese

introduction

Jonathan Romney
and **Adrian Wootton**

Robert De Niro's slo-mo cruising into a Little Italy bar to the sound of 'Jumping Jack Flash' in Martin Scorsese's *Mean Streets*... Michael Madsen as Mr Blonde carving himself a slice of copper's ear to the sound of Stealers Wheel in *Reservoir Dogs*... Over Vietnam treetops, 'copter blades swirling to The Doors' 'The End' at the start of *Apocalypse Now*... The screaming tones of the credit sequence to *Do the Right Thing*, with Rosie Perez body-slamming to Public Enemy... Kenneth Anger's fetishistic camera measuring every sheened inch of a leather boy's jacket, to the oiled tones of Bobby Vinton's 'Blue Velvet'... and in Wim Wenders' *Kings of the Road*, two German cinephiles slapping 'Just Like Eddie' on the Dansette, pop, crackle and all...

For nearly half a century, the repertoire of memorable pop moments in film has been mushrooming, until they can be fairly said to outnumber the more traditional canon of musical epiphanies on screen – Dirk Bogarde's sodden expiry to Mahler in *Death in Venice*... Anton Karas'

zither incarnating Vienna's spirit of place in *The Third Man*... the jangling lamentations that accompany Gary Cooper's slow walk to meet his fate in *High Noon*... the psychotic shriek of Bernard Herrmann's strings in *Psycho* as Ma Bates wields her knife over an unsuspecting Janet Leigh (who's surely humming another Hitchcock hit, 'Que Sera Sera', in that shower)...

Selecting your own personal high points in pop film history is rather like pressing buttons at random on some huge mental jukebox – you never know what tunes are going to come up. Landing on the image of the jukebox as a metaphor for this book's subject was the last, fortuitous stage in its preparation, but that image crystallises many of the concerns that our contributors and interviewees repeatedly allude to. As many of them point out, selecting one forgotten number from among the B-sides of the unconscious instantly takes you back to the place and age you were when you first heard it (the tag-line for *American Graffiti* says it all: 'Where were you in '62?'). Moreover, every viewer comes to the cinema carrying his or her own jukebox ready loaded, waiting only for the film-maker to hit the right buttons.

But the celluloid jukebox is in itself an anachronistic image. At the end of the twentieth century, it's arguable that nearly every note of music ever recorded and released for public consumption is currently available commercially, or potentially releasable (see the current prevalence of CD boxed sets, which allow completists

Where were you in '62? - American Graffiti

to acquire unfamiliar tracks or alternative versions of familiar ones). It seems there's no longer anything to discover, nothing that can be left unheard, nothing left to languish tantalisingly in the margins. If all this is available, however, it won't be on jukeboxes, even less on celluloid. With the advent of CD-i and CD-ROM, the very conditions under which we hear sounds and see pictures are set to change irrevocably. Beyond the changes in consuming habits entailed by the jump from vinyl to CD, and from celluloid to videotape, the advent of digital technology enables viewers and listeners not only vastly to increase the amount of material available to them, but also to multiply the possible permutations of their consumption. Beyond the 'shuffle' facility on CD players, beyond the 'alternate takes' offered by laser discs, CD-ROM promises not only to knit together sound and vision in unprecedented ways (starting with the very fact of storing them in a single medium), but also to make the audience into the selective players they have never been before. (A timid opening is the possibility, on David Bowie's 1994 *Jump* CD-ROM, of creating various different edits of his 'Jump They Say' video.) Massively expanded possibilities of visual and audio remixing are not far away. How long before we can re-edit De Niro's *Mean Streets* entrance to a Nino Rota theme or design our own image loops of the *Psycho* stabbing to, say,

Philip Glass or Handel's 'Water Music' – *and* have Freddy Krueger do the deed?

The main aim of this book, however, is not to herald a new technological utopia in which we all become sound-and-vision remixers in our own personal editing suites cum chill-out rooms. Nor are we yearning nostalgically for a golden age in which every image was not only definitive and unique, but new, never before seen. Clearly, one of the side products of the boom in CDs and in home video, with the vast repertoire it makes available, is a culture which enshrines the 'classic', a worship of cinematic and musical 'golden oldies'. Above all, we're not out to identify a canon of exemplary uses of pop – although certain directors and films (Scorsese, Wenders, Richard Lester's *A Hard Day's Night*, Franc Roddam's *Quadrophenia*) seem to recur more often than most. We're most concerned in this book to ask how the jukebox repertoire of pop cinema has evolved and where it's going.

This study is not, for the most part, a historical survey – although Mark Kermode's essay goes some way to providing one. However, there is one mythical starting point we can imagine, the Year Zero from which we've come an unthinkably long way. The great founding myth of pop film is the release in 1955 of *The Blackboard Jungle*, whose credit sequence featured Bill Haley and his Comets' 'Rock Around the Clock' – to such incendiary effect on its teenage audiences at the time that both in Britain and the US cinema seats were ripped out and questions asked in the House. *The Blackboard Jungle* imported definitively into the cinema the notion of generation outrage, thereby facilitating (indeed, necessitating) a further wave of youth movies that placated and domesticated raging teen hormones – from the Frankie Avalon/Annette Funicello beach blanket romps to

Summer Holiday, in which the MGM musical was reinvented as a church youth club outing under the aegis of Britain's own Reverend Cliff.

The Blackboard Jungle, however, represented a never-to-be-repeated moment in pop movie culture – perhaps the only moment in cinema history when people got up from their seats and danced. It was a moment in which cinema – the reeled-off repetition of an already fixed image – suddenly became *live*, as if satanically imbued with the animation and *event*-fulness of Haley's credit sequence song. It would never happen again (or rarely, and then only in exceptional, ritualised circumstances – as in the fetishistic audience participation cults that grew up around *The Rocky Horror Picture Show* and *The Blues Brothers*). Thereafter, cinema would again become what it has always essentially been – a deferred experience, not live but recorded, telling you what you'd missed by *not* being there.

Some of the films that have been released in Britain during the preparation of this book (1993-4) give an idea of how far we've come since the sound of avuncular, kiss-curled Haley terrorised the ushers at the Huddersfield Essoldo, and where we've got to now. For film has largely become its own jukebox – or, more accurately, its own vending machine. It is comparatively rare these days for an entire movie to be scored by one composer, when so many parties – producers desperate to get a film financed, record companies hoping to push an artist, publishers anxious to squeeze more mileage out of a one-time hit song – stand to profit from using a ready-made repertoire of recorded product. It's increasingly hard, faced with a film and its soundtrack CD, to tell which product is really supporting which. And because so much of a rapidly expanding 40-year-plus repertoire is constantly being used, making sense of these films and their music requires our skills not only as viewers, but as CD shoppers too – we have to know our way around film music's new Megastore culture.

Few uses of pop in film achieve what that Bill Haley song once did – theoretically, at least – that is, to appeal directly to the viscera, bypassing the viewer's cultural judgment. Nowadays, no use of pop in film can signify without being filtered through our knowledge of the cultural codes which

When Mod was God: *Quadrophenia*

govern no longer just film, but pop itself. There are rare examples. Arguably, Quentin Tarantino's use of the Revels' surf number 'Comanche' for Bruce Willis' big revenge sequence in *Pulp Fiction* appeals not at all to our knowledge of surf music and the way it's been used in film. It works purely as score – because of the dynamics, because the rasping sax *is* a chainsaw (the same is not true of 'Stuck in the Middle With You' in *Reservoir Dogs*, which works on the principle of radical incongruity). Likewise, the success of Wet Wet Wet's recording of 'Love is All Around' – fifteen weeks at the top of the UK charts in summer 1994, following its use in *Four Weddings and a Funeral* – depends entirely on a 'pure' emotional response, or as near such a thing as is possible; bring to the film any knowledge of the song's origin as a bizarre anomaly in the Troggs' recording career, and an already glutinous performance becomes altogether ludicrous. (It's worth noting, though, that the minute the song achieved No. 1 status, it instantly became impossible to react 'innocently' to its use in the film.)

What is remarkable, though, is how most of the films now using pop songs appeal to specific areas of knowledge, to the viewer's adherence to distinct genres of music or film – as if each film exclusively addressed habitués of one particular rack in a megastore whose clientele is fragmented as never before. Martin Scorsese's and Wim Wenders' use of pop – in films such as *Mean Streets* and *The Goalkeeper's Fear of the Penalty* – arguably addressed the universal significance of rock culture to an entire generation, the one that fully awoke to both vinyl and celluloid cultures in the 60s. Now, however, the fragmentation of the pop market is reflected in the way that individual films or genres invoke not a universal audience, but a series of 'micro-communities', each one possessing, or aspiring to possess, its own cultural consensus. (The success of Wet Wet Wet, or of Bryan Adams' 'Everything I

Do', from *Robin Hood: Prince of Thieves*, can be seen as a nostalgic throwback to a time when 'everybody' knew and loved/loathed a particular song.)

The power of Jonathan Demme's AIDS film *Philadelphia* to unify its audience in empathy depends partly on the rhetoric of its custom-built soundtrack – which assumes the acceptance, by a generation in their thirties and forties, of Neil Young and Bruce Springsteen as spokesmen for the liberal conscience in the post-Woodstock, post-Live Aid 'compassion culture'. A more complex historical and cultural knowledge is addressed by Robert Zemeckis' extraordinarily successful *Forrest Gump*. When Zemeckis uses a Doors song in a Vietnam sequence, he is not merely using it to tell us the date. Rather, he is drawing on an audience's knowledge of Michael Herr's now enshrined claim, in his book *Dispatches,* that Vietnam was 'a rock 'n' roll war'; their knowledge of that premise's illustration in Coppola's *Apocalypse Now;* their knowledge of the further elaborations of the 'rock war' myth in *Good Morning, Vietnam* and Oliver Stone's war cycle. Every number in *Forrest Gump* – which boasts a staggeringly long playlist – comes loaded with a cultural overdetermination that belies any notion of a song's 'innocent' use. The film's massive success suggests that from here on cinema as imagistic jukebox can only go further into hyperdrive.

A whole school of rap movies – or more generally of movies with black characters that allude to the stereotypes of 'gangsta rap' – has risen up in the wake of *New Jack City*, making the hip-hop soundtrack not only a stamp of supposed authenticity but also a failsafe commercial opportunity, mandatory material for inner-city-blues dramas (*Menace II Society*), generic thrillers (*Sugar Hill*), and sports movies (*Above the Rim*) alike. At one remove are parodies such as

CB4 and *Fear of a Black Hat*, rap satires which depend on a viewer's awareness of rap-genre codes in general, and also of narrowly time-specific ones (with the result that *Fear*'s sequence parodying PM Dawn videos looked like yesterday's news by the time of the film's British release).

A new perceived audience – the teen/early twenties 'slacker' generation, or 'Generation X' – has been addressed variously. In *Dazed and Confused*, Richard Linklater disinterred and reanimated the long discredited dinosaurs of 70s mainstream rock (the terminally uncool likes of Foghat, Aerosmith and Peter Frampton), at a stroke revealing the hitherto unsuspected ancestry of the grunge generation depicted in his previous film *Slacker*. More duplicitously, the bigger-budget *Reality Bites* – a prime example of a project where film and soundtrack CD form part of one and the same marketing initiative – looks like a conscious attempt to call into being its own target demographic, a generation of media-literate post-teens adept at reading and at ironically participating in MTV culture and its corpus of pop-history knowledge (using U2, Crowded House, the Knack, and – once again – Peter Frampton).

Possibly the most complex – and the most literate – attempt in recent years to appeal to an audience's pop culture knowledge has been Iain Softley's *Backbeat*, an account of the Beatles' early years as a cover band. The film is remarkable for the energy with which the band's performance revivifies rock standards long since preserved in aspic. The soundtrack becomes all the more extraordinary once you know that

the authentic-sounding reconstructions are performed by a band comprising members of Nirvana, Sonic Youth, REM and the Afghan Whigs; the music takes on a curiously stereophonic aspect, so that the Beatles' Hamburg residency – one of those mythical starting points in which rock legend abounds – also miraculously becomes a key moment in the pre-history of a current generation.

Two less successful attempts to capture a moment in British pop may nevertheless provide some clues to the future. *The Young Americans* and *Shopping*, tentative stabs at giving 90s British rave culture a visual representation, could both have been conceived in the heyday of the 50s London gangland thriller; both have immensely powerful dance music soundtracks that simply fail to find their correlative in the films' weary narrative, B-movie iconography and stereotypical characterisations. Nevertheless, both films' attempt to use the new generation of dance tracks clearly represents a nostalgic desire to get the pop movie back to where it began – to directly addressing rhythm itself as the nerve centre of youth culture, as *The Blackboard Jungle* once briefly did. Where these films failed, it may be that future club music soundtracks may achieve the unthinkable and get cinema audiences dancing again, if not ripping seats.

Clearly, a project such as this book is addressing too vast and fluid a topic not to leave an enormous number of gaps. It's best, then, to define what we're not attempting rather than to make claims for a grand strategy. First, we're addressing a comparatively narrow range of films, defining 'popular music' here as including rock, pop, soul, blues and rap, but not jazz and country, since those two areas have their own peculiar iconographies and mythologies. By necessity, then, we're not attempting to be encyclopedic, nor guaranteeing to acknowledge everyone's idea of a classic movie – a case in point being Andy Medhurst's overview of the British pop film, which pointedly excludes more obvious reference points in favour of a marginal canon (Terry Dene, Mike Sarne *et al.*). We are also largely excluding music video and television, areas which involve quite another set of specific considerations. In addition, we have decided to limit our scope largely to fictional and narrative films, partly because rock documentaries have already been the study of extensive surveys, partly because of our belief in pop itself as a form of fiction-making; nevertheless we do address questions of documentary in our own essays. We have also found ourselves unable to deal as much as we would have liked with pop music's inheritance from the tradition of mainstream film scoring. It should therefore be taken as read that certain key figures underlie the book as inescapable touchstones – foremost among them Ennio Morricone, who pioneered the absorption of pop instrumentation into scoring practices.

The range of essays is designed not to exhaust the topic of pop film, but at least to give the widest possible sense of its diversity. Mark Kermode's piece introduces the book with an overview of pop cinema and of the nostalgia factor as its key function. Specific areas of cinema are addressed by Kodwo Eshun, who examines the legacy of the 70s blaxploitation cycle in defining the images and narratives of contemporary rap-based cinema; by Jane Giles, in her geography of the underground in which counter-cultural impulses in music and film strike an uneasy and often perverse allegiance; and by Andy Medhurst, in his sceptical overview of that 'impossible' genre, the British pop movie. A number of essays address the question of star persona and its place in pop cinema. A key point in David Toop's essay on pop performers who have become quasi-mainstream soundtrack composers in their own right is the fact that film scoring confronts performers most used to occupying the limelight with the sudden prospect of invisibility. This is a question also explored by Ben Thompson's account of the perilous manoeuvres involved in artists crossing between the not always compatible realms of pop and film stardom – a crisis acutely illustrated by Death and Morton's potted cartoon history of the Cliff Richard film canon.

The question of persona also plays a large part in those essays that look at pop film's purchase on the real world. Mike Atkinson argues that the pop biopic throughout its history is caught up in an unanswerable dilemma: that the pop star's persona is predicated on the very fact of being larger-than-life to the point of being unrepresentable. Jonathan Romney examines the nature of the backstage in pop documentary as a purportedly 'real' space which is nevertheless the prime site for staging fictions about a star's persona. And Adrian Wootton's essay examines the failures of rock documentary – depictions of live rock concerts and hagiographies of dead legends – while tentatively mapping an escape route from the cul-de-sac of cliché.

The final contribution, by Mark Sinker, inverts the book's frame of reference by looking at the idea of film from the point of view of music; he traces the idea of pop *as* film from the three-minute movie of the Shangri-Las single to the LP-as-imaginary-soundtrack, as practised by Barry Adamson.

In our interview section, we've thrown open the question of pop film to a quorum of leading contemporary practitioners of music and film. Inevitably, the logistics of time and availability have meant that we weren't able to speak to everyone we would have liked to, and it's only for that reason that this section displays a preponderance of directors over musicians, and a shortfall of European representatives. We hope we can correct the balance in a future forum. We also look forward to seeing its debates extended in a three-month programme of films and events at the National Film Theatre, London, and other UK venues in 1995.

The book concludes with a reference section comprising a select bibliography and a filmography compiled by Tise Vahimagi, whom we'd like to thank for his invaluable input.

September 1994

Il maestro Morricone (photo: Claude Mayet)

twisting the knife

Mark Kermode

**Pop music [in movies] is like a knife.
You twist it and nostalgia comes pouring out.**

Steve Woolley, producer [1]

The relationship between rock music and movies is both long-standing and multifarious. At its best, pop music can inspire and enliven directors; it can accompany, counterpoint, boost or ironically comment upon their visual work in a unique and sometimes spine-tingling manner. It can create an instant period location, establishing with just a few choice chords, haunting vocal phrases or distinctive drumbeats an

Blackboard Jungle has gone down in history as 'the first rock film',[3] acknowledging the awesome power of Haley's music to capture a critical moment in American social history. Hot on the heels of Brooks' crowd-pulling, seat-ripping success came Frank Tashlin's *The Girl Can't Help It* (1956), an audacious Technicolor spectacular bursting with wit and invention, and featuring on-screen musical offerings from (among others) Gene Vincent and the Blue Caps, Eddie Cochran, Julie London, Fats Domino and Little Richard. Meanwhile Fred F. Sears directed the

More than any other art form, pop music is a disposable, transient product which reflects, mimics and occasionally shapes the *zeitgeist*

authentically rich milieu from over five decades of social history. Perhaps more than any other art form, pop music is a disposable, transient product which reflects, mimics and occasionally shapes the *zeitgeist*. As such, pop music can serve as a film's memory, instantaneously linking it with its audience, tapping into a nostalgic past, or fixing the film firmly in the present.[2]

When Richard Brooks decided to use Bill Haley and his Comets' 'Rock Around the Clock' as the theme tune to *The Blackboard Jungle* in 1955, he lent the film a sparkling air of 'now-ness' which no amount of scriptwriting or directing could have achieved. Despite the fact that the film featured no pop music other than in its opening and closing credits, *The*

incongruously aged Bill Haley in *Rock Around the Clock* (in which Haley and co. perform the title song not once but twice) while Edward L. Cahn entered the fray with *Shake, Rattle and Rock!*, both pictures drawing substantial teen audiences in 1956. Producer Sam Katzman put Haley back on the big screen in the same year's *Don't Knock the Rock*, a shameless rock 'exploitation' movie, again directed by Sears, which was lambasted by critics while pulling enthusiastic young viewers by the thousands. What is significant about this limp but seminal trio of rock movies is that although none of them could be called 'good' films (unlike *The Blackboard Jungle* or *The Girl Can't Help It*) their musical content is so quintessentially representative of a critical moment in youth history – the birth of the 'teenager' – that they have grown in stature over the years into classic celluloid time-pieces. The same is true of much of the Elvis Presley movie catalogue; nobody took *Jailhouse Rock* seriously in 1957, but it is now regarded as something of a cultural landmark. All these films have gained a nostalgic appeal as a result of their seminal pop content – they got the music right, and that was enough.

The Graduate

Modern examples which have similarly captured their moment (and to which time will surely be kind) include such diverse fare as John Badham's disco classic *Saturday Night Fever* (1977), Chris Petit's grim post-punk road movie *Radio On* (1979), John Hughes' *Some Kind of Wonderful* (1987) with its prominent American college radio soundtrack, and Spike Lee's *Do the Right Thing* (1989), which uses a radical rap/blues background, much imitated in subsequent years. Most recently, former *Rolling Stone* critic Cameron Crowe has risen to prominence as the director of *Singles* (1992), a visual jukebox of a movie built upwards from a collection of songs by bands from the then thriving Seattle scene. A hit with both critics and audiences on its initial release, *Singles* has already become enshrined as *the* document of 'grunge', a briefly flaring musical movement now bearing the official stamp of 'last year's thing'. That Crowe should tap this musical vein at precisely the moment that its international youth currency was highest is a testament to his astute judgment. Remember, for every *Singles* or *Saturday Night Fever* that captures a historic musical moment, there are a hundred *Roller Boogie*s which back a losing pop fad, and promptly disappear into the ether, never to be seen (or heard) again.

Picking exactly the right brand of contemporary music to give a film 'now' appeal (which will hopefully mature over the years into nostalgic magic) has proved a hit and miss affair in the years since *The Blackboard Jungle*. From the offerings of the 60s and 70s several titles stand out as milestones. Among them are Mike Nichols' *The Graduate* (1967), in which a tale of twisted young love is played out over a classic backdrop of Simon and Garfunkel songs, most memorably 'Mrs Robinson' and 'Scarborough Fair'; Antonioni's *Blow-Up*, his 1966 take on Swinging London, which featured a legendary appearance by The Yardbirds performing 'Stroll On', and his 1969 film *Zabriskie Point*, in which The Grateful Dead, Pink Floyd, The Youngbloods and the Kaleidoscope clash in a historic soundtrack whose original sleevenotes proclaim, 'It is more than just a case of a film of today demanding the music of today. Contemporary music doesn't merely tell a story or set a mood; it *is* the story. It *is* the mood.' There was also Dennis Hopper's *Easy Rider* (1969), which perfectly captured the aural flavour of a new breed of youth rebellion, epitomised by Steppenwolf's 'Born to Be Wild'; and Donald Cammell and Nic Roeg's *Performance* (1970), in which Mick Jagger becomes the living embodiment of 'the shock of the new', to the strains of Randy Newman, The Last Poets, Buffy Sainte-Marie and Jagger's own 'Memo from Turner'. Each of these very different films succeeded in capturing and crystallising the moment of their creation, in large degree because of their efficacious use of pop music.

While the use of pop music to fix a film in the 'now' is a risky business (long production times mean you actually have to *predict* rather than respond to the charts), the retrospective use of pop is a far safer and often more artistically rewarding process. Hear a classic pop song years after its first chart appearance and the chances are you'll be able to remember exactly where you were and how you felt at the moment of its first blossoming. Like everyone else, film directors frequently remember times and places by their associations with contemporary pop songs, and freely admit to the influence this has upon their work. Martin Scorsese has said of the pop-laden soundtrack to *Mean Streets* (1973) – which *Time Out* described as 'one of the few [movies] to successfully integrate rock music into the structure of the film'[4] – that it consists entirely of songs which he remembers from his own New York youth (most notably The Rolling Stones' 'Jumping Jack Flash' and The Ronettes' 'Be My Baby') and which for him still evoke exactly the milieu he was attempting to portray. In the nostalgic horror yarn *Christine* (1983), adapted from Stephen King's best-selling novel, John Carpenter explored this magical power of pop music to conjure a bygone age. Here, the eponymous '58 Plymouth Fury allows its ghoulish memory to seep into (and transform) the modern world via its radio, which plays nothing but wall-to-wall 50s favourites. This is no golden oldie radio broadcast, of course – the car is simply singing to itself, reinvoking the past with hits from yesteryear.

British producer Steve Woolley is particularly down-to-earth in his assessment of the function of pop music in movies, which he describes as the cheapest form of period scenery, or 'wallpaper', available to a film-maker: if you can't afford the sets, slap on a distinctive period tune and the audience will imagine the rest.[5] Classic illustrations of Woolley's 'wallpaper' theory include Franc Roddam's elegy to 'mod', *Quadrophenia* (1979), a drama set in 1964 in which the on-screen appearance of modern-day buses and cinemas showing *Grease* are easily plastered over by a soundtrack blaring Booker T. and early Who. For all their period costumes and costly props, the big-budget fantasies *Back to the Future* (Robert Zemeckis, 1985) and *Peggy Sue Got Married* (Francis Coppola, 1986) also relied heavily on 50s pop to illustrate their time-travelling motifs. Other recent musically located period pieces include Rob Reiner's *Stand By Me* (1986), Peter Medak's *Let Him Have It* (1991) and Robert Shaye's *Book of Love* (1990), all of which hark back to the 50s; Michael Caton-Jones' pot-boiler *Scandal* (1988) and Bruce Robinson's *Withnail & I* (1986), which revel in the unmistakable sounds of the 60s; and Richard Linklater's *Dazed and Confused* (1993), Howard Zieff's *My Girl* (1991) and Jim Sheridan's *In the Name of the Father* (1993), an unlikely trio which all rely heavily on 70s hits to establish an authentic sense of cultural history.

The Wanderers

In car entertainment: *American Graffiti*

Whitney Houston in *The Bodyguard*

The quintessential 'musical wallpaper' movie, to which all of the above owe a heavy debt, is George Lucas' 1973 hit *American Graffiti*. Set during the last summer night of 1962, the film follows the angst-ridden antics of a group of teenagers in the San Joaquin Valley, marauding together for one last time before college (and approaching adulthood) puts an end to their carefree youths. It seems significant that, although there had been 'retro' rock movies before, *American Graffiti* was the first major hit to capitalise fully upon a 'pop heritage' soundtrack. Until that point, pop music in movies had served primarily to give them a contemporary edge, and to lend them saleability in the drive-in market. Now, it seemed as if the genre was coming of age and starting to feel nostalgic for its own childhood. Crucially, despite its extraordinary pop-packed soundtrack, *American Graffiti* is *not* a drive-in movie; rather, it is a *remembrance* of a drive-in movie, a nostalgic homage to the jukebox cinema culture which had already receded into the past. Considering that so many budding young directors who came to the fore in the 70s and 80s had childhood memories of the late 50s and early 60s, it is perhaps hardly surprising that this was the period for which cinema seemed to pine. (In the 80s, the slew of 'rocking' movies which began with *American Graffiti* gave way to a series of 50s sci-fi remakes – *The Thing, The Fly, The Blob* – all of which similarly suggested relived youths for the middle-aged directors.)

1963 was also the setting for Philip Kaufman's *The Wanderers* (1979), which expands upon Lucas' use of pop oldies to create a richly evocative portrait of a lost era, and something of an unsung high point in the marriage of pop and movies. Set in the Bronx at a time when America was undergoing massive social upheaval (Kennedy's assassination and the full-scale escalation of the Vietnam War were on the horizon), *The Wanderers* chronicles an Italian greaser street gang's confrontation with imminent

The 80s saw a previously unparalleled explosion of the 'pop promotion' gimmick

obsolescence. Intelligently using such period tracks as The Four Seasons' 'Walk Like a Man', 'My Boyfriend's Back' by The Angels, Dion's 'Runaround Sue', and The Surfaris' 'Wipe Out', Kaufman marvellously blends aloof irony and loving admiration in his depiction of the gang's street-crawling escapades. Yet The Wanderers' greaseball lifestyle is under attack, and Kaufman expresses the threats to their existence through music. The arrival of proto hep-cat Nina, who unwittingly causes a rift in the gang, is signalled by a mellow refrain from Mel Martin's 'Stranger on the Shore' which interrupts the pounding rock and roll rhythms associated with the gang. More bizarrely, appearances of the surreal, zombie-like Duckie Boys (who seem to represent an amorphous fear of the future) are accompanied throughout by discordant, atonal electronic wails and free-form drumming, which in one scene actually enter into an aural battle with Dion's 'The Wanderer'. At the end of the movie, Richie, by now a hero-out-of-time, follows Nina to a darkened club where a silhouetted Bob Dylan plays 'The Times They Are A-Changin'' – Richie, the rock-and-roller, cannot enter to follow the object of his desire. He is literally locked out of the future.

More recently, directors have moved from the innocence of that pre-'63 period to an obsession with the catastrophe of the ensuing years, and the advent of the Vietnam War. Unsurprisingly, pop songs have again featured strongly in the depiction of this period. Whereas war movies were once played out against glorious orchestral themes (*The Dam Busters, The Battle of Britain, 633 Squadron*), period pop songs were now used to provide clashing, ironic discord to the on-screen action. The Vietnam War has been repeatedly depicted on screen as having been fought to the nihilistic strains of Jimi Hendrix and The Doors. Coppola's 1979 epic *Apocalypse Now* opens ominously (and ironically) to the droning tones of The Doors performing 'The End'. Seven years later, Oliver Stone's *Platoon* would be trailered using images of bloody and explosive jungle combat overlaid upon the jarringly sweet and tender sounds of Smokey Robinson's 'Tracks of My Tears'. Even Barry Levinson's flimsy *Good Morning, Vietnam* (1987) labours the well-worn point that while American radio was blaring 'I Feel Good' the country was gearing itself up for national and international humiliation. In 1991, Mark Rydell's *For the Boys* exemplified this trend, charting the changing nature of war from World War II to Vietnam by following a pair of singers entertaining the troops through the years. After early 40s footstompers, the darkest scene found Bette Midler wailing the Beatles' melancholic tune 'In My Life' in the middle of a Vietnamese battlefield, before watching her son get ripped apart by a bomb. (This use of bleak musical irony was not restricted to Hollywood. The 1989 British movie *Resurrected*, in which Falklands veteran Kevin Deakin is persecuted by his own comrades, used the mindlessly anthemic Rod Stewart song 'Sailing' as a grim overture to acts of hideous brutality.)

If it is indeed true that the makers of these movies are gradually working their way through the traumas that affected them in their youth, we can expect a slew of movies set in the 70s to begin trickling onto our screens in the near future, with appropriate musical accompaniment. Quentin Tarantino's bizarre choice of 70s bubblegum pop as a striking counterpoint to the (sometimes hideous) modern-day action of *Reservoir Dogs* suggests that musical memories from the director's youth can be used to do far more than merely create a historical background. Like Scorsese, Tarantino is musically literate, and understands the magical, nostalgic power of pop. Like Philip Kaufman, he knows that the exact placement of a song within a movie can shape and change the nature of the on-screen story, and that the relationship between music and action does not have to be harmonious.

Just as importantly, the success of MCA's *Reservoir Dogs* soundtrack album, with its pappy hits (interrupted regularly by the monotonous tones of Steve Wright welcoming us to 'K Billy's Super Sounds of the 70s'), provides much needed proof that this lucrative area of marketing is not entirely artistically bankrupt. Sadly, in recent years there has been a notable trend toward the youth promotion of often unremarkable films via rock and pop music tie-ins. Although this is nothing new, the 80s saw a previously unparalleled explosion of the 'pop promotion' gimmick with often artistically bankrupt results, thanks largely to the rise of music video as a primary marketing tool. Ever since Joe Cocker and Jennifer Warnes hit the top twenty in 1982 with 'Up Where We Belong' (a theme song co-written by legendary scorer Jack Nitzsche), for which the much played video was essentially an advertisement for *An Officer and a Gentleman*, producers and distributors have been loathe to overlook such potential free publicity. By the time Tony Scott's *Top Gun* (1986) passed into movie lore as the quintessential pop-promo 'feature',[6] the 80s had already become the decade of the 'pop soundtrack', with *Flashdance* (1983), *Ghostbusters* (1984), *Footloose* (1984), *Beverly Hills Cop* (1984) and *St Elmo's Fire* (1985) all benefiting from associated hit singles.

The relationship between pop music and film throughout this heady period was clearly symbiotic from a marketing standpoint. Revamped hits from yesteryear provided not only the theme tunes, but the very titles of such variable celluloid fare as John Hughes' *Pretty in Pink* (1986), Rob Reiner's *Stand By Me* (1986) and Garry Marshall's *Pretty Woman* (1990). Soundtrack placements also had the power to revitalise flagging careers. When 'Kokomo' was featured in the Tom Cruise vehicle *Cocktail* (Roger Donaldson, 1988), the Beach Boys scored a US number one, despite having been dropped by their record company; and Simple Minds finally broke big in the United States when 'Don't You Forget About Me' (not, in fact, one of their own songs) was used in John Hughes' *The Breakfast Club* (1985).

The ubiquitous use of pop songs to market movies also had a profound (and in some respects damaging) effect upon the soundtrack albums market. By the time Elvis Presley, Cliff Richard and the Beatles began to use cinema to broaden their

Breathless moments: Madonna in *Dick Tracy* (photo; Peter Sorel)

promotional bases, the incidental film soundtrack album was well established, finally coming of age with the arrival of the generation of composers spearheaded by John Barry, Jerry Goldsmith and Ennio Morricone. After an initial period of critical uncertainty, in which pop soundtracks were considered the illegitimate offspring of incidental movie music, the genre grew in stature in the late 60s thanks to two landmark releases. In 1967, Mike Nichols asked Simon and Garfunkel to score his film *The Graduate*. Suffering from a lack of time and inspiration, the duo offered Nichols only one new 'work in progress' song, 'Mrs Robinson'. Not to be defeated, Nichols simply licensed several other already recorded songs, which he had been using as guide tracks, thus creating, almost by accident, the seminal pop-soundtrack album. Two years later, Dennis Hopper's road movie *Easy Rider* became the yardstick by which all future 'pop compilation' soundtracks would be judged. The quintessential 'underground breakthrough' movie, *Easy Rider* was made independently for relatively little money. However, with efficient distribution, Hopper's cult classic achieved an extraordinary mainstream popularity, due in some degree to its hip rock soundtrack, which brilliantly melded the counterculture sounds of the 60s – Hendrix, the Byrds, Steppenwolf – into an evocative document of a dying decade.

In the wake of such artistically coherent pop soundtracks came a plethora of less accomplished rack fillers. By the mid-70s, the soundtracks market had pretty much divided into two competing camps, 'scores' versus 'songs', with the latter stealing the lion's share of sales. This trend continued throughout the 80s, and still thrives today; while the score album of James Cameron's 1991 *Terminator 2: Judgment Day* (which omitted the associated Guns N' Roses single) was considered a major hit when it went platinum, the pop soundtrack to Mick Jackson's 1992 *The Bodyguard* (which took *Top Gun*'s pop-promo experiment to new heights) has long since breezed past the triple platinum post.

However ill-fitting the inclusion of a pop song may be in an incidental score, it is surely preferable to the wholesale ditching of a composer's work in favour of a pop soundtrack. Director Michael Radford publicly denounced Virgin at the 1984 BAFTA awards after they had stripped Dominic Muldowney's evocative score from his British-made film *Nineteen Eighty-Four* and replaced it with some hideous techno groaning by the Eurythmics.[7] The very next year, director Ridley Scott was forced by Universal executive Sidney Jay Sheinberg to scrap Jerry Goldsmith's orchestral score for the Tom Cruise fantasy *Legend* (1985), in favour of a soundtrack by Tangerine Dream. Even though Scott had worked with Goldsmith throughout the production of *Legend*, and European reviewers had praised his music, Sheinberg insisted that a more 'accessible' sound was needed to attract the youth audience.

Recent years have also seen the rise of a bizarre phenomenon in which two, or even three, music albums from the same film are released simultaneously, one featuring the score, another the songs, and yet another languishing under the weirdly conceptual banner of 'songs inspired by the movie'. Tim Burton's *Batman*, Warren Beatty's *Dick Tracy*, Ralph Bakshi's *Cool World* and Anthony Hickox's *Hellraiser III* all produced multiple soundtracks. More bizarrely, the 1994 British blockbuster *Four Weddings and a Funeral* spawned a soundtrack album in which the entire incidental score is reduced to a five-minute medley, while a wide-ranging collection of classic pop love songs packs out the rest of the album. Almost none of these songs appears in the movie but, cleverly intercut with snippets of dialogue from the film, they have served as an extraordinarily successful promotional item.

As the film soundtracks market, in all its bizarre permutations, continues to expand, the use of pop music as a promotional tool will undoubtedly play an increasing role in the selling of movies, particularly to a teen audience. Like the films themselves, the pop soundtrack albums which these movies produce will range from the inventive to the inane, from the creative to the crass. Although some more puritanical soundtrack collectors view pop soundtracks as inherently heretical, there is a now strong need for the positive critical appraisal of such inventive works as MCA's *Reservoir Dogs* soundtrack, or the long awaited original Vangelis *Blade Runner* score (released 1994), which again straddles the divide between pop and 'incidental' music. Equally, with irrelevant contemporary pop songs clumsily adorning so many forgettable studio blockbusters, the time is ripe to remind ourselves just how exquisitely a well-chosen pop soundtrack can enhance a director's vision. In the right hands (and indeed the right place) a pop soundtrack can lend a movie a depth and resonance which no other medium can achieve.

NOTES

1. Steve Woolley in *Mojo*, June 1994, p. 52.

2. The future is a much harder milieu to capture, and its effective musical evocation on film has rarely been pop-based. While Richard Stanley broke the mould in 1990 by effectively using a heavy-metal/goth soundtrack for his sci-fi shocker *Hardware*, the music of successful cinematic futurism has generally been 'incidental', from Bernard Herrmann's *The Day the Earth Stood Still*, with its clashing strings and wailing theremins, to the lush synthesised sweeps of Vangelis' *Blade Runner* score.

3. Marshall Crenshaw, *Hollywood Rock: A Guide to Rock'n'Roll in the Movies* (London: Plexus, 1994), p. 41.

4. *The Time Out Film Guide: Third Edition*, ed. Tom Milne (Harmondsworth: Penguin, 1993), p. 447.

5. Steve Woolley, *op. cit.*

6. Of the pop hits associated with *Top Gun*, Berlin's 'Take My Breath Away' was the most successful, achieving a lengthy stay at the UK number one spot, and providing a regular outlet for the 'promo' video which itself was little more than a trailer for the film.

7. See Cynthia Rose, 'Ministry of Virgin Truth', *New Musical Express*, 1 December 1984.

John Travolta in *Saturday Night Fever*

long black limousine :
pop biopics *Michael Atkinson*

'Is everybody in? Is *everybody* in? Is everybody *in*? The ceremony is about to begin,' intoned Val Kilmer at the opening of Oliver Stone's rose-bespectacled mastodon *The Doors* (1991); and, even though the words were Jim Morrison's, it was quite obviously the film itself that was pure ceremony. Like any film genre worth its rock salt, the pop music biopic is a self-fulfilling ritual, contrived of tropes and significations propagated in the hothouse of cinematic hyperbole and thriving jauntily at a respectable remove from the reality on which it is based. Unlike most, it traffics in a culture myth that is not only dead, a lie or buried in history, but is our most ferociously beloved bedtime story – the grandstanding, fire-breathing music genius/god courting Untimely Death by way of his or her essential extra-ordinariness. Ever since the baseball movie *The Pride of the Yankees* (1942) converted the ordinary biopic – *Disraeli*, *Wilson*, *The Story of Alexander Graham Bell* – into love-and-death pop idolatry, our modern pop heroes, who do little more than sing, play guitar and exude raw, churlish magnetism, must die at their stories' ends like ailing kings. Room must be made, time and time again, for new and younger dynasts.

Val Kilmer in *The Doors*

It's a ceremony of the innocent, certainly, and as such, movies from *The Glenn Miller Story* (1953) to *La Bamba* (1986), no matter how fanciful and hagiographic, express a truth about pop culture: that the life-affirming three-and-a-half-minute jukebox ditty does in fact often end with a plane crash (or at least an overdose), that the Mach 1 rise to glory so often endured by pop stars has death and menace written all over it, and yet no one ever seems to heed the heritage. (*Per capita*, the life expectancy of pop stars must be shorter than, say, that of nuclear power workers.) It's the American Dream distilled down to its grain-alcohol essence, instant splendour and celebrity twinned inexorably with disaster.

They did it their way: Chloe Webb and Gary Oldman as *Sid and Nancy* (left)

21

The Buddy Holly Story; Gary Busey

Backbeat: Ian Hart as John Lennon

At the same time, there's nothing more Romantic and, if it was good enough for Keats, it's good enough for Buddy Holly. Pop music, or more specifically rock 'n' roll, is both an essentially cinematic beast and the frankest manifestation of life force that modern culture has ever produced – which may amount to the same thing. Thus its biopics create and then lament the frustrated dreamtime of our collective fantasies, which, with the creation of youth culture after World War II, have never before been more powerful or seductive. The 90s guitar group Radiohead was right: everybody wants to be Jim Morrison. Few of us want to die at 28, however, and therein lies the paradox no true cultural obsession can live without.

Perhaps the question isn't whether we all want to be rock 'n' roll stars so much as that we all *can* be; pop biopics have always adored the deathless tale of a guileless rube stumbling into success and attaining godhood by virtue of unschooled talent and good will, and eventually falling victim to Fame, the System, or just plain Fate. On a very real level, this is pure Americana, the arena of cheap apocalypse; wherever a pop idol crashes and burns, it's always an American phenomenon, thanks to one man – Elvis, who cut his first Sun record less than a year before generational archetype James Dean smacked up his Porsche on Highway 41. If Dean cut the mould, Elvis sold it to the world. The hayseed Christ of pop music, the Greatest Story Ever Told, the King of kings, Elvis served as the prototype for every pop myth imaginable, biopics included. Even if it took more than twenty years for the crush of iconolatry, wealth and drug abuse to boomerang back at him, the classic trajectory of Elvis' life is still clung to popularly as a modern tragedy – as if he was *meant* to die sometime before getting fat, middle-aged and campy, didn't, and we'll just pretend he did.

Mysteriously, no major Elvis biopic has ever been produced, outside of a handful of American TV movies and spirit-of-Elvis guest appearances in postmod-ish industry offspring such as *Heartbreak Hotel*, *True Romance*, *The Dark Half* and *Death Becomes Her* (which

Angela Bassett as Tina Turner: *What's Love Got to Do With It?*

also gave us an ageless Jim Morrison). Though undeniably pivotal and totemic, Elvis' story may be too archetypal: modest country schmuck to instant sensation worshipped by millions, to lonely despot slumped dead over his gold-plated toilet, successful but empty and wasted by fame. It's the same story, one way or another, at the core of *The Buddy Holly Story*, *The Doors*, *La Bamba*, *Lady Sings the Blues*, *Sweet Dreams*, *Sid and Nancy*, *Backbeat*, *The Rose*, etc.; it's just the true story of pop culture, true because it's ours, we made it and we live by it. (Its prevalence shows no signs of waning; we can only speculate as to who might play Kurt Cobain in his inevitable biopic – call it 'Nevermind' – Brad Pitt? Ethan Hawke? Leaf Phoenix?) Still, it's impossible to overtell the story, and Elvis as an icon may be too familiar, a face, name, voice and swagger so ubiquitous in the universal consciousness that we don't need a major movie of his life any more than we need one of our own. The paradigm survives, of course, and in essence we watch Elvis live and die over and over again in other people's tales, like the wax Gary Gilmore being executed, and revived, every half-minute at Madame Tussaud's. The King is dead, long live the King.

To the naked eye, the Elvis legend seems simultaneously chintzy and debauched, and it's somehow fitting that TV movies, the kitschiest and least self-important movie breed in America, have felt most comfortable exploring Elvis – you can imagine the man watching them himself, a gun in his lap. *Elvis*, *Elvis and Me* and *Elvis and the Beauty Queen* (starring Kurt Russell, Dale Midkiff and Don Johnson, respectively) all regard the premier pop saga with the misty, maternal sentiment of supermarket tabloids, the sort that report live Elvis sightings even to this day. The most thorough, John Carpenter's *Elvis* (1979), lavishes more angst upon Elvis' relationship with his dependent mother (Shelley Winters) than upon the

King's various jailbait romances (as the other two movies do) or the frighteningly hollow nature of absolute fame, which TV could never have the wisdom to examine. All three movies are tinged with rue, without ever being explicit as to why. It's assumed we know the rest of the story, and we do, all too well.

The pop music biopic didn't begin with Elvis; it just suddenly had more at stake, just as rock always seemed to be more immediate, more dangerous, more a matter of life or death, than jazz. The pop biopics dealing with pre-Elvis

What they did – how they played – mattered most; who they were, and why they were popular, mattered least

phenomena – such as *The Glenn Miller Story*, *The Benny Goodman Story*, *Young Man with a Horn* – centre on either hit songs or tearful comeback chronicles, and we're never asked to understand their protagonists as charismatic pop idols. What they did – how they played – mattered most; who they were, and why they were popular, mattered least. With Elvis, the dimensions of pop expanded nova-like to nearly every neglected corner of the media quotidian, and fans didn't merely buy records any more, they were *fans*, hungry, crazy and dizzy with sexual awe.

Kurt Russell in *Elvis*

Background: *The Doors*

Do you know me? Roger Daltrey in *Lisztomania*

Suddenly the nature of pop music changed, from simple entertainment to something that could control your life. The stories, and lives, of its artists took on a Rimbaldian intensity. Glenn Miller was never seen as musically compensating for a tortured off-stage existence, and although Gene Krupa and Lillian Roth battled with dope and booze behind the scenes in *The Gene Krupa Story* and *I'll Cry Tomorrow*, it was just a lost weekend or two, and there was light at the ends of their respective tunnels. After Elvis, one could not have fame without paying for it with flesh and blood. (You'd have to pay for salvation that way, too – take a big step backward and you're looking at Christ himself, the first foredoomed pop idol.) It was a phenomenon Ken Russell tried to comment on, in his particularly semi-toxic manner, in *Lisztomania* (1975), which immolates itself trying to demonstrate that musical fame has stayed more or less the same over the centuries, when in fact the kind Roger Daltrey knows about is no older than the 45rpm single – or perhaps just as old.

Like a true last temptation, the onus of responsibility for a pop star's doom must lie with him or her – if only subtextually – or it's pointless. Even climbing aboard an airplane is a choice made at the end of one's rainbow, as in the various versions of that doomed plane trip in *The Buddy Holly Story* and *La Bamba*. Both Holly and Richie Valens could have gone by bus, but such was the nature of their role in popular history that if they had, another plane would have crashed, somewhere, sometime. (Valens even had portentous dreams about plane crashes for years before.) One wonders when a Big Bopper biopic will be produced, providing us with a fully triangulated vision of that same air passage, the same damnation, that same ill-fated day when, as Don McLean said, the music died.

All modern pop biopics are by nature hagiographic, but, haunted by the ghost of Elvis, they are also inevitably tempted by the forces of darkness. The bitter destiny balances the music's natural élan. And without the buoyancy of youthful privilege, the crashes and ODs and asphyxiations would have no resonance. So pop biopics are often pilgrims' progresses, for the most part brimming with hope, and the more mundane the pre-stardom lives seem, the more remarkable the rise and fall. This pattern best fits the agrarian tincture of country/folk music, exemplified by George Hamilton as Hank Williams in *Your Cheatin' Heart*, David Carradine as Woody Guthrie in *Bound for Glory*, Sissy Spacek as Loretta Lynn in *Coal Miner's Daughter* and Jessica Lange as Patsy Cline in *Sweet Dreams*. Here, the Elvis mountain-boy cliché has its purest expression: dirt-poor Ozark hillbilly sings like a mockingbird, gets noticed, becomes simultaneously sanctified and cursed by his or her Nashville ascendancy. What's fascinating in these films' use of the Elvis myth is the tension between the idolised stage persona, which in its attainment of musical sublimity is beyond reproach, and the violent yet mundane chaos of their real lives. This conjures up a sense of classical tragedy as well as the inevitable creep of nasty housewife gossip; the dialectic between larger-than-life demigod and next-door victim of spousal abuse is irresistible, especially to Middle America.

Each brand of music has its own narrative zone, however Elvisised. If country is the land of misused homemakers-turned-songbirds, then jazz, in the contemporary biopic, is a frontier of racial spite and wholesale self-destruction. Compare *St Louis Blues* with *Leadbelly*, *Lady Sings the Blues* and *Bird*, and you'll see hagiography slowly turn sour in the gut. As these are the only notable examples of black pop biopics (with *What's Love Got to Do With It?* the subgenre's sole tale of triumph), it's safe to say that Hollywood remains racial light years from the well-paved inroads of Motown. Gordon Parks' *Leadbelly* (1976) is fraught with post-Confederacy rage, just as it deepens the stakes paid for iconhood. Huddie Ledbetter's particular ring of Movie Hell — years spent on the chain gangs

of Depression-era Texas and Louisiana — gave his music, and his biography, instant cachet of a calibre unseen anywhere else, while simultaneously sanctifying the man as a free-range Johnny Appleseed *à la Bound for Glory*. A spoonful of bitter honesty helps the hero worship go down, and so *Lady Sings the Blues* (1972) and *Bird* (1988) travel the dark corridor of junkiedom, implying that like a poet's madness, smack-fuelled dissolution is the price you pay for jazz glory.

In *Lady Sings the Blues*, Billie Holiday is a black cross between Anne Sexton and Patsy Cline — it's implied, mostly by Diana Ross' performance, that Holiday's terminal combat with heroin deepened her singing, gave it resonance. Sidney J. Furie's film mutates the facts of Holiday's life into a three-act soaper; better is Ross, who establishes a precedent (see *Bound for Glory*, *Coal Miner's Daughter*, *The Buddy Holly Story*, *The Doors*, etc.) by singing Holiday's vocals herself. In pop terms, the honourable and brave practice of recreating an artist's vocal achievements anew musters an aesthetic Catch-22 — if Holiday paid such high stakes for her art, what did Ross pay? If Holiday is worthy of a sentimental, teary movie of her life because of her singing, why isn't Ross? (Perhaps Ross will be, some day: the scenes of Ross' impersonator doing Ross doing Holiday will be fascinating.) But Holiday's voice is not duplicated so much as approximated; her biopic is a dream version of her life, and while we're there the real Billie Holiday doesn't even exist. This is a principle violated years later in *What's Love Got to Do With It?* (1993), which closes with footage of the real Tina Turner strutting her stuff; whatever empathy we have with Angela Bassett throughout the film is summarily obliterated in the presence of the real McCoy.

Death is to rock what lightning strikes are to summertime

Sissy Spacek in *Coal Miner's Daughter*

Perhaps rock 'n' roll was ricocheting too freshly and frenetically around the popular consciousness for full-scale biopics to be made before *The Buddy Holly Story* (1978), which stands as the first true rock biography. An unassuming pie-plate of latent 50s nostalgia, Buddy Holly's drama came with the shrugging break-up of the Crickets; it wasn't much and that was OK. All that was necessary was our knowledge of Holly's premature death to charge even the most mundane recording studio squabble with poignancy. Gary Busey's Holly seemed to have just come off an iron-pumping jag, but the film's modesty fits Holly's own and the real story did the real work. *La Bamba*, coming nine years later, matched this formula meticulously, draining Richie Valens (Lou Diamond Phillips) of any serious dramatic fire – his delinquent brother has more problems, and more reason to escape the *barrio*. Richie has the plane crash, after all; who needs more than that? When the good die young, the whole world mourns.

Death is to rock what lightning strikes are to summertime, and the only sure reason why Dennis Wilson, Brian Jones, Keith Moon, John Bonham and Ricky Nelson are not already the subjects of movies is the sometimes formidable price tag of music rights. (Big-budget Joplin and Hendrix biopics are in the works.) Todd Haynes' infamous *Superstar: The Karen Carpenter Story* (1987), in which he depicts the Top 40 life and bulimic death of Karen Carpenter using animated Barbie Dolls, remains a hostage to lawsuits by both Richard Carpenter and Mattel. Fictionalising the descent is a popular alternative: in *The Rose* (1979), a thinly disguised tour of duty through Joplin territory, Bette Midler's rock mama careens toward the boneyard on a river of original songs and belted covers of Motown faves, mixing her own brand of stage attitude generously into the Janis legend. *Eddie and the Cruisers* remakes the 'his-death-was-a-sham-he-just-disappeared' Jim Morrison myth (complete with copious references to the Lizard King's poet-of-choice, Rimbaud) with Springsteenish songs by John Cafferty and the Beaver Brown Band.

Alex Cox's *Sid and Nancy* (1986) has the raw strength to become a biopic prototype – as if anyone else's life might ever resemble that of Sid Vicious.

Perhaps the best that could objectively be said about Vicious is that he was in the right place at the right time – once; otherwise, he was an impenetrably dim working-class sod whose lack of talent or ambition left him completely unprepared for the demands and indulgences of fame. No one was as vulnerable, or succumbed as easily. Vicious and Nancy Spungen were hardly 'candles that burn twice as bright but half as long' – they were merely innocents ploughed over by the steamroller of pop history. Arguably the greatest of all pop music biopics, *Sid and Nancy* hits the gutter early on and loiters there for the duration, splitting the burden of ruin between punk fame and the most harrowing of dysfunctional relationships. In his way, Vicious constitutes the nether edge of the Elvis paradigm; by virtue of his worthlessness, he's the Greatest Punk, the ultimate negation of pop values. His death, and Nancy's (that is, suicide *and* murder), represent not a Faustian pact with the devil but with the culture's own anger. If anyone has been sacrificed for rock 'n' roll, it's Sid and Nancy.

Though still sporadically produced, rock biopics have reached a state of happy self-fascination, maturing alongside the baby boomer generation, who finally want their own childhood myths re-enacted for them in 35mm. Jim McBride's *Great Balls of Fire!* (1989) was a conspicuous failure, not because of Dennis Quaid's Daffy Duck-like performance, but because the time for a Jerry Lee Lewis bio had long since passed. No one cared by 1989, and one couldn't be sure audiences would ever have cared – Lewis' only claim to notoriety was marrying his 13-year-old cousin. There was no premature death, no tragedy, no Calvary for Jerry Lee. *What's Love Got to Do With It?* was another story, fraught with crucifixions, and was therefore a minor hit. While Angela Bassett's Turner looked as if she spent six hours a day in the gym, she still suffered through her career arc weathering Ike,

rock's most renowned wife-beater, in the classic Susan Hayward manner. What's interesting about the film is its built-in triumphant ending, for which Turner herself has been amply celebrated. She seemed destined for a Holidayesque finale, but walked across the street in bare feet instead. It's truly a tale for the 90s.

Perhaps the most lavish and blindly worshipful pop biopic of all is *The Doors*, a misty-eyed counter-culture valentine in which the tragedy of Jim Morrison's over-indulged life is seen as some sort of homage to the Old Gods. Stone stages concerts as if they were gargantuan pagan orgies, literally superimposes dancing shamans over Morrison's drugged-up stage shenanigans, and likens the man more than once to the earthly avatar of Dionysus. *The Doors* manages to be more pretentious about Morrison than he was about himself, and sometimes, at least, Stone seems to know it. ('Did you have a good world when you died?' Val Kilmer reads from Morrison's poems. 'Enough to base a movie on?') All the same, perhaps moderation is not what the Jim Morrison story required; he was the closest thing rock has yet had to a Poe, and if Stone overdid the Gothic New Age mythopoeia, it was in the service of expressing what Morrison meant to his fans. (Stone's dreaminess is not uncommon – see Danny Sugarman's biog *No One Here Gets Out Alive*, in which the author unequivocally admits to believing Morrison to be 'a god'.) *The Doors*, and Kilmer's scarily accurate portrayal, make one point crystal-clear: that Morrison, whatever else he may or may not have been, was Elvis with the backwoods bashfulness removed, leaving only the raw sexuality. More than anyone, even Mick Jagger, Morrison represented the ideal of hedonism in the hearts of teenagers everywhere. The will to fuck that had been in the music all along was, finally, standing right there on the stage, in black leather pants.

Morrison was Elvis with the backwoods bashfulness removed, leaving only raw sexuality

While sex motivated rock, death became its proudly displayed battle scar. The two needed each other, which may be why John Lennon had to die before any of the Beatles got straight biopics of their own. If the Beatles seem to have fallen out of the loop with regard to biography, it may be because each survived youth and fame to lead successful subsequent careers. A dreadful TV movie, *John and Yoko: A Love Story* (Sandor Stern, 1985), was the first biopic of a single Beatle, coming five years after Lennon's murder; it served only as a forum for dozens of Beatles recordings, an opportunity afforded this low-budget quickie by the good offices of Michael Jackson, who owns the rights to the songs. Lennon's legacy was approached with great savvy in both Christopher Münch's *The Hours and Times* (1992) and Iain Softley's *Backbeat* (1993), both using the same actor, Ian Hart. Neither film was able to use the Lennon-McCartney songs, a handicap breezily circumvented by featuring no music at all or early cover tunes, respectively. Münch's film may be the cleverest and most thought-provoking movie yet to take on a pop legend, exploring a single weekend early in the Beatles' career and using it to speculate upon the sexual tensions between Lennon and manager Brian Epstein, as well as to explore Lennon's tentative relationship with worldwide fame. Shot for next to nothing and in black-and-white, *The Hours and Times* seeks to attain a truth about its subject, not glorify him. Lennon is on the cusp of the best years of his life; Münch lets the audience conjure the tragedy themselves.

There's no such subtext in *Backbeat*, in which Hart's Lennon is the young proto-punk art student of the Hamburg days. Instead, the tragic art belongs to bassist Stu Sutcliffe, who went from being a piece of unnecessary Beatle furniture and latent Lennon lover to art martyr, dead in his twenties of an aneurysm. It hardly seems much of a loss compared to Lennon's death decades later, and appropriately *Backbeat* only comes alive when Hart is on screen. Curiously, both films speculate on the possibility of Lennon being at least semi-gay, using the biopic strategy for varying subtle what-if scenarios. Hardly scandal-mongering, both films do this with genuine sensitivity, and if the proposition has little basis in fact, the films still make up a text unique to the genre – mourning the loss of a rock star, and the universal youth he signified, by wondering aloud if at the beginning he was drastically different from how we remembered him, or very much the same.

But Lennon had already starred in his own biopic. What is *A Hard Day's Night* (1964) if not a semi-fictionalised version of the Beatles' lives? Few viewers then or now have bothered to recognise what an odd, metatextual creature Richard Lester's movie is, what with the Fab Four playing themselves – internationally worshipped pop idols named John, Paul, George and Ringo constantly besieged by fans and fame – ambling through life as if it were a Mack Sennett comedy. Sure, Babe Ruth played himself in *The Pride of the Yankees*, but that whole film was not structured around the bristling contradictions between biography, documentary and outright fiction. *A Hard Day's Night* could be, and is, all three, and may be the best biopic any rock star will ever get, in so far as it captures its protagonists at the height of their powers, gives them all the best lines and cancels any question of likeness or musical impersonation.

If so, what about *ABBA: The Movie*? What about Arlo Guthrie playing himself in his self-created folk tale *Alice's Restaurant*? Sonny and Cher in *Good Times*, The Monkees in *Head*, Bob Dylan in *Renaldo and Clara*, Prince in *Purple Rain*? What about the bizarre transformation from glitter rockers to superheroes in *KISS Meets the Phantom of the Park*? Or star-manipulated 'documentaries' like *Bring on the Night* and *In Bed with Madonna*? If not biopics *per se*, then surely films like these participate in the same current of cultural dreaming. In the mass consciousness, reality matters less than spectacle, and even the shrewdest of pop stars can get lost between the two. If they didn't, it wouldn't be rock 'n' roll.

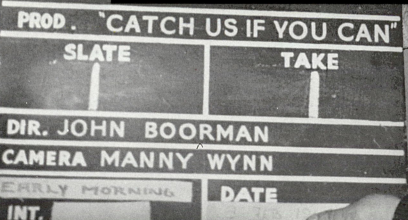

pop and film:
the charisma crossover

BRUTO

PROD. "CATCH US IF YOU CAN"

SLATE | TAKE

DIR. JOHN BOORMAN

CAMERA MANNY WYNN

EARLY MORNING | DATE

INT.

Three-minute Screenplay: Junction of Doom

Pontius Pilate (David Bowie) has been cryogenically frozen in a vat of Quaker Oats. He wakes, showers to rid himself of porridge residue and unzips a beautifully cut suit from its protective carrier. He puts the suit on, admiring himself in the mirror to the sound of Tina Turner's 'Private Dancer', and walks down a hotel corridor. The barman (Tom Waits) serves him a drink, accompanied by a wry observation on the fleeting nature of human love. The bell-hop (Sting) carries his luggage across the foyer, but Pilate does not tip him. He pays his bill in crisp notes, and the desk clerk (Madonna) gives him a sly look. Outside is a sweltering street in the Deep South. On the street corner, a madman (Mick Jagger) quotes from the book of Leviticus. A car pulls up – a small, battered family saloon, perhaps a Honda Civic. At the wheel is Elvis Presley (as himself). Elvis shifts into the passenger seat and Pilate gets in. The car pulls away, kangarooing slightly. The two men are looking for something, but they don't know what. The radio plays Millie's 'My Boy Lollipop'. At the first intersection, Presley and Pilate collide with a bus-load of famous actors. At the moment of impact, the camera focuses on the face of the driver (Cliff Richard). As the credits roll, Bob Dylan reads the Desiderata.

Ben Thompson

Sympathy for the folk devils:
Jagger in *One Plus One*
Cliff Richard in *Expresso Bongo*

There is no mystery about the mutual attraction between film-makers and pop stars. Big pop names will – in theory at least – supply both charisma and crowds, and films offer them the chance to appear multi-faceted at the same time as prolonging their working lives beyond the whim of teen allegiance. So why are the fruits of this apparently felicitous union so often the object of ridicule and contumely?

Sometimes the reason is obvious: pop stars get film parts for which their abilities as actors do not qualify them, and on the big screen there is no place to hide. But sometimes

Dave Clark, take five. John Boorman directs *Catch Us If You Can* (left)

the situation is more complicated than that. In-built hostility to celebrity overreach might stop us accepting someone in a film whom we have happily embraced on disc or on video. Feedback from one career to another can also be damaging. Even if Sting or Roger Daltrey were truly great actors, people would still hate them in films for their musical crimes. Madonna could star in the most erotic Hollywood film ever made, and commentators intimidated by her successful exploitation of her sexuality as a pop star would still claim, as they did about *Body of Evidence* (1992), that 'people laughed at her sex scenes'.

The two types of career do not share the same dynamic and, as Ringo Starr knows only too well, a ticket to ride in one world is not necessarily transferable to the other. A pop persona works in a different way from a film persona: it is more complete, which means it is harder to submerge, and keeps popping up at the wrong moment. When David Bowie is unconvincingly buried alive at the end of *Merry Christmas, Mr Lawrence*, the dramatic impact of his cruel demise is still more cruelly softened by thoughts of 'The Laughing Gnome'. This is part of the reason so few pop luminaries – Kris Kristofferson, Cher excepted – have ever made the transition to authentic film stardom, and this separation of identity has only been achieved at some cost to their credibility as musical performers. It's not that pop fame and film fame are incompatible, just that they interact in an extremely complex way.

A Brief History

Pop and film have been together from the beginning. In pre-pop 'race movies' starring Louis Jordan or, even earlier, Bessie Smith, the star crossover seemed perfectly natural. One of the first defining moments of rock 'n' roll came from film, as teenagers possessed by the devil rioted in the aisles to Bill Haley's 'Rock Around the Clock' over the credits of *The Blackboard Jungle* (Richard Brooks, 1955). By *The Girl Can't Help It* (Frank Tashlin, 1956), the rock 'n' roll cameo was established, as was the suitability of the burgeoning music industry as a case for film treatment – sympathetic or otherwise. It was only a short step for

pop stars to take lead roles. Not just Elvis but Tommy Steele, Pat Boone, Cliff Richard, Frankie Avalon, Adam Faith and others made it a standard career move in Britain as well as America.

From *Jailhouse Rock* (Richard Thorpe, 1957) to *G.I. Blues* (Norman Taurog, 1960), Elvis showed the way, as primal raunch was sanitised into social responsibility. But Cliff Richard, moving with deceptive ease from the hoodlum's brother of *Serious Charge* (Terence Young, 1959) to the budding entrepreneur of *Summer Holiday* (Peter Yates, 1963), was not far behind. The Beatles of Richard Lester's *A Hard Day's Night* (1964), however, were not using film as a stepping stone to respectability. 'I fought the war for your sort,' an irate commuter chides as they invade his railway carriage. Ringo Starr replies, 'I bet you're sorry you won.' Lester's flashy new visual style helped the Beatles move on to the next phase of their career, just as they were defining what it meant to be a pop group. Anything the Beatles could do, the Dave Clark Five could not quite as well, and in John Boorman's weirdly compelling *Catch Us If You Can* (1965) they confirmed the emerging truth that inferior pop stars make better film actors.

Elvis practises his primal raunch: *Jailhouse Rock*

Help! (Richard Lester, 1965) left the Beatles feeling like extras in their own film, so they made *Magical Mystery Tour* themselves. Shown on British TV at Christmas 1967, it elicited a profoundly unfavourable reaction. Paul McCartney defended it feistily – 'The Queen's Speech was hardly a gasser' – and added, 'It is better to be controversial than to be boring'[1] (a message he would have forgotten by the time he got round to making *Give My Regards to Broad Street*, 1984). On the other side of the Atlantic, *Head* (Bob Rafelson, 1968), the intended cinematic coming of age of ersatz Beatles, the Monkees, ensured itself eternal cult status by alienating an even higher proportion of its prospective audience.

Psychedelia broke up narratives and widened the generation gap, as well as nourishing the notion of rock star as Dionysian figure. This idea found its purest cinematic expression in the casting of Mick Jagger and David Bowie in *Performance* (Donald Cammell/Nic Roeg, 1970) and *The Man Who Fell to Earth* (Nic Roeg, 1976) respectively. In America, the rock 'n' roll and film industries huddled together in the fading embers of the counter-culture. James Taylor and Dennis Wilson broke the speed limit but no acting records in *Two Lane Blacktop* (Monte Hellman, 1971), Kris Kristofferson ambled out of the soundtrack of *The Last Movie* (Dennis Hopper, 1971) and into a starring role in *Cisco Pike* (Bill Norton, 1972), and Sam Peckinpah cast him and Bob Dylan in *Pat Garrett and Billy the Kid* (1973). Meanwhile David Essex gave Brit-grit a good name with *That'll Be the Day* (Claude Whatham, 1973) and *Stardust* (Michael Apted, 1974) but The Who (with a little help from Ken Russell) lost it with *Tommy* (1975).

The rock star as film *auteur* was never meant to be. Performers who remained true to flighty musical muses over the span of several decades proved unable to translate that spirit on to film. Neil Young's *Journey Through the Past* (1973) and *Human Highway* (1980) (both directed

pseudonymously as Bernard Shakey) and Bob Dylan's *Renaldo and Clara* (1978) all endure as landmarks of maverick hubris but little else. Bowie's inability to sustain a film career after the success of *Merry Christmas, Mr Lawrence* (1982) prefigured the inabilities of Prince and Madonna, the 80s megastars he influenced so much, to build on their twin triumphs, *Purple Rain* (1984) and *Desperately Seeking Susan* (1985). All three consoled themselves by excelling at promo clips, but however energetically they blurred the line between cinema and video, there was no getting away from their sense of themselves as matinee idols manqués. True matinee idol status was reserved for Whitney Houston, who resurrected her recording career and broke box-office and soundtrack sales records by playing a pop star in *The Bodyguard* (1992). This was a performance worthy of Elvis. As he was in *Clambake*.

The Stars Speak

Mick Jagger: 'Acting is just as natural as singing – you can either do it or you can't.'[2]

Tom Waits: 'Moving from music to films is like going from bootlegging to watch repair.'[3]

Elvis Presley: 'Just as soon as I could get out of those film contracts, I wanted to get back to live performance.'[4]

What The Big Bopper Might Have Said About It All If He Was Still Alive

Casting pop stars in films is like trying to catch a bird... They are themselves and not themselves in varying proportions. The identity confusions this promotes are often a source of frustration, but they can just as easily be fruitful and interesting.

Formerly known as Prince: *Purple Rain*

Background: *Head*

An officer always keeps his head: David Bowie in *Merry Christmas, Mr Lawrence*

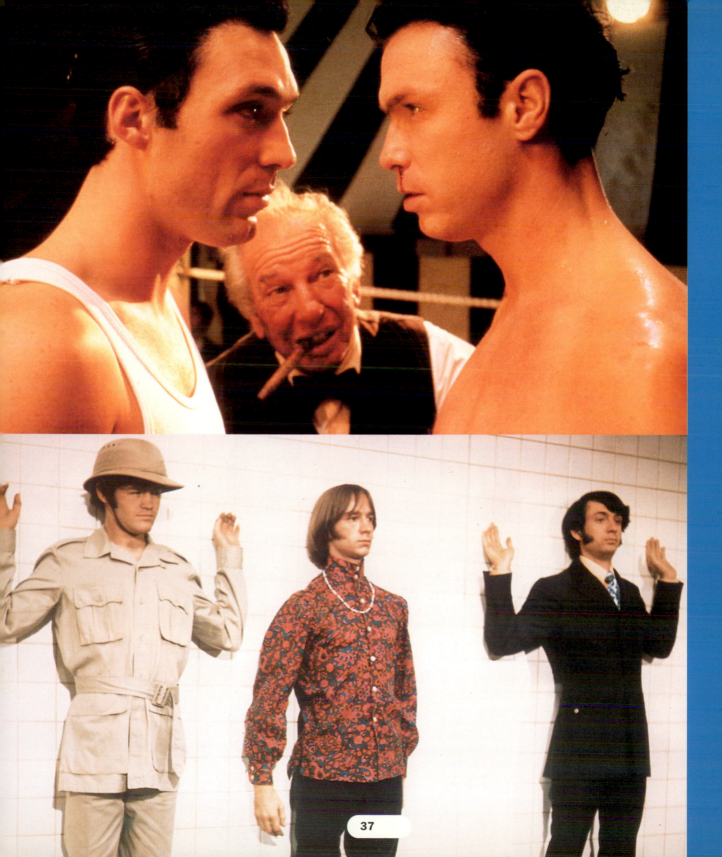

Brothers in harm: the Kemps as *The Krays*

They get the funniest looks from the people that they meet: the Monkees in *Head*

Four Areas of Intrigue

1. *The Age of Innocence*: There wasn't one. The cinema's idea of rock 'n' roll started out as cynical as it was ever going to get (the idea of a new branch of the entertainment industry more venal than itself was just too good to resist), and while films like *The Girl Can't Help It* often captured the excitement of early rock 'n' roll, they did so through a filter of condescension and contempt that would not really be removed (and then not for good – mentioning no names like Ken Russell) until Richard Lester met the Beatles. Compared with the ideas about the relationship between music's production and its consumption in *Expresso Bongo*, Malcolm McLaren's Svengali fantasies in *The Great Rock 'n' Roll Swindle* (Julien Temple, 1980) are the work of a playground innocent.

2. *Pre-pop film stars playing variants of a pop self not yet formed*: cf. Meat Loaf in *The Rocky Horror Picture Show*; David Essex, 'hitching a roller coaster ride in search of fish and chips and freedom' in *That'll Be the Day* and then meeting a dreadful end in *Stardust*; Hazel O'Connor in the criminally underrated *Breaking Glass* (Brian Gibson, 1980). Subsequent real-life pop careers were shot through (in Hazel's case, fatally) with memories of a celluloid preface. Where careers were well under way but move up a gear with cinematic assistance – cf. Jimmy Cliff in *The Harder They Come* (Perry Henzell, 1973), Prince in *Purple Rain* and Madonna in *Desperately Seeking Susan* – the serendipity can be spectacular.

3. *Aspirational Casting*: In which an established star or stars take a role because they want to tell us something, but end up telling exactly the opposite. Diana Ross as Billie Holiday in *Lady Sings the Blues* and Kylie Minogue as a bad girl with a heart of gold in *The Delinquents* spring to mind – the only message these two films got across was that their two stars were both surprisingly good at acting – but these transparent career moves pale into respectability compared to the Monkees in *Head*. In their desperation to prove that they were hip to what was happening in the psychedelic underground, the Monkees forgot that they were in fact a great pop group and buried themselves six feet down – 'Changing your image, darlings?' observed a passing waitress. 'And while you're at it, why don't you have them write you some talent?'

4. *Paying your dues*: The seeming modesty of a judicious blend of cameo and low-budget major roles can actually represent the ultimate in long-term status enhancement (if things go wrong, though, life can get ugly, especially if you are Adam Ant). Debbie Harry showed the way, but will never top her supreme cameo performance in John Waters' *Hairspray* (1988). The ultimate dues-payer is Tom Waits, whose bulging portfolio of drunkards and low-rent psychopaths has inspired a generation of rock character turns from Nick Cave to Lyle Lovett. For those with an eye to the main chance, John Waters, Jim Jarmusch and Robert Altman are directors to court. If Alex Cox calls, you're not in.

Rappers Annexe

No one seems to have a problem with rappers having film careers (the same applies to Country singers and the French). The relationship between what they do and what they are is subtly different from that of a conventional pop star: their day job is all about delivering lines anyway. When I asked LL Cool J about his role as Michael Gambon's son in Barry Levinson's *Toys*, he said, 'There's no growth in doing that [hip-hop characterisations], I *already* do that.'

Original gangsta: Ice-T in *New Jack City*

Ice Cube had already proved him wrong. His Doughboy in John Singleton's *Boyz N the Hood* (1991) was a remarkably successful translation of a musical to a screen persona. In establishing that black anger and corporate profit do not have to be mutually exclusive, rappers had facilitated the emergence of a new generation of black directors, so it was only fair that they should reap some of the benefits.

Ice-T has done this apparently without effort, but his establishment of a thriving career as an all-action hero (*New Jack City*, *Trespass*, *Surviving the Game*), after a shaky start in some terrible breakdance movies, has actually been an exemplary achievement. At a press conference in London in 1993, he told a rapt audience how it was done. 'I'm not an actor – I have absolutely no idea how to act – I just read the script. If the script says open the door, I open the door, and the director tells me how wonderful I am.' Asked how he chose his roles, and whether he was satisfied with them, he replied, 'Not being an actor by trade, I have the luxury of being able to pick which movies I do. So I try to do the kind that I'd go to see myself. I am not trying to do any super-dramatic stuff – you could give me a cool movie about something stupid and I might like it. I'm a B-movie fan; I like action movies, I like horror movies. I like shit that's not good. If I read a script and it says, "You're a schoolteacher but you might get an Oscar", I'm like, save that Oscar – I want to go shoot some shit up.'

Save That Oscar – I Want to Go Shoot Some Shit Up

It's not just rappers who make good criminals. The pop star/gangster interface is the exception to the general rule of charisma-cross opprobrium. Early identification between rock and roll stars and delinquency is probably a part of this. But shared outsider status and the common need to present a face to the world seem to enable even the least convincing pop stars to pass muster as celluloid gangsters. Phil Collins' *Buster* – the biopic of 'Great Train Robber' Buster Edwards – might have been reprehensibly sanitised, but that was what the film demanded, and

Spandau Ballet's Kemp brothers were memorably nasty in *The Krays*. Quasi-gangsterdom gave Elvis his best role in *King Creole* (1958); Kris Kristofferson got his big break as a reluctant drug dealer in *Cisco Pike*; and Jimmy Cliff produced one of the most electrifying performances in the whole pop film canon as Ivan, the reggae hopeful turned outlaw, in Perry Henzell's *The Harder They Come*.

Jagger and Richard

Performance made explicit the link between rock stardom and gangsterhood. Turner, Mick Jagger's rock star archetype, mingles identities over Notting Hill hallucinogenics with Chas, James Fox's East London gangster on the run. 'Comical little geezer,' Chas observes prophetically, 'you'll look funny when you're fifty.' Jagger's is one of the definitive rock star on film performances, and it is instructive to compare it with an earlier one: Cliff Richard's, as Bongo Herbert in Val Guest's *Expresso Bongo* (1959).

Both were London films, and both were controversial at their own time. *Expresso Bongo* revelled in its seamy Soho setting – the strip-club scenes passed the censors on the grounds of their 'documentary' style, and Laurence Harvey's dialogue as fast and sometimes dirty-talking manager Johnny Jackson was just too quick for them. The release of *Performance* was delayed for two years, because Warner Bros thought it was 'evil'. Jagger's is certainly an effectively louche personification of sensual licence. He carries off his blues song with great aplomb, and the 'Memo from Turner' sequence, in which he slicks up and invades the hood's life as an equal, is the best rock video of all time, eight years before such things were invented.

By Turner's own prescription – 'The only performance that matters is the one that achieves madness' – it is Cliff Richard's embodiment of manufactured teen idol Bongo Herbert that carries the honours. Cliff plays Bongo as a noble savage – 'I've got the rhythm, kind of natural like!' The unnerving blankness of his performance impressed people then as well as now. Isobel Quigley wrote in the *Spectator*, 'He is either such a clever actor that he actually persuades one he isn't acting, or else a boy of such transparent and alluring simplicity that the whole of *Expresso Bongo* has rolled off him like water off a duck's back.'[5]

All around him is infectious cynicism (Wolf Mankowitz was said to have toned down some of the dialogue from his original stage play, but this film is still the nearest there is to a British-set *Sweet Smell of Success*). The barbs just keep on coming – 'Recordings, variety bookings, why, he'll even open up shoe shops for cash'; 'A chip on your shoulder, an H-bomb in your pants – it's you against the world, baby, and the world loves you for hating it' – but Cliff refuses to be stung by them. His resolute asexuality in all his dealings with mildly predatory love interest Yolande Donlan is kookier and more disturbing than anything Mick Jagger and Anita Pallenberg can cook up for James Fox in *Performance*. 'Bongo is under age,' someone tells Jimmy Jackson. 'To me,' he replies, 'he looks all of a sudden very grown-up.'

**Individuals and Community –
In Praise of Oncoming Vehicles**

The charisma-swap debate tends to focus on questions of individual identity, but collective crossovers can be just as intriguing. The Ramones in *Rock n' Roll High School*, for example – driving down Fifth Avenue, eating chicken vindaloo – are not 'acting' in any sense other than that in which they always are, but theirs is still a pivotal film performance. And anyone who has seen the semi-legendary robot replicants scene in Hanna

Barbera's *KISS Meets the Phantom of the Park*, in which a mad scientist tricks a theme park full of kids into accepting, nay embracing, an inauthentic KISS, will have been forced to think long and hard about the divide between fantasy and reality.

In *Take It or Leave It*, Madness play themselves in their early days. The impact of this shockingly honest saga of instrument and record theft, fare-dodging, fights and musical incapacity is somewhat mitigated by the fact that some members of the band appear to be struggling not to laugh, but there are still some poignant insights into the development of a group identity ('You said we were playing up here in the bedroom, not out in the poxy garden').

The mother of all nuts-and-bolts portrayals, however, is Slade's in *Flame* (1974). The story – of a group plucked from working-men's-club obscurity and groomed for stardom by a suave London executive (played by a young Tom Conti with a disturbing hint of Al Pacino), only to break up quickly under the pressures of fame – is a basic one. But the background of cramped dressing rooms, unsavoury canal tow-paths and squalid pirate radio station interiors has the pungent whiff of authenticity, and the band's collective acting performance is a triumph of West Midlands naturalism. Rarely, if ever, have the uncomfortable

Cliff Richard's resolute asexuality is kookier and more disturbing than anything in *Performance*

Flame (right and background)

truths of most pop and rock lives – if you've got drums you're the drummer, if you've got a van you're the roadie – been so clearly and compellingly on display.

Slade in Flame: Noddy Holder – Eye-witness Testimony

'Originally it was our manager, Chas Chandler's, idea. He'd always planned our career in stages, and once we'd had success with records and touring he thought it would be a good idea to do a film. We got quite a lot of scripts in. There was a rough draft for a spoof of the Quatermass films – *The Quite a Mess Experiment* it was going to be called – that was quite funny, but Dave Hill, our guitarist, wasn't quite into doing it at all because he got eaten by a triffid in the first reel. And because none of us had any acting experience we thought it would be best if we were a band, so in the end we decided to go more for a documentary approach.

'The director Richard Loncraine and the writer Andrew Birkin sent a script which was not really what being in a band was like, it was more like people that weren't in a band's idea of what being in a band was like. But they came with us for several weeks on our American tour and learnt about our backgrounds. We told them stories about ourselves and other bands and they amalgamated them into a script, so Flame was a cross-section not just of us, but of a lot of bands at the time. Everyone had these experiences with crooked promoters, small-time managers etc. Although we were thought of as a 70s band, we set the film in the late 60s because that was the time when all this sort of thing was most rife. The characters they wrote were basically our characters – the names had been changed to protect the innocent – so we didn't really have to act.

'When the film came out, I don't think people knew what to make of it. Everyone expected a slapstick sort of thing – lots of costumes and running about with speeded-up film – but we'd obviously taken it seriously and tried to give a realistic picture of how things were. We wanted to make a real nitty-gritty, down to earth, working-class movie. There were some good actors in it too, Kenneth Colley, Tom Conti – it was his first film.

'The critics were very nice about it. Even Barry Norman gave it a good review on *Film 74*. But the fans were a bit baffled because we didn't give them the glamour. It wasn't all tomfoolery in the dressing room; there were some very heavy scenes, and a lot of it was filmed heavier than it came out because we were worried about getting an X certificate.'

Unfortunately, what remained was still too close to the proverbial bone for the fans and *Flame*'s critical kudos never translated into commercial success. Sadly, a later project involving Zucker and Abrahams, The Two Ronnies, Slade and a plot which sounds strangely similar to the former team's later *Top Secret!*, came to naught. With the benefit of hindsight, what does Noddy Holder think of *Flame*? 'Well, the last time I watched it – on Channel 4, about six years ago – I thought, "Bloody hell, this is quite good".'

Moral: You can either be a bit less than yourself, a bit more than yourself or exactly yourself.

Motto: 'All you need to succeed in this business is one success after another!'[6]

NOTES

1. Alex Hendry and Douglas Marlborough, 'Show Was Mistake says Beatle Paul', *Daily Mail*, 28 December 1967.

2. Anne Nightingale, 'Jagger – They Take Their Frustrations out on Me', *Daily Sketch*, 8 July 1969.

3. David Schiff, 'Tom Waits and his Act', *Rolling Stone*, October 1988.

4. Madison Square Garden press conference, 8 June 1972, released on *This is Elvis: Original Motion Picture Soundtrack* (RCA/Victor, 1981).

5. Isobel Quigley, 'Funny and Musical', *Spectator*, 4 December 1959.

6. Wolf Mankowitz, via Laurence Harvey, in *Expresso Bongo*.

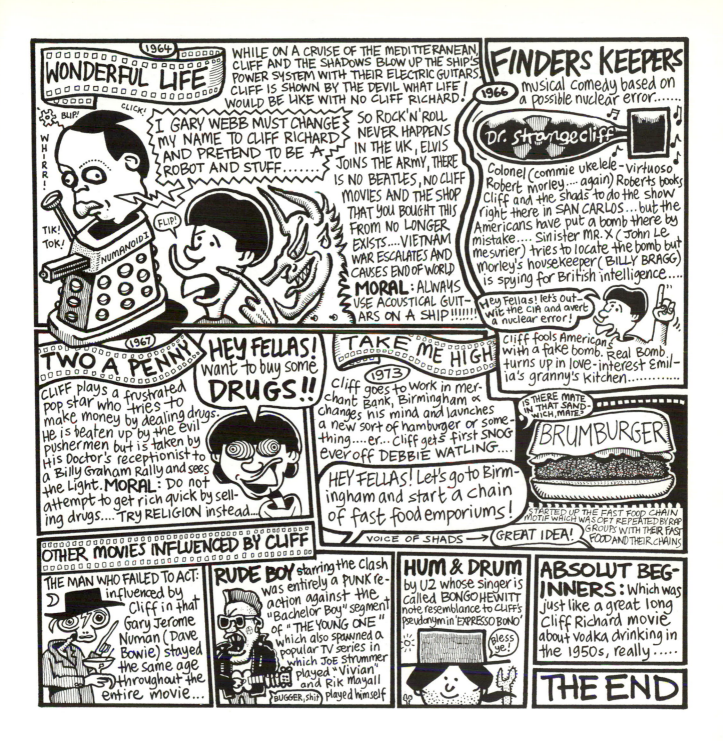

WONDERFUL LIFE — 1964

WHILE ON A CRUISE OF THE MEDITTERANEAN, CLIFF AND THE SHADOWS BLOW UP THE SHIP'S POWER SYSTEM WITH THEIR ELECTRIC GUITARS. CLIFF IS SHOWN BY THE DEVIL WHAT LIFE WOULD BE LIKE WITH NO CLIFF RICHARD!

BLIP! CLICK! WHIRR! TIK! TOK! FLIP! NUMANOID!

I GARY WEBB MUST CHANGE MY NAME TO CLIFF RICHARD AND PRETEND TO BE A ROBOT AND STUFF......

SO ROCK'N'ROLL NEVER HAPPENS IN THE UK, ELVIS JOINS THE ARMY, THERE IS NO BEATLES, NO CLIFF MOVIES AND THE SHOP THAT YOU BOUGHT THIS FROM NO LONGER EXISTS....VIETNAM WAR ESCALATES AND CAUSES END OF WORLD **MORAL**: ALWAYS USE ACOUSTICAL GUITARS ON A SHIP!!!!!!!

FINDERS KEEPERS — 1966
musical comedy based on a possible nuclear error.......

Dr. Strangecliff

Colonel (commie ukelele-virtuoso Robert morley.... again) Roberts books Cliff and the shads to do the show right there in SAN CARLOS... but the Americans have put a bomb there by mistake.... Sinister MR. X (John Le mesurier) tries to locate the bomb but morley's housekeeper (BILLY BRAGG) is spying for British intelligence....

Hey Fellas! let's out-wit the CIA and avert a nuclear error!

Cliff fools Americans with a fake bomb. Real Bomb turns up in love-interest Emilia's granny's kitchen.............

TWO A PENNY — 1967

CLIFF plays a frustrated pop star who tries to make money by dealing drugs. He is beaten up by the evil pushermen but is taken by his Doctor's receptionist to a Billy Graham Rally and sees the Light. **MORAL**: Do not attempt to get rich quick by selling drugs.... TRY RELIGION instead...

HEY FELLAS! want to buy some **DRUGS!!**

TAKE ME HIGH — 1973
Cliff goes to work in merchant Bank, Birmingham & changes his mind and launches a new sort of hamburger or something....er... Cliff gets first SNOG ever off DEBBIE WATLING....

HEY FELLAS! Let's go to Birmingham and start a chain of fast food emporiums!

VOICE OF SHADS → GREAT IDEA!

IS THERE MATE IN THAT SANDWICH, MATE?

BRUMBURGER

STARTED UP THE FAST FOOD CHAIN MOTIF WHICH WAS OFT REPEATED BY RAP GROUPS WITH THEIR FAST FOOD AND THEIR CHAINS

OTHER MOVIES INFLUENCED BY CLIFF

THE MAN WHO FAILED TO ACT: influenced by Cliff in that Gary Jerome Numan (Dave Bowie) stayed the same age throughout the entire movie...

RUDE BOY starring the Clash was entirely a PUNK reaction against the "Bachelor Boy" segment of "THE YOUNG ONE" which also spawned a popular TV series in which Joe Strummer played "Vivian" and Rik Mayall played himself

BUGGER, shit!

HUM & DRUM by U2 whose singer is called BONGO HEWITT note resemblance to CLIFF'S pseudonym in 'EXPRESSO BONO'

bless ye!

ABSOLUT BEGINNERS: Which was just like a great long Cliff Richard movie about vodka drinking in the 1950s, really.....

THE END

as above, so below:
30 years of underground cinema and pop music

A Black Day for Mankind

Kenneth Anger always considered movies evil, famously describing the day that cinema was invented as 'a black day for mankind'.[1] Anger's *Scorpio Rising* (1963) marks probably the first significant collision of experimental film-making with the so-called scourge of the twentieth century: Pop Music. *Scorpio Rising* is informed by juvenile delinquent and rock 'n' roll-themed commercial B-movies, a trend that began in the mid-50s when film producers wised up to the market force of teenagers.[2] Anger juxtaposed several benign pop tracks with a devilish montage of swastika-sporting, drug-snorting biker boys and biblical movie clips, creating an anarchic collage that simultaneously revered and yah-booed the orthodoxies of both film and music. For example, Kris Jensen's heartbroken song 'Torture' (plus the sound of an animal screaming) informs images of a bespectacled type (*à la* Piggy from *Lord of the Flies*) being sadistically debagged by his gang at a Walpurgis night party, intercut with clips of Christ seemingly looking on.

Anger's film also anticipates the direction of youth-oriented movies, which favoured the ever-more sensational subjects of Hell's Angels[3] and drugs[4] during the mid to late 60s. Because of its homoeroticism and some extreme imagery, *Scorpio Rising* was practically unshowable in public during America's panic-stricken 60s;[5] and so at this point, rather than being absorbed by the mainstream, the movie fed back into the underground, where it set a precedent for the use of pop music in experimental film-making.

Notes on the Underground and the Mainstream

If the mainstream is a place dominated by conformity and commerce, then the underground is theoretically its alternative, a lawless space for countercultural experimentation in literature, art, fashion, music, cinema and sexuality. But does this mean that the models of the underground are any different from those of the mainstream? Some of the distinctions and similarities are as follows:

While the mainstream promotes popular culture, the underground is exclusive, producing cults with relatively small but vociferous followings.

In the underground, the personal is political and experimental work is often overtly autobiographical. It is also in a perpetual state of flux, unlike the mainstream, which advocates closure. Underground work characteristically cross-references between mediums: literature; art; theatre; fashion; dance; politics; film; music. The underground demands a specialised knowledge and shared appreciation of its various sources, which can combine like the eclectic jumble of a teenager's bedroom in a frenzy of cult references.

For better or worse – and usually for commercial reasons – music stars have long brought their pre-tested appeal to film as actors. One of the most significant similarities between mainstream and underground is the maintenance of a star system, incorporating both actors and directors. The underground version of the star system is ironic, informed by both exclusivity *and* the concept that anyone can be an actor, musician, director, artist.

Cross-overs between underground and mainstream occur in the independent sector, when an individual 'defects', is appropriated, or when an alternative movement is absorbed by the establishment.

This essay charts the relationship between underground film and pop music across the thirty years following *Scorpio Rising*, showing how the aesthetic of experimental film became absorbed in the commercial industries of pop videos and music television, but identifying a source of sustained opposition to the mainstream.

Jane Giles

The Blank Generation

In the same year as *Scorpio Rising*, Antony Balch made the hallucinatory experimental short *Towers Open Fire* in collaboration with William S. Burroughs. Balch's later *The Cut-Ups* (1967) is a more overt cinematic equivalent of Burroughs' literary technique, with a hypnotic soundtrack by Brion Gysin. Balch's films mark the influence of drugs on experimental film aesthetics; B-movies were also then occupied with mind-expanded visuals and backed by garage music, the authentic underground sound of America.[6] Towards the late 60s, Kenneth Anger's films became more overtly mystical and used experimental music soundtracks. *Invocation of My Demon Brother* (1969) employs the relentless sound of Mick Jagger's Moog synthesizer, while the incarcerated Bobby

Beausoleil (with his Freedom Orchestra) provided the music for one of the versions of *Lucifer Rising*. Although *Scorpio Rising* is a landmark film, montage did not become the dominant form in music-oriented underground film-making. It was Andy Warhol's blankly fascinated cinematic portraits that set the East Coast scene. Whereas Jean-Luc Godard intercut rehearsal footage of the Rolling Stones with dramatised revolution scenes in *One Plus One* (also known as *Sympathy for the Devil)* (1968), Warhol's unblinking documentary *The Velvet Underground and Nico* (1966) stares in fan-like wonder for seventy minutes at the enigmatic band rehearsing.

A heritage of juvenile delinquency, garage music's aesthetic, the instant star appeal of glam rock, pop art, folk devils and moral panics, informed *the* subculture of the 70s: punk. A snot-nosed kid brother to the political and aesthetic Situationist movement of the late 60s, punk was quintessentially underground, an eclectic, polymorphous, perverse

movement that cross-referenced music, art, politics, clothes and the moving image. In 1976, the Sex Pistols played at the Screen on the Green cinema in Islington, supported by the Clash and the Buzzcocks plus the films *Scorpio Rising* and *Kustom Kar Kommandos*. Several New Wave bands used a backdrop of film projected during their performances: Cabaret Voltaire famously adopted a split screen (industrial films showing to the left, hardcore pornography to the right) while Throbbing Gristle opted for one of their own movies, the devastating *After Cease to Exist* (Coum Transmissions, 1976), in which an acolyte succumbs to castration at the hands of TG singer Cosey Fanni Tutti. Punk was a force that said anyone could be a musician. Or a movie star, or a film-maker. This is a common enough narrative theme, but, free from the tyranny of so-called talent, punk seemed to be genuinely breaking down the barriers between performer and audience.

Like Warhol, Derek Jarman had long been documenting the flaming creatures of his milieu on Super 8, when he filmed the Sex Pistols at Andrew Logan's St Valentine's Day party in 1976. Julien Temple prepared for *The Great Rock 'n' Roll Swindle* by shooting *Sex Pistols Number One* and *Sex Pistols Number Two* on Super 8. Don Letts' *Punk Rock Movie* was also shot on this format, which aesthetically captured the feeling of the movement. Most punk films of this period were documentaries; concentrating on live music footage, the sensationalist subject matter seemed to preclude the need for a story, while the movement itself was rapidly changing and resisted definition. Just as impresario manager Malcolm McLaren had suckered EMI into coughing up advances for the Sex Pistols' music, which duly charted, *The Great Rock 'n' Roll*

Brian Jones in *One Plus One*

The Clash in *Rude Boy*

Swindle (1979) was produced with funds from major film companies Warner Bros and Twentieth Century-Fox; the film had a commercial release with relative box-office success. As punk influenced and became absorbed by commercial industries, the *cinéma vérité* documentaries gave way to feature films that fell within the independent production and distribution sectors and employed conventional narrative structures.[7]

Superstars

Warhol's films developed from anthropological gazing to campy fiction, influencing the work of Amos Poe and the New York underground film-makers of the early 80s. Echoing Warhol's stable of superstars, punk characters and actors appeared in films that were not usually about the movement itself, but fictionalised the exhausted hysteria of a generation washed out after the New Wave. The much sought-after star of this scene was the Lounge Lizards' enigmatic saxophonist John Lurie. Blessed with wasted looks and a desirable, drop-dead cool attitude, he personified the movement. Lurie featured in *The Offenders* (Beth and Scott B, 1979), *Permanent Vacation* (Jim Jarmusch, 1980), *Underground USA* (Eric Mitchell, 1980), *Subway Riders* (Amos Poe, 1981) and Jarmusch's influential *Stranger than Paradise* (1984), co-starring Richard Edson, drummer for Lydia Lunch's band Teenage Jesus & the Jerks and Sonic Youth. Although he took a leading role in Rachel Amodeo's nostalgic, low-budget *What About Me?* (1993) alongside Dee Dee Ramone, Richard Hell and Johnny Thunders, Edson – like Lurie – also became a familiar bit-part actor with appearances in mainstream films.[8]

Such was the 'fate' of several other outsider stars.[9] Europe's independent sector embraced Nick Cave, the emaciated post-punk vocalist with an intimidating Lydonesque stare whose star quality was immediately apparent to a generation of intense young men. Cave made his film debut in the startling prison drama *Ghosts ... of the Civil Dead* (John Hillcoat, 1988), contributing music, dialogue and a show-stopping performance as the psychotic

inmate Maynard. (In contrast, Cave's role as an albino rock star in Tom Di Cillo's *Johnny Suede* (1991) marked one of those embarrassing bad-choice lows of his career.) Then resident in Berlin, Cave and his new band The Bad Seeds performed his song 'From Her to Eternity' in Wim Wenders' *Wings of Desire* (1987).[10] Uli M. Schuppel's *The Road to God Knows Where* (1990) is a straightforward on-the-road tour movie, doggedly tracking the Bad Seeds in the style of the fan's-eye documentaries of the early 80s. Cave's only work with underground rather than independent film-making has been his participation with Blixa Bargeld, Yello's Dieter Meier and Nina Hagen in *Dandy* (Peter Sempel, 1988), a dated, feature-length experimental film which seems to sap the energy of its subjects.

Cinema of Transgression

The New York underground scene of the mid-80s seemed energised; the Super 8 scene was liberated by the accessibility of video as both a shooting medium and a format for alternative distribution. The work of a number of post-punk film-makers constituted a 'Cinema of Transgression' – a wave of taboo-breaking experimental cinema with cutting satirical humour and extreme visions of sex or violence. The titles alone of Nick Zedd's *Geek Maggot Bingo* (1983), *They Eat Scum* (1985), *Whoregasm/I Shit on God* sum up the spirit of the movement. Richard Kern's intelligent, provocative short films exemplify this 'Cinema of Transgression'. Collectively known as the 'Deathtrips', they range in style from *Stray Dogs* (1985), a straightforward black comedy in which writer David Wojnarowicz plays the anti-social fan of a suave painter, to the orgiastic *Submit to Me Now* (1987). Kern frequently collaborated with post-punk musicians such as Sonic Youth, Jim Thirlwell, Henry Rollins and Lydia Lunch.

Lunch had previously worked with underground film-makers Beth and Scott B on the controversial *Black Box* (1978), a visually near-impenetrable study of sexual terrorism. Lunch co-wrote and acted in two films for Kern, *The Right Side of My Brain* (1984) and *Fingered* (1986). These operate around cycles of female abuse and violent relationships, with Lunch as both the victim and the victimiser who supplies a quasi-poetic explanation to the visual horrors. Lunch is exceptional in her uncompromising resistance to the mainstream (or its resistance to her), continuing to work prolifically within alternative production, exhibition and publication contexts, while remaining unable to find backing for her feature script *Psychomenstrum: The Case of the PMT Murders*. Kern is also unable to find a niche within the commercial sectors – his slick, sensationalist, ironic style has been by and large rejected by the pop promo market.

Promos

In the UK, the 80s saw the emergence of the New Romantic movement, which had a strong influence in both music and film. But while Derek Jarman's films occupied a central position in the subsidised production, distribution and exhibition sectors, the early Super 8 works of Steve Chivers, Cerith Wyn Evans, John Maybury and Holly Warburton were barely seen. Although this work now constitutes an undocumented gap in the underground, its Gothic, glossy style fed easily into the twin commercial forms of pop promos and advertising. Promotional music films had existed in some form since the 30s, but the format was reinvented in the 80s following the emergence of music television and video, where new technologies were in the hands of a generation of directors familiar with the key titles of avant-garde film-making.

With every type of band now making promotional films, several independent record labels set up their own film companies. The US label Ralph Records had set a precedent, specialising in challenging avant-garde music films, such as the Residents' *Third Reich and Roll* (1978) and *Hello Skinny* (1980). In Britain, Mute Records set up a film division to handle their

A Resident

48

promotional needs and address the growing video market for concert films. Mute's *Halber Mensch* (Sogo Ishii, 1985) is an imaginative coalition of experimental film and music in which a spatial and conceptual environment is created for the industrial noise of Einstürzende Neubauten. Mute's alternative label The Grey Area pioneered soundscapes and led quickly to the creation of Fine Line, a dedicated soundtracks division dealing in the film music of composers such as Simon Fisher Turner and Mick Harvey. Out of Josh Collins' UK Toe Rag music studios, and nightclub The Fratshack, have come no-budget video-distributed short films such as *The Vengeance of Voodoo Annie* and *Hot Carumba* (1993). All their films feature Toe Rag bands, such as the Slingbacks and the Easy Lays, but are the irreverent antithesis of pop promos. Influenced multifariously by comic books, the sexploitation shorts of Irvin Klaw and Harrison Marks, *Carry On*, Hammer horror and the skinny budgets of Troma Inc., Collins' demented movies hark back to the first films of John Waters, eschewing art and commerce in favour of fun and shock value.

The Gay Punk Sensibility

Like Anger, Warhol and Jarman, John Waters and Pedro Almodóvar emerged from the underground having immortalised their outrageous friends in Super 8 shorts and no-budget 16mm features. These film-makers share what can be seen as a gay punk sensibility, an anarchic 'bad taste' aesthetic informed by their sexuality. John Waters' glam-trash-garage movies of the early 70s are proto-punk par excellence; in *Pink Flamingos* (1972) Divine infamously competes for the title of 'filthiest person alive' by eating dog shit. A 25-stone tranvestite disco diva, Divine liberated the screen for performers such as the transsexual singer Jayne (formerly Wayne) County, infamous for such punk anthems as 'If You Don't Want to Fuck Me (Baby Fuck Off)', who featured in Rosa von Praunheim's *City of Lost Souls* (1983). Pedro Almodóvar became active in the *movida*, the Madrid avant-garde of the late 70s, and shot his sensationalist Super 8 short *Fuck, Fuck, Fuck Me*

Tim in 1978 while performing with his punk group Almodóvar and [Fabio] McNamara. The band can be seen performing 'Suck It to Me' in Almodóvar's feature *Labyrinth of Passion* (1982).

Derek Jarman's low-budget *Jubilee* (1978) was the UK's first punk feature; with a keen sense of history, the film dramatised the anarchic politics, sensibility and sexuality of the movement. Jarman continued to collaborate with musicians, filming the shorts *Broken English* for Marianne Faithfull (1979), *TG: Psychic Rally in Heaven* (1981), *The Queen is Dead* for the Smiths, and a video commission for the Pet Shop Boys' stage show. Like Anger, Jarman also had an enduring fascination with Magick – or, as Aleister Crowley described it, 'the science and art of causing change to occur in conformity with the Will'.[11] Jarman's medium-length experimental film *In the Shadow of the Sun* (1972-80) pushes Super 8 images of ritual to abstraction through an optical printer and uses a hypnotic soundtrack specially composed by Throbbing Gristle. By the late 80s, TG had become Psychic TV; Dave Lewis uses their music in his paganish short films *Dead Cat* (1989), which features Derek Jarman and Genesis P. Orridge, and *The Wanderer* (1990). In 1994 Lewis helped complete Jarman's final film, *Glitterbug*, a montage of Super 8 fragments exemplifying the hoarding, diary-like quality of underground work which clashes frame against frame and creates an excess of meaning.

Supposedly laid-back and anti-commercial, the grunge music of the 90s has informed a string of lifestyle features that remain unpolished but teeter willingly the way of the establishment.[12] However, grunge's sister, Riot Grrrl music, has spawned its own teenage underground superstar, Sadie Benning. Daughter of avant-garde film-maker James Benning, Sadie made the idiosyncratic Pixelvision technique her own, using the Fisher Price toy film camera which produces grainy images within a black border. Edited

Edited on video, Benning's clutch of no-budget experimental shorts are like personal diaries stuffed full of dolls, desire and death

on video, Benning's clutch of no-budget experimental shorts are like personal diaries stuffed full of dolls, desire and death.[13] Aesthetically, Benning's work brings us full circle, intimately connecting with *Scorpio Rising* via Derek Jarman. Her films have a dense, fragmentary structure of both sound and image.

Benning admits that she has watched MTV for as long as she can remember: 'I've been sucked into it most of my childhood. It has really helped a lot of my generation to see imagery in a totally different way. Kids my age have been so bombarded with images they have less patience and have become more like timebombs.'[14] She inflects meaning into found footage, for example by erotically charging the scene in which a malevolent Patty McCormack strokes her mother's face (in the film *The Bad Seed*), extracted in *It Wasn't Love*. Pop music is used ironically (a cross-dressed Benning pictures herself lip-synching to Fats Domino's 'Blueberry Hill') but also sincerely, as she thrashes around to her beloved Riot Grrrl music (Bikini Kill *et al.*). And crucially, Benning's highly personal films are informed by her queer sexuality. But despite being the toast of the festival and experimental circuits, Benning seems to shun not only publicity but also the feature budgets being offered to her by even like-minded independent production companies. While Anger developed 'a case of enormous, petrified, extremely sour grapes over the subject of Hollywood',[15] Benning sees it as a place where people are watered down, and dedicates her films to 'Bad Girls Everywhere', to people like herself.

What differentiates the underground from the mainstream is not so much its embrace of cultural diversity and the clashing of these forms, or even an extremity of subject matter. In the age of MTV, where every other pop promo looks like an underground film montage, what counts is the tenacity of the outsider who works against cultural assimilation and against compromise. It is therefore unsurprising that the work of greatest resistance should be that informed by a gay sensibility. The work of Kenneth Anger, Derek Jarman and Sadie Benning is not just outside of the mainstream, but constitutes the cutting edge of experimental film-making. Each one has used their counterparts in music to inflect and underscore the dense, fragmented and intensely personal imagery of films which work to challenge conformity and effect change.

NOTES

1. Quoted in Tony Rayns, 'Lucifer: A Kenneth Anger Kompendium', *Cinema*, no. 4, 1969.

2. Such as *The Blackboard Jungle* (Richard Brooks, US, 1955); *Untamed Youth* (Howard W. Koch, 1957); *High School Confidential* (Jack Arnold, 1958); *"Beat" Girl*, also known as *Wild for Kicks* (Edmond T. Gréville, 1959).

3. Hunter S. Thompson's book *Hell's Angels* was published in 1966; films of this genre include *Wild Angels* (Roger Corman, 1966); *Hot Rods to Hell* (John Brahm, 1966); *Devil's Angels* (Daniel Haller, 1967); *Born Losers* (Tom Laughlin, 1967); *Hell's Angels on Wheels* (Richard Rush, 1967); *Easy Rider* (Dennis Hopper, 1969).

4. For example, *The Trip* (Roger Corman, 1967); *Riot on Sunset Strip* (Arthur Dreifuss, 1967); *Psych-Out* (Richard Rush, 1968); *Head* (Bob Rafelson, 1968); *Wild in the Streets* (Barry Shear, 1968).

5. *Scorpio Rising* was banned for obscenity in several states of the US, along with Jack Smith's *Flaming Creatures* and Jean Genet's *Un Chant d'amour*, and exhibitors of the uncertificated prints were prosecuted.

6. For example, *Psych-Out* (Richard Rush, 1968) features music by the Strawberry Alarm Clock and The Seeds.

7. Such as *Rude Boy* (Jack Hazan, 1980); *Rock 'n' Roll High School* (Allan Arkush, 1979); *Out of the Blue* (Dennis Hopper, 1980); *Order of Death* (Roberto Faenza, 1983); *Repo Man* (Alex Cox 1984); *Suburbia or The Wild Side* (Penelope Spheeris, 1983); *Sid and Nancy* (Alex Cox, 1986); *Straight to Hell* (Alex Cox, 1987); *Dogs in Space* (Richard Lowenstein, 1986).

8. John Lurie appears in *Paris, Texas* (Wim Wenders, 1984), *Down By Law* (Jim Jarmusch, 1986) and *Wild at Heart* (David Lynch, 1990). Edson appears in *Desperately Seeking Susan* (Susan Seidelman, 1985), *Do the Right Thing* (Spike Lee, 1989) and Oliver Stone's *Platoon* (1986), among others.

9. Former New York Doll David Johansen camps his villainous way through *Freejack* (Geoff Murphy, 1992) with Mick Jagger, while Black Flag's Henry Rollins is cast against type as a cop in *The Chase* (Adam Rifkin, 1994) and the cyberpunk movie *Johnny Mnemonic* (Robert Longo, 1994). Since Jarmusch's *Down By Law*, Tom Waits has also lent his 'sensitive alcoholic' image and gravelly voice to *Bram Stoker's Dracula* (Francis Coppola, 1992) and *Short Cuts* (Robert Altman, 1993).

10. While his use of the Bad Seeds perfectly caught the spirit of mid-80s Berlin, it is ironic that Wenders never used the most influential avant-garde German musicians of his time, Kraftwerk (whose 1977 hit 'Autobahn' was surely some sort of soul-mate for Wenders' road movies). Wenders was largely enamoured of *non-German* alternative music, and later commissioned songs from Cave for the soundtrack-heavy *Until the End of the World* and *Faraway, So Close!*

11. Quoted in Tony Rayns, *op. cit.*

12. For example, Richard Linklater's *Slacker* (1991) and *Dazed and Confused* (1993); Cameron Crowe's *Singles* (1992); *Clerks* (Kevin Smith, 1994); and *Reality Bites* (Ben Stiller, 1994).

13. *Me and Rubyfruit*, *Living Inside* (both 1989), *Welcome to Normal, Jollies* (both 1990), *It Wasn't Love* and *Girlpower* (both 1992).

14. 'Girls, Videos and Everything': Sadie Benning profiled by Cherry Smyth', *Frieze* 8, January/February 1993.

15. 'Dedication to Create Make Believe': Kenneth Anger interviewed by Tony Rayns, *Time Out*, no. 91, 1971.

from blaxploitation to rapsploitation

Kodwo Eshun

The era of the blaxploitation movie was brief – roughly, from 1971 to 1974 [1] – yet it produced legendary soundtracks that still dominate our aural memories of the 70s. The musical presence of *Shaft* and *Superfly*, for example, completely overshadows that of other, more lauded genres of the period such as the road movie, the conspiracy thriller and the white vigilante flick. Lesser known soundtracks, such as Marvin Gaye's score for *Trouble Man* (1972), James Brown's for *Black Caesar* (1973) and Earth Wind and Fire's for *Sweet Sweetback's Baadasssss Song* (Melvin Van Peebles, 1971) have become cult classics, little heard yet much feted.

Part of the reason for this was that chart writer/producers such as Isaac Hayes and Curtis Mayfield were scoring entire films for the first time. Hayes, for instance, could extend the symphonic arrangements he was already working with on his 1969 album *Hot Buttered Soul* into the open territory offered by the film score. Working with arranger Johnny Pate, Mayfield turned his previously gospel-driven harmonies into a string-suffused music for *Superfly* (1972). The music swathes the film's anti-hero Priest as if he were walking inside the scenario set up by Mayfield's falsetto vocal. His songs, hovering above pizzicato violins and weeping guitar lines, are like invisible second films, options that Priest cannot take. This kind of score had more in common with John Barry or Ennio Morricone than with the jittery jukebox economy of *Mean Streets* or *The Harder They Come*. Because of its own success, blaxploitation proved to be the exception rather than the rule in the black music soundtrack.

By 1976 producer-writer Norman Whitfield had foregrounded the jukebox principle in the radio intercom that programmes the music for Michael Schultz's *Car Wash*. Disco heralded the birth of DJ culture. The soundtrack fragmented into diegetic snatches heard in car radios, parties, nightclubs. Where theme tunes had once sprawled through entire films, now they could be heard only during the closing and opening credits. By the 80s, the film score came in two parts – a signature track written by a major rap producer, and the rest of the score arranged as unobtrusively as

possible by composers such as Herbie Hancock or Michel Colombier.[2]

This polarisation is a far cry from the music-led sequences popularised by blaxploitation, such as *Shaft*'s famously relaxed saunter through Times Square. The chikka-chikka guitars are like strobe lights, and the sliding horns are at once sirens and aural zoom lenses. They relieve Shaft of his cop status so that he's free to walk through Harlem as a regular guy. Where the fast edits and close-ups of a film like *Trespass* (Walter Hill, 1992) brutally restrict rap to tinny snatches from a car radio, in blaxploitation even the swiftest chase sequence lingers and dawdles, subordinated to the score arrangements. Strings play right to the last note, fading out slowly only after a series of dramatic crescendos.

As Greil Marcus points out in his book *Mystery Train*, all blaxploitation films were an answer to Coppola's *The Godfather*. For the soundtrack to *Black Caesar*, James Brown dramatically expanded his usually compressed funk, tempering the harsh polyrhythms of his band the JBs with arpeggios that suggested dynastic fate. In its title, plot and lead role, *Black Caesar* played like a brilliantly contorted rerun, right down to lines such as 'Every time you speak Sicilian, it's like you're in a dubbed-in movie.' It was the archetypal exploitation movie, in fact, and Brown's music played an integral part.

Tommy Gibbs, played by Fred Williamson as the Godfather of Harlem aka the Boss aka Black Caesar, speaks Sicilian with the energy of the excluded. He double-crosses the Mafia for the right to exploit the area. He steps out on the Harlem streets dressed in a top coat and flat-brimmed hat, flanked by his guys. People

Richard Roundtree (left) in *Shaft*

nod, exchange glances. Guitar riffs strike up, flicking back and forward. 'Ain't it cool to be the Boss,' James Brown yells on the soundtrack, anticipating the crowd's response. The clipped yet gentle percussiveness of the guitars interlocks with languid brass punctuation, creating an inexorable forward movement, as if destiny is with the Boss.

When the theme comes up again it is scathingly severe. Williamson comes out of Tiffany's with a present for his former best friend's wife and crosses a busy street in the afternoon sun. A blind man bumps into him, shooting him through the waist. Suddenly the camera is twenty floors up, looking down at him; then it returns to street level, and as Williamson turns, the camera wheels with him. On the soundtrack the horns take off, chasing each other in a fluid vortex, lifting as he collapses. The action hovers, suspended as the brass section strafes this stumbling guy. Then the guitars return, but this time they're rolling over him, crushing him. The same lines, 'Ain't it cool to be the Boss', return, but now Williamson is surrounded by uptown shoppers, nearly all white, who stare shocked as he clutches his stomach. 'Look at me/Know what you see?/You see a bad mutha!' goes

the song; damned by the riffs that celebrated him, Williamson staggers into an achingly slow screen death. Eventually he is stoned to death by some kids who do not recognise him; his epitaph is the crashing drums and the screams of James Brown singing, 'And you try hard and you die hard and no one really gives a good damn.'

While Brown relaxed his usual throttle-choked riffs, Marvin Gaye's score for *Trouble Man* (Ivan Dixon, 1972) went the opposite way, suspending the aerial, sepulchral soul of his 1971 LP *What's Going On* into a hollowed-out, cavernous space of reverbed strings. On the sleeve to the *Trouble Man* album, Gaye thanked the Motown Engineering Department for their 'immeasurable electronic excellence'. The film's hero Mr T drifts through in a series of dispassionate errands, while Gaye's wordless sighs blend into mentholated Moog refrains. Years ahead of their time, these synthesizer passages were the most dramatic example of Gaye's experimentation during the early 70s.

In *Black Caesar*, James Brown had used flugelhorns and bassoons for a sense of dynastic flourish. More dramatically, Maurice White of Earth Wind and Fire scored *Sweet Sweetback's Baadasssss Song* (1971) as a scorching duel between gospel and

Car Wash: Antonio Fargas (left)

jazz, the sacred and the secular, heaven and the street. White's rippling pools of doubled-up electric piano were the aural analogues of slow-motion photography, dragging Sweetback's feet as he limped through the orange and yellow solarisations and reverse superimpositions with which Van Peebles psychedelicises the Watts district.

Usually cited as the first blaxploitation movie, *Sweet Sweetback* plays like a barely updated slave narrative, with its hero running from the cops, out of Watts and into the Mexican desert. Even though he gets away from the cops, a vengeful swarming chorus of gospel voices keeps up with him, mocking him fiercely. The film uses a conventional prodigal son motif, which the gospel undertones of Mayfield and Willie Hutch's score for *The Mack* (Michael Campus, 1973) also acknowledge. Director-star Melvin Van Peebles played Sweetback as a virtually mute hustler for hire, a Passive Macho type closer to the protagonist of Warhol's fatalistic *My Hustler* than to the predatory desperation of *Superfly*'s Priest or *Black Caesar*'s Tommy Gibbs. The snarling Earth Wind and Fire chorus supplies what some early critics naively saw as purposeful radicalism and also anticipates the criticism which would rain down on the genre it launched.[3]

If *Sweetback* signals the start of the blaxploitation wave, then Michael Schultz's 1976 *Car Wash* heralds its end and the beginning of Disco. The straight life which blaxploitation's anti-heroes dreaded even more than the Law here returns with a vengeance. The ghetto has shrunk to a concrete forecourt and hustling is as outmoded as militancy. Setting up an intercom radio in the forecourt,

Norman Whitfield, ex-Motown producer of The Temptations' psychedelicised soul (the label's last *auteur*, after Gaye and Wonder), synched the film's soundtrack to the playlist of radio DJ 'The JB', which programmes the Deluxe Car Wash routine. *Car Wash* sometimes feels like an allegory of Motown behind the scenes, with the buffed cars standing in for assembly-line pop manufacture. The post-Philly sheen of Rose Royce's theme tune is Motor Town music on the verge of a metronomic mutation, poised between the steady beat of MFSB and of Giorgio Moroder's Donna Summer productions. The assembly line of Motown pop is about to be superseded by post-Fordist robotics and drum-machine time. Hence the truculent despondency of Rose Royce's chorus 'Work and work and work...'. *Car Wash* hears its own redundancy in disco. When the character Hippo sells his most prized possession, his transistor radio, for sex, the film is looking forward to another passion which will weld the boombox to the MC in a furious declaration of rap as teen identity. Nine years later, in Schultz's *Krush Groove* – an exercise in instant self-mythologising by the Def Jam rap label – the 17-year-old LL Cool J will gatecrash an audition, scream 'Box!' and throw down a vicious version of 'I Can't Live without My Radio'.

Krush Groove parodies the fear of obsolescence which haunts *Car Wash* by having Run-D.M.C. rapping instead of working properly; they play their box in church, only to be told by the pastor, 'It's a lot of screaming noise. It's not a record... And what's this I hear about you two quitting your jobs at the car wash?' In 1976 the weeping guitar and rimshots of Rose Royce's 'Disco Dance' are as much ergonomic regulator as a spur to

In *Car Wash*, the straight life which blaxploitation anti-heroes dreaded even more than the law returns with a vengeance

dancing. On the radio, 'The JB' has a George Clinton curl to his croon that points away from this fate towards the radiophonic pranksterism of Parliament's *Mothership Connection* album from the same year: 'The JB is rapping in your ear/The JB is not on your radio/Your radio is not really on/Too hot for ya!'

Rap's tautological pleasure in rapping for its own sake updates disco's love of dancing as its own reward. Def Jam reinvented the teenage time of antagonism by severing rap's connections to disco and aligning itself with rock. Run DMC open the film by declaring themselves the Kings of Rock, and their piston hammer beats inaugurate Year Zero for hip-hop. Out went the Marvel Comics drag of old school rapper Grandmaster Flash and in came the Reign of New Black Rock. *Krush Groove* owed more than one might expect to Prince's similarly self-mythologising *Purple Rain* (1984), but Prince's rock was the other side of Def Jam's, as frivolously, foolishly Royalist as the rap label was fundamentally and puritanically Roundhead. The one was faux metal, as critic Chuck Eddy would call it, a shiny stadium-buffed lite metal that couldn't be further from Hendrix's fluid phallic aqua frequencies. The other was rockdrill rigour and brutalism.

With his fanatic claim that he'd die without his radio, LL Cool J in *Krush Groove* had announced DJ culture; but Radio Raheem would embody it. Raheem, the first Boombox Martyr, would die for the sins of Duracell in Spike Lee's *Do the Right Thing* (1989). This is where volume returns to mark what Michel Chion calls 'territorial ambience'.[4] The film's setting, New York's Bed-Stuy district, was not a ghetto or a hood, but a fragile community. The Public Enemy track 'Fight The Power', which Raheem plugs himself into, is as schizophonically dense as Run-D.M.C. had been cavernous and sparse; Run-D.M.C. boomed, Public Enemy bombed. Raheem brought the noise that already crackled uneasily between Bed-Stuy's different 'ethnic' frequencies. The film's community DJ Mister Senor Love Daddy couldn't reconcile all these into his

'Radio We Love – Home of the Voice of Choice'. His hall of fame worked on what Benedict Anderson calls 'unisonant' time, invoking and hailing an imagined simultaneous community.[5] Raheem projects panic tempo. His radio is a warning and a shield, an incitement and a siren, defensive and provocative. *Do the Right Thing* multiplied James Brown's antiphonic gridlock (Public Enemy had taken their name from his anti-drug track 'Public Enemy No. 1') into hypervigilant awareness. (As a diegetic set-up, the use of radio in rap movies made blaxploitation's off-screen anthems seem dated. In his 1989 film *I'm Gonna Git You Sucka*, Keenen Ivory Wayans satirised that invisible off-screen music for the MTV age. In one scene, Jim Brown walks down the street, and a raggle-taggle of musicians, the band Fishbone, follows him playing a raw version of the *Superfly* theme.)

But hip-hop's hypercapitalist lust was still blaxploitation by other means. Where blaxploitation movies had characters overdosing on heroin, Wayans' film has them dying from an excess of gold chains, 'OG-ing' – which makes a link with Original Gangsterism. In *New Jack City* (Mario Van Peebles, 1991), these materialist appetites appear without the satirical slant Wayans gives them. Drawing on a variety of sources – *Black Caesar*, De Palma's 1983 *Scarface* and Abel Ferrara's hip-hop *noir* in *King of New York* (1989), Van Peebles refitted blaxploitation for the 90s. Ice-T's theme song was sharp, deliberately hollow. After starring in first-wave rapsploitation movies, Ice-T had reinvented himself as the heir to blaxploitation by sampling from Mayfield's 'Pusherman' (from *Superfly*) in 1988 and collaborating with him a year later. His 1990 album *OG (Original Gangster)* went on to affirm all the scenarios Wayans had mocked. And his

I'm Gonna Git You Sucka

theme for Dennis Hopper's *Colors* – which sampled John Carpenter's *Halloween* theme – had stepped into the kill-crazy heads of the Bloods and the Crips gangs with an understated articulation.

At blaxploitation's height, former sports stars such as Jim Brown and Fred Williamson, as well as the real pimps who played themselves in *The Mack*, introduced a halting non-actors' delivery and a bitterly harsh edge that impressed the audience who would one day invent hip-hop as much as, if not more than, the films' music.[6] Similarly, Ice-T's impact in *New Jack City* is not so much in his theme tunes as in his presence as an actor, translating rap cadence into on-screen language, and revelling in his ironic casting against type as a cop. His articulation – emphatic, plosive and sardonic – now feeds back into material for other MCs.

New Jack City relocates Teddy Riley's 'new jack swing' music style into an uptown nightclub setting. Gang boss Nino Brown (Wesley Snipes), heir to De Palma's Scarface, throws a party at the Spotlite Club with Riley's group Guy performing in suits and flat-brimmed hats, while his 'family' watches from behind a one-way glass window.[7] Swing was returning to the initial meaning of 'new jack' that journalist and the film's co-writer Barry Michael Cooper had given it; Cooper saw swing's retooled R&B harmony as the soundtrack for smart crime, the music for an 80s upwardly mobile Reaganite aesthetic that left *Superfly*'s coke dealings looking prehistoric.[8]

Swing was now a corporate black pop. A year later, Damon Wayans' character in *Mo' Money* (Peter Macdonald, 1992) ditched a life of scams for one of office cons. As he swooped through carpeted corridors, Janet Jackson and Luther Vandross' 'The Best Things in Life are Free' played, a Jimmy Jam and Terry Lewis swing production that was speedy to the point of giddiness, its panicky euphoria underscoring 90s entryism. *Boomerang* (Reginald Hudlin, 1991), with its use of 'End of the Road' – a thirteen-week number one US hit by Boys II Men – made the same point for Eddie Murphy's upscale ad agency romance.

New Jack City brought back vocal harmonies that had only existed on screen in retro movies such as *The Cotton Club* (Francis Coppola, 1984) and *A Rage in Harlem* (Bill Duke, 1991). It was as if harmony created a space that Van Peebles' film could not otherwise conceive. In a self-contained interlude, Stevie Wonder's 'Living for the City' became an on-the-corner *a cappella* performance for the swing groups Troop and Levert; as the song progresses, the film moves seamlessly from spring to a winter blizzard. It makes a grandiloquent elegy for the hopes and hype of the new crack economy, and Wonder himself extended it further in the crack-house sequence of Spike Lee's *Jungle Fever*, which he scored in 1991.

But such highly choreographed sequences self-consciously harked back to the visual juxtapositions of blaxploitation, especially to *Superfly*'s six-way split-screen sequence. There the tributaries of coke were traced from manufacture to user, from Harlem through to the whitest parts of Manhattan, the frame splitting further at each step, while Mayfield's elegiac 'Pusherman' provided an ironic commentary.

In the New Jack Age, the very shape of soundtracks had changed. The long orchestral sequences that Hayes, Gaye and others had routinely composed for blaxploitation had shrunk to a single sequence. Ice-T's theme for *Colors*, and Dr Dre's for Bill Duke's *Deep Cover* (1992), each has its moment, then disappears until the closing credits. With the rap and swing industries vertically tied into soundtracks, songs are used in fragmented snatches heard in car radios and house party sequences. Hence the Bomb Squad's original score for Ernest Dickerson's *Juice* (1992) and Dr Dre's production and music supervision for 1994's *Above the Rim* work better on album than they do in the films.

Only the Hughes Brothers' 1992 *Menace II Society* tried to find a way round ending up as long-form music videos by factoring in all kinds of off-screen warps of sound – strafing noises, reverbed scratching, skids, engine whooshes – with no diegetic correlatives.

The sound here works much as it does in the action films of James Cameron, John Tiernan or John Woo, constantly pulverising the frame with the unsettling impact of unseen threats – stray shards of sonic danger in the air rather than in a locatable source. Perhaps *Menace II Society* shows how fragmentation might yield a new kind of soundtrack experience.

NOTES

1. See Jim Pines, *Criminal Records*, official programme to *Shots in the Dark* Festival, 1984.

2. In *Jungle Fever* (Spike Lee, 1991) and *Deep Cover* (Bill Duke, 1992), respectively.

3. See Ed Guerrero, *Framing Blackness* (Philadelphia: Temple University Press, 1993), pp. 87-103.

4. See Michel Chion, *Audio-Vision*, ed. and tr. Claudia Gorbman (New York: Columbia University Press, 1994), p. 87.

5. See Benedict Anderson, *Imagined Communities: Reflections on the Origin and Spread of Nationalism* (London: Verso, 1983), p. 30.

6. Hear, for example, Snoop Doggy Dogg's *Doggy Style* (Death Row/Interscope Records, 1994), which features a homage to the bubblebath scene from *Superfly*.

7. Here Van Peebles seems to be quoting a similar scene in Sergio Leone's *Once Upon a Time in America*. *New Jack City* directly samples *Sweet Sweetback* and De Palma's *Scarface* among others. The film itself is later quoted on the Nas track 'The World is Mine', from *Illmatic* (Columbia, 1994).

8. See David Toop on Barry Michael Cooper, in *Rap Attack 2* (London: Serpent's Tail, 1991), p. 181.

Deep Cover

it sort of happened here:
the strange, brief life of the british pop film

n recent years critics and academics have rewritten the history of British cinema, rediscovering previously neglected strands and genres like Gainsborough melodramas, Hammer horror and vulgar comedy and championing them against the old orthodoxies which valued documentary realism, literary adaptations and genteel good taste. The British pop music film, however, has as yet found few advocates. Everyone loves *A Hard Day's Night*, some are prepared to put in a word for the earlier Cliff Richard films, but beyond those well-worn paths lies uncharted territory. I confess that I began researching this piece harbouring secret fantasies of being that lucky explorer who returns with wild-eyed tales of fantastic hidden riches – perhaps *Dateline Diamonds* (Kiki Dee, Kenny Everett and the Small Faces in a pirate radio jewel-smuggling plot) or *The Ghost Goes Gear* (the Spencer Davies Group in a haunted house) would turn out to be lost masterpieces.

Alas, no. The British pop film has captivating moments – it would take a harder heart than mine not to revel in the lurid, cack-handed kitsch of *Gonks Go Beat*, which tells of the science-fiction-coated rivalry of Beatland and Balladisle and is also the only known film to team Ginger Baker and Arthur Mullard – but it is a genre largely composed of intriguing misfires and downright schlock. The reasons for those misfires are, however, very revealing, since the real value of the British pop film is the light it sheds on a culture in transition and transformation.

Andy Medhurst

What I want to do here is to use some specific British pop films (deliberately avoiding the overdetermined Cliff and Beatles films in favour of more symptomatic obscurities) to prise open the cultural tensions, contradictions and anxieties of the historical moments that produced them. The main focus will be on the late 50s and the mid-60s, since it's my contention that after those years pop and

cinema ceased to interrelate in any sustainedly meaningful way. There may well be interesting things to say about *Glastonbury Fayre*, Slade in *Flame* or (heaven help us) *Confessions of a Pop Performer*, and indeed I'll be making reference where relevant to films from the 70s and 80s, but after the mid-60s the pop film was at best only marginal to what remained of British cinema.

Prologue: Bad Timing and Grammar-School Hepcats

It's May 1956. Elvis Presley's 'Heartbreak Hotel' and 'Blue Suede Shoes' have just entered the British singles charts, inaugurating the modern world. A British film is released in which a youthful rebellion against authority is sparked off by popular music. Great timing.

Except that the film, *It's Great to be Young*, is not full of splendidly surly Teds fired up by Bill Haley and Elvis into havoc and mayhem, but instead concerns the painfully polite inhabitants of a suburban grammar school, who barricade themselves in the gym because the headmaster objects to them using the school orchestra to play the occasional slice of big-band jazz. Scrubbed and sexless, these are kids who wear their school uniform at weekends, who say 'twerp' and 'chump' and 'blighter', and whose main aim is to persuade the head to reinstate their jazz-loving music teacher, played as a living embodiment of elbow patches by John Mills – phew, such rebels.

Taken on its own terms, *It's Great to be Young* has a kind of blithe, fresh-air, consensual charm (it's very much a film of its time, a mid-50s comedy of compromise), but the fact that its release coincided with the eruption of Elvis points up one of the cruel, recurring truths of the British pop film. The production time needed for feature film production means that between conception and release a film can find itself horribly stranded by changes in the cultural landscape. In the light of the rock-and-roll revolution breaking out all around it, *It's Great to be Young* is irritatingly coy, indelibly conformist, irretrievably English. As its whiter-than-white kids go into their neutered jitterbug and sing, with a stunning lack of conviction, 'Rhythm is Our Business', you wonder if the British will ever be able to make a film which dealt adequately with the raw, erotic, seismic ecstasy of the new music.

The Late 50s: New Stars, Old Stars

Once Britain had begun to produce its own home-grown rock-and-rollers, once the market for such a thing was arguably established, the film industry was bound to muscle in, seeking its share of the teenage spending money which so excited and worried the sociological commentators of the day. The resulting films are tentative and confused, cinematically impoverished and musically ineffective, but they have a retrospective fascination as examples of British film and British pop trying to find some common ground – two cultural industries seeking an uneasy alliance, two sensibilities sniffing each other's hind

quarters, two constituencies never quite speaking the same language but carrying out a conversation nevertheless. Four of these earliest British pop films repay particular attention – *The Tommy Steele Story* (1957), *The Golden Disc* and *The Duke Wore Jeans* (both 1958), and *The Lady is a Square* (early 1959).

Tommy Steele was Britain's first pop star, in the Presley sense of the term, and *The Tommy Steele Story*, released with ferocious speed only eight months after his first hit record, was appropriately the first British pop film. To some extent, then, it had carte blanche to map out the new terrain, but what it was most concerned with was seeking to negotiate a space between its specific topic of British pop and two established film genres, the rags-to-riches biopic and the Hollywood musical.

As biopic, it sketches its hero's rise to fame, retelling the tale which Steele's ruthless managers had already circulated so assiduously through the press that it had taken on the status of modern urban myth. Bermondsey teenager Tommy learns the guitar during the boredom of a long illness, joins the merchant navy, discovers a knack for entertaining at sea, is offered work performing in a Soho coffee bar, is snapped up by an agent, has hit records and provokes a national outbreak of Tommy-mania. The tone is breathless and gauche, terms which equally well describe *The Golden Disc*. Here the star is Terry Dene, briefly Steele's rival as Britain's top pop pin-up, and though the narrative has less grounding in biographical fact, its trajectory is remarkably similar, as the pudgy and less-than-macho Terry climbs from coffee-bar attendant to chart-topper.

The Golden Disc has a particular fascination with the workings of the pop industry, Terry's stardom being sponsored by a group of older and conspicuously middle-class friends who open the coffee bar, a record shop and a record label in rapid succession. The naivety with which this is done is retrospectively laughable, but the fact that so much of the film is blatantly concerned with the economics of pop points to a broader cultural assumption – that pop

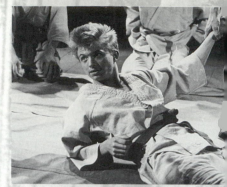

was a gimmick to be sold like the hula-hoop, that it had no intrinsic merits or deeper resonances, and needed only shrewd manipulative management to turn it into profit made from the dupes on the street. *The Golden Disc*, then, has almost Frankfurt School undertones, which will later become overtones with the filming of the satirical stage musical *Expresso Bongo* (1959). There the witless economic determinism of *The Golden Disc* blossoms into a fully-fledged conspiracy theory of rampant cynicism, as svengali agent Laurence Harvey transmutes idly pouting Cliff Richard into teen-dream Bongo Herbert. This exploitation narrative remains a strong thread in the British pop film, though many romantically conclude with the shyster manager thwarted and talent triumphant. Its belated finest hour came with *The Great Rock 'n' Roll Swindle* (1979), where the audience is asked to revel in Malcolm McLaren's hustling as the real success story of the Sex Pistols – *Expresso Bongo* with safety pins.

The Tommy Steele Story and *The Golden Disc* also share a common problem of genre: can this new music be accommodated within the traditional shape of the musical? Early Hollywood pop films faced similar dilemmas, the most graphic demonstration of colliding codes being the title number of *Jailhouse Rock*, where Elvis' primeval bump-and-grind is hemmed in by dozens of pseudo-convict chorus boys. The British films avoid such images, though this was due not so much to shrewd cultural decisions on the part of the film-makers as to the fact that the all too evidently minuscule budgets precluded elaborate production numbers. Besides, by centring the narratives on the processes of performance, numbers can be presented in relatively 'logical' terms – on stage, in the recording studio, with no need for anyone but the singers themselves to be there.

The Duke Wore Jeans was Steele's second film (produced, it's worth noting, by the team that were

Sid Vicious in *The Great Rock 'n' Roll Swindle* (photo: Tiberi June, 1978)

Svengali agent Laurence Harvey transmutes idly pouting Cliff Richard into teen-dream Bongo Herbert

simultaneously working on the first *Carry On* films) and is worth consideration for how it exemplifies the British pop film's stampede towards showbiz. If pop was a flavour-of-the-month fad, then how could its performers' careers be sustained? There's a beautifully telling moment in *The Tommy Steele Story* when Tommy's family hear that he is to undertake a tour of variety theatres – Tommy's mother's face is electrified with delight, awe and most of all relief. 'Variety!' she cries, thrilled and reassured that her son is moving into proper grown-up showbiz. *The Duke Wore Jeans* is the outcome of such a shift, since it is only on the merest nodding terms with late-50s pop, preferring to set Tommy in a Ruritanian mistaken-identity fantasy that is part Ivor Novello operetta and part Danny Kaye musical comedy.

It is, frankly, almost unwatchably bad, but its existence underlines the prevailing belief that longevity within pop was a contradiction in terms and that the way forward was the one marked 'all-round entertainer'. From later, post-Beatles vantage points, such a move could be mocked as a craven complicity with the establishment, and George Melly in his

Jiving, drivelling scum: *"Beat" Girl*

pop history *Revolt into Style* (published in 1970) does just that, identifying Steele's films as emblematic of what he calls the 'castration' of early rock 'n' roll; but in the late 50s any ideas of pop generating creative independence or rock as rebellion were hard to imagine. So Tommy strode into family entertainment, cheesy grin and architecturally improbable quiff intact, off on the road that led to *Tommy the Toreador* and *Half a Sixpence*.

The Damned, whose anti-social and simmeringly sexual challenges to authority are musically underlined, the beat-crazy kids evicted by David Farrar in *"Beat" Girl* with the treasurable line 'Get out of my house, you jiving, drivelling scum', and the rock 'n' roller who is one of the platoon in *Carry On Sergeant*, answering orders with 'I dig' – the creation of a new comic stereotype is always a pointer to significant cultural change.

Compared to *The Lady is a Square*, however, Steele's films still exuded a virtually Presleyesque subversiveness. *Square* (the abbreviation is carefully chosen) starred Anna Neagle, still gamely prolonging a career that had begun in the 1920s, as a benefactress of classical music horrified to find that her butler has a second career as a pop star. Worse still, he has designs on her daughter. All is resolved in a climactic concert where the bopping butler, played by the oleaginous Frankie Vaughan, follows his pop numbers with a rendition of a Handel oratorio. Once again, pop is a fad, good taste wins out, and Anna is so relieved that she even goes in for a spot of prim, condescending jiving at a post-concert supper.

The thrust of these early pop films is clear enough. Pop is OK as long as it can be moulded into an updated rise-to-fame, putting-on-a-show musical (with Tommy Steele as Mickey Rooney and Terry Dene as Judy Garland), but it's not a pastime for intelligent adults. Let's pretend it was just an amusing diversion and cream off its stars for a more grown-up showbiz career – to which direction the films themselves form a significant launching-pad. For any sense of subcultural threat, any hint that pop was proving an outlet for feelings too strong and too disquieting to be rechannelled into family fun or bought off by an indulgent smile from the likes of Neagle, you need to look beyond the pop film itself to see how music featured as an index of wider moral panics about youth. Space precludes considering these in detail, but key examples would include the teenage gangs in *Violent Playground* and

The Mid-60s: Which Way to Pop?

Pop, of course, outlasted the hula hoop, and thanks to the success of the Cliff Richard musicals, the potential profitability of the pop film was plain to see. The mid-60s saw a reckless profusion of British pop films, though many found themselves caught out by shifts in musical taste similar to that which had scuppered *It's Great to be Young*, and even though the once inevitable Steelean slide into showbiz could be increasingly refuted, most still found it hard to rid themselves of the long shadows of the Hollywood musical, for all its patent unsuitability in the context of pop's new thrills. The film which irrevocably sundered that connection was *A Hard Day's Night*, but in this section I want to look at a clutch of less celebrated mid-60s films which sought out various solutions to the continuing dilemma of how to put British pop on film.

What a Crazy World, released in July 1963, attempted to link pop with older cultural traditions without delivering it into the bland hands of mainstream showbiz. Set in the East End, and redolent of the theatricalised Cockneyisms of Joan Littlewood, it posits pop as the inheritor of music hall, casting popsters Joe Brown and Marty Wilde as street-wise London lads, carving out a space for fun and frolics in a world of street markets, council estates and dole offices. The intriguing possibility

Cliff hits the skins: *Expresso Bongo*

of a pop/music-hall connection (which Tommy Steele also intermittently explored) was that it opened up a potential space for a pop based on Englishness. That is, I acknowledge, a dangerous term, trailing behind it all manner of nationalistic and ethnocentric connotations, but it does help to locate *What a Crazy World* in a tradition that has sought to avoid second-hand Americanisms in favour of a pop that addressed more pertinently English structures of feeling.

The fact that it was released into the maelstrom of nascent Beatlemania meant that the film stood little chance of substantial success (Brown and Wilde were yesterday's men after the scorched-earth impact of Merseybeat), but *What a Crazy World* remains fascinating, a neglected thread in that strand of white pop Englishness which later wove

clearly, was to emulate the Cliff Richard musicals – lots of wide-screen colour, well-behaved heterosexual romance, sunshine and teeth – and consequently the male leads are John Leyton and Mike Sarne, well-laundered blond boys who had big hits a couple of years previously, while the girls all try to be Una Stubbs.

Fifty minutes into the film, however, Freddie and the Dreamers appear. Hardly the most radical exponents of mid-60s beat (and those of you following the pop/music hall connections should note that Freddie's entire act is based on Arthur Askey), they nonetheless connote an entirely different pop world from Leyton and Sarne, and in trying to hold the two together the film collapses. The concluding number (at that staple device of British pop films, the talent contest) goes even further, trying to yoke together a Cliff-like

Its original conception, clearly, was to emulate the Cliff Richard musicals – lots of wide-screen colour, well-behaved heterosexual romance, sunshine and teeth

itself from the Kinks and the Small Faces through the Jam and Madness to the Smiths and Blur.

A film caught out even more drastically by changing pop times was *Every Day's a Holiday* (October 1964). Set in a holiday camp where various clean-cut youths work as redcoats and waitresses, it's a film pulled apart by the strain of trying to reinvent itself during its actual period of production in an attempt to keep up with the volatile shifts in taste affiliation of the eventual target audiences. Its original conception,

love song, a Hollywood-musical rousing finale, and vocal and instrumental stylings filched via the Rolling Stones from rhythm-and-blues. It's horrible, but the film has an awful allure as a textbook demonstration of getting it wrong by trying too hard to keep up, of the slowness of film production outsmarted by the faster footwork of pop.

More convincing were two films starring the pre-*Blow-Up* David Hemmings - *Live It Up* (summer 1963) and *Be My Guest* (spring 1965). There's an interesting

The punk and the princess: Mike Sarne in *Every Day's a Holiday*

undertow of mod culture in these two, partly evinced by the time and trouble the scooter-riding Hemmings takes over his appearance, and made more concrete by the casting of Steve Marriott (imminently of the Small Faces) as a member of Hemmings' pop group. The earlier film is still unsure of its subcultural moorings, so the mod elements rub shoulders with the collarless Beatles jacket worn by another group member and the presence of the extravagantly peroxided Heinz, the homoerotically charged protégé of record producer Joe Meek, who wrote and supervised the music for the film. This collision of Meek, mod and Beatles (with some Shadows dance steps and Kenny Ball and his Jazzmen in post-Trad attendance) is then grafted on to yet another rags-to-riches plot, but the film has a shrewder grasp than most of its kind of that sheer sense of escape, of a youthful future, which pop offered to its devotees.

Be My Guest, mindful of the topicality of the mods and rockers riots, moves the same central characters to Brighton, though regrettably little is done with this fruitful location apart from the title song showering Beach Boys harmonies all over exhilarating shots of a car speeding along the seafront, and the moment where an excitable entrepreneur (organising the inevitable talent contest) proclaims, 'The Mersey Sound can move over, from here on in it's the Brighton Beat.' Otherwise, the recipe is much as before, though the styling is more unambiguously mod, and the luckless Heinz has been despatched. There's a standard plot of managerial duplicity versus youthful truthfulness, and it all winds to its expected conclusion of love and talent vindicated.

Neither film is in any way ground-breaking, but they do have a B-picture vitality, an unpretentiousness which keeps them fresh, full of numerous incidental pop-cultural pleasures of dress, dialogue and decor. The staging of the numbers stays rigidly conventional, however, the kind of static on-stage set-piece that was one of the many casualties of the new approach pioneered by *A Hard Day's Night*.

The first pop film to fully absorb the lessons of Dick Lester and the Beatles' breakthrough was *Catch Us If You Can*. It was released only a few weeks after *Be My Guest*, but its sensibility is that of a different era. The fact that the Dave Clark Five were less well-known and individuated than the Beatles curiously enhances the film's impact; they're more malleable, more usable as iconographic shorthand for the liberating jolt of nowness that permeates the film. The stock narratives and Rooney-Garland conventions that dogged the likes of *Be My Guest* are thrown away, the sociology of *What a Crazy World* vanishes in favour of pure semiotics. Even *A Hard Day's Night* had half a foot in kitchen-sink naturalism, but *Catch Us If You Can*, especially in its first startling thirty minutes, goes all out for the shiny plastic immediacy of the moment. It is, in short, where the pop film becomes the Pop film.

It is also, then, when the pop film assumes the marginal status that it will subsequently occupy. The sacrificing of narrative also meant the sacrificing of audiences, as the Beatles found to their cost with the bemused and hostile

response that greeted *Magical Mystery Tour*. Yet after this radical mid-60s break, there was no going back to the more accessible naiveties of *Live It Up* or *The Golden Disc*, not, that is, if the resulting films were to have any shred of credibility. The British pop film, in all its endearing awkwardness, was pretty much dead.

The most important reason for its demise, however, lay outside the specific formal evolution of the genre. The reason the pop film became surplus to requirements was that (and I should whisper this, given the subject-matter of this book) television always did pop better anyway. Pop TV had no need to try to shoe-horn the music into outdated formats, it had less rules to break and more freedom to move, it was quick, cheap and immediate, just like the music itself. The pop film was quicker than any other genre in poaching personnel and learning tricks from TV – the screen rhetoric of a film like *It's Trad, Dad!* (1962, Dick Lester's first feature) is entirely televisual – but its attempts to keep pace were doomed to failure. How could a film that took months to produce compete with the right-here-right-now buzz of *Ready Steady Go*? The truly cinematic option, the arty Pop Art knowingness kickstarted by *Catch Us If You Can*, led only to a declining spiral of self-referentiality and pretension, a hermetically sealed, gestural cinema that imploded into *Performance* – a key film of its times, to be sure, but scarcely worth five seconds of Mick Jagger singing 'Honky Tonk Women' on *Top of the Pops*.

Postscript:
Council-flat Travoltas and Postmodern Picaresque

Although I have just tried, with rather strenuous rhetoric, to bury the pop film in a mid-60s grave, honesty compels me to admit that the genre has limped on ever since. My general conviction, however, remains the same (with the possible exception of the punk films of the late 70s and early 80s), so I'll conclude with two snapshots of later films that bear out the arguments outlined above.

The Music Machine (1979) was the British *Saturday Night Fever*, and is the kind of film you think somebody must have made for a bet. It's a shameless return to cash-in

exploitation, a scandalously inept attempt to ride a trend, a woeful interweaving of inner-London laddish comedy, limp teen romance and wannabe-Americanisms, and I mention it here mainly for the way it so spectacularly shows that the old avenue of quick-buck pop film-making really cannot be opened up again. As such, of course, it deliciously feeds that desire for pop film kitsch that rather dried up after *Gonks Go Beat*, especially at the moment where the celebrity judge of the disco dancing competition is revealed to be Esther Rantzen. Beyond the confines of camp, though, it should be left to stand as an awful warning.

If *The Music Machine* was sheer folly, at least *It Couldn't Happen Here*, the 1988 film starring the Pet Shop Boys, was a *folie de grandeur*. It's the answer to two questions: firstly, is it possible to make a successful pop feature film in a pop

The Music Machine was the British Saturday Night Fever, and is the kind of film you think somebody must have made for a bet

video age, and secondly, what would happen if we continued the line of *Catch Us If You Can* up to the late 1980s?

The answer to the first question is, to be very English and very Pet Shop Boys about it, yes and no. Just as pop TV made the old-model pop film redundant, so pop video has now redefined the way we think about pop and moving images. To readjust our soundbite ears and channel-surfing eyes to almost ninety unbroken minutes of pop imagery is difficult and perhaps unwelcome – but in any case, *It Couldn't Happen Here*, for all its cinematic sweep, is a film that will always be seen primarily on tape, and its episodic structure makes it very easy to edit from the armchair, turning it into pop videos despite itself.

As for the second question, *It Couldn't Happen Here* not only clearly belongs to that tradition of non-narrative, sensibility-driven music cinema, but the eagerness with which it parades its lineage can become rather wearing. It's typically postmodern in the way it invites comparisons with and offers pastiches of other, older texts. You can tick the references off one by one – *Catch Us If You Can* and *Magical Mystery Tour*, of course; other iconic Pop Art texts like *The Prisoner*;

camp downmarket British culture signalled by the casting of Barbara Windsor and Gareth Hunt; slices of Jarman and slabs of Ken Russell; even (to slip into the pretentiousness the film so invites) the 1950s opera films made by Michael Powell. So picaresque, so knowing, so English. It's the film an art student with a taste for the melancholia of the seaside might make after going to a Peter Blake exhibition, but who would want to see it apart from her or his classmates?

The truth is that we simply don't have any use for pop films any more. They're like 78s in a CD world. Just think, if they had been a group of the 50s or 60s, Take That would already have been herded through their first full-length feature film, but now we can drool over their long-form videos instead – quicker, more convenient, freeze-frameable and with no demeaning over-extended stories for Mark, Robbie, Gary, Howard and the luscious Jason to half-heartedly enact. The pop film may not be dead, but it is terribly unnecessary. It no longer needs to happen here.

Dancin' fools: *Catch Us If You Can* (top), and *The Music Machine*

rock musicians and film soundtracks

David Toop

For pop musicians who have the skill to orchestrate moods within the pragmatic confines of commercial music, film scoring is a logical career development in the move from pubescent desires to broader adult themes. Scratch the surface of a film composer and there may be traces of the pop star, abandoned by the audience, or the composer/arranger who never wished to be (or never came close to being) a pop star in the first place.

But a major shift of emphasis takes place when a pop musician enters the film soundtrack world. Pop music is public. In most cases, a persona is required in order to 'present' the music to its market, and to varying extents persona and music can become indivisible. Film scoring is an invisible activity, however. Even composers as prolific, successful and publicly known as Ennio Morricone or John Williams have no 'personality' profile. Only by regular performing and television appearances can the soundtrack writer rise above cult magazines and industry recognition. For most film composers this is a perfect balance between commercial success and anonymity, but for reformed pop stars the need for a public persona may be too strong for film scoring to develop into a consistent career. Like a rock audience, the cinema audience is in the dark, but in the cinema the creators are nowhere to be seen.

The template of the pop star turned film composer was drawn by John Barry. With his band, the Seven, John Barry recorded his first single at the dawn of British rock and roll. 'Zip Zip', released on Parlophone in 1957, was a dinner-jacketed attempt to xerox the energy of American rock, yet for Barry popular music offered career potential rather than the short-term lure of celebrity. His mother was a classical pianist, his father ran a chain of cinemas in the North-East of England, so from an early age he was imbued with the dual training necessary for soundtrack composing.

As a boy, he made war with toy soldiers on the living room carpet, an underscore of Sibelius playing on the gramophone to set a mood. His understanding of the importance of mood to drama was evident in Barry's third single, 'Big Guitar'. A twangy guitar instrumental, this track was influenced both by the Duane Eddy sound and by a late 50s fashion for television Westerns.

A new piece of furniture for many British families during this period and a potent symbol of modernity, television was an important transmitter of early rock and roll. Through shows such as *6.5 Special* and *Drumbeat*, Barry's professionalism was channelled into an ability to write theme tunes as well as simple pop songs. After 'Big Guitar' he began to experiment with Latin and African rhythms, jazz harmonies, electronic instruments (the Clavioline) and his famous 'Stringbeat' arrangements, inspired by the Dick Jacobs string arrangements on Buddy Holly singles. By the early 60s, Barry was recording pieces such as 'The Challenge' and 'The Aggressor', both film music themes in spirit, lacking only a film to support them, as well as recording cover versions of actual film themes such as Elmer Bernstein's 'The Magnificent Seven' and Nino Rota's 'Rocco's Theme'.

He had also scored his first film, a flimsy youth culture period piece from 1959 starring Adam Faith (the teen idol frontman for much of Barry's early chart success) and Shirley Anne Field. The first musical score for a UK feature to be released in LP form, *"Beat"Girl* illustrates why Barry was destined for screen composing. Having paid for postal tuition with Stan Kenton's arranger Bill Russo, and heavily influenced by the experiment-lite of West Coast jazz, Barry was impatient to incorporate a broader sweep of musical material than the classic three-minute pop tune could support. 'I think I'm one of the few people who started off wanting to be a movie composer,' he has said. 'I think you'll find most movie composers drifted into it in a strange way. Because my father had eight cinemas and I was brought up from four years old on Mickey Mouse, it was something I positively wanted to do.'[1]

The Hot Spot

Yet retaining the pop band format of twangy guitar, bass guitar, drums, keyboard and horn section led to his lengthy career as a leading composer for Hollywood. Barry's arrangement of 'The James Bond Theme' for the first Bond film is still a gripping example of the art of orchestration. Although the story behind this composition has yet to be clearly explained, Barry's contribution of a single track to Monty Norman's score for *Dr. No* in 1962 was followed by an invitation to compose the entire soundtrack of most of the Bond films that followed. The gift for using simple, arguably Mickey Mouse elements to evoke dramatic tension was perfect for the high-camp, somewhat creaky techno-fetishism of the series. Despite the fact that Barry progressed to more

Performance

complex screen composing, some of his best moments have occurred in Bond scores (particularly *Goldfinger* and *You Only Live Twice*). The pragmatism of the bandleader looking for a hit single may be an unromantic antidote to the myth of pop inspiration, yet, as Barry himself is happy to admit, there are strong links between this necessary process and a film composer's subservience of personal desires to the requirements of the director.

A move from the backroom of pop to the Moviola, accompanied by flirtations with solo records and even pop stardom, has characterised

the careers of a number of pop musicians turned soundtrack writers. Jack Nitzsche, for example, collaborated with Sonny Bono, Lee Hazlewood and Phil Spector, all of whom contributed significantly (in Spector's case, spectacularly) to the evolution of recording studio techniques, unique arrangements and an original sound for 60s pop. Nitzsche took what he had learned, which could be described as a basic foundation in pop as art and sound as content, and applied the lessons to records by Jackie DeShannon, Buffalo Springfield and Neil Young. In 1968 he worked with Randy Newman on Cammell and Roeg's *Performance,* and later composed scores for *One Flew Over the Cuckoo's Nest* and *Blue Collar* (with director Paul Schrader pitching in with lyrics for the opening credits song, performed by Captain Beefheart), as well as supplying bought-in material for *The Exorcist* and writing basic guidelines, as if they needed them, for the diverse talents (Miles Davis, John Lee Hooker, Taj Mahal, Earl Palmer *et al.*) who played on Dennis Hopper's neo-*noir* feature, *The Hot Spot*.

Two of these scores are particularly interesting in this context. Both *Performance* and *Blue Collar* featured the slide guitar playing of Nitzsche's friend Ry Cooder. For *Blue Collar*, Nitzsche artfully used

blues and soul as an ambience, drawing out solo slide guitar passages into evocative atmospheres. This prefigured the kind of desolate, ambient blues that Cooder played in his own scores for a series of Walter Hill films during the 80s; the appealingly avant-garde mood music created with Jon Hassell and drummer Jim Keltner for *Trespass* (1992); and, most influential of all, his desert guitar soundtrack to Wim Wenders' *Paris, Texas* (1984). As for *Performance*, this included a song entitled 'Gone Dead Train', written by Nitzsche and performed by Randy Newman, another square peg in the music industry who moved into film composing with scores such as *Ragtime*, *The Natural* and *The Paper*.

The use of pop song as soundtrack was seen by Hollywood as a device to maximise the cinema audience and create a youth cinema to match the ascendancy of rock in the latter half of the 60s. There had been rock and roll films, surf films, biker films and any number of other genres which were propelled by a soundtrack of cameo performances and featured songs. Roeg stepped outside genre conventions, using rock songs to add deeper undercurrents to the narrative of a film which already defeated audience expectations.

One of the pioneers of this technique was Kenneth Anger. As the Jimmy Page score for *Lucifer Rising* and Mick Jagger's Moog music for *Invocation of My Demon Brother* demonstrated, Anger shared Roeg's awareness that rock stars and their music possessed an iconic significance in the 60s and early 70s that could gloss over poor acting or thin musical content. A sledgehammer of irony, Anger's deployment of pop tracks by Bobby Vinton, Ricky Nelson, The Crystals and others in *Scorpio Rising* (1963) inspired Martin Scorsese, and surely David Lynch, who later repeated and amplified Anger's choice of Bobby Vinton's 'Blue Velvet' as the utopian dream sound of suburban psychosis. In *Mean Streets* and *GoodFellas*, Scorsese used pop music as a Greek chorus, an off-screen commentary which gave the audience a clearer sense of passing time than his insulated characters and which indicated some intriguing links between the conservatism of romantic nostalgia and the capacity for violence.

You gotta have Faith: 'Beat' Girl

Cotton Comes to Harlem

This exploitation of songs as a subtext ran contrary to the straightforward use of songs as a line drawn under screen action. More typical were Paul Simon's wistful songs for *The Graduate* (1967), which provided Hollywood with the perfect prototype of pop/cinema synergy. The songs eased the audience through chunks of narrative and areas of emotion without further need for explication; if they were the right kind of songs, they gave viewers the feel-good mood that would generate a box-office hit; finally, they turned into hit singles and a best-selling soundtrack album, thus presaging the cross-marketed audio-visual products of Bryan Adams and Whitney Houston in the 90s. As *The Graduate* album sleevenotes made clear, 'Simon and Garfunkel express – in this picture score and independently in their music – those

'proper' composer. The job could also resolve some of the structural problems of pop stardom. Fashions in songwriting, arranging, instrumental performance and production techniques can change as quickly as the heel of a shoe or the width of a trouser leg. Success rarely lasts long, and after the adulation dies few pop stars manage to maintain a musical career at a level they consider anything more than humiliating. So film scores can be an escape route with potentially lucrative consequences and perhaps a few statuettes awarded as a mark of respect.

In this knowledge, most musicians blessed with sufficient talent and professionalism to compose scores on demand harbour ambiguous feelings about their good

Commissioned to score *Shaft*, Isaac Hayes created a sound that would influence action films for two decades

audible qualities of the young generation that have so far removed it from conventional American life as to create a recognized "gap".'[2]

In other words, pop and rock song soundtracks were just another aspect of Columbia's success in marketing youth rebellion. Just as Simon and Garfunkel could be found on the CBS Records *The Rock Machine Turns You On* compilations of the late 60s, so they were signed up to carry this exercise into the cinemas. For musicians, a composer credit on a movie conferred validation. This was as near as most rock stars would ever come to being a

fortune. Vangelis, for example, has downplayed his ability to write the type of *Chariots of Fire* melody that can lift banal sequences into a quasi-mythic realm, uplift audiences and send box-office receipts skyrocketing. His 1982 *Blade Runner* score, for example, is a schizophrenic mess of inspiration and cliché. Big romantic tunes sit at a glossily aloof remove from the dystopian drama played out on screen; only occasionally does Vangelis allow his music to be absorbed into the sound design to become the fourth world, lo-tech/hi-tech hybrid that the images and story demand. Understandably, though often regrettably, composers are reluctant to vanish into the texture (or wallpaper) of sound design. The hierarchical nature of film marketing already relegates them to a tiny credit at the bottom of the poster. For musicians who have already enjoyed the ego gratification of a rock or pop career, this reluctance to disappear can lead to some serious misjudgments of cinematic needs.

Within some genres, however, a less homogeneous musical approach enhances the dual nature of certain films as both self-contained works and carriers of pop products (hit singles, fashions, dance crazes, cameo appearances by pop stars, etc.). The so-called blaxploitation trend which swept Hollywood in the early 70s was typical in its creation of opportunity and nemesis. Launched in 1970 by Ossie Davis' film of Chester Himes' novel *Cotton Comes to Harlem*, the genre was defined the following year by a Gordon Parks film, *Shaft*. Isaac Hayes, composer of the *Shaft* soundtrack, had been one of the leading backroom talents at Stax Records during the 60s. A gifted pianist and saxophonist who could write hit songs, arrange and produce, Hayes broke out of the backroom in 1969 with an unusual album entitled *Hot Buttered Soul*. A platinum seller for Hayes, *Hot Buttered Soul* featured an eighteen-minute version of 'By the Time I Get to Phoenix' that was stretched into an epic. His narration underpinned by a sustained organ chord, Hayes addresses his audience: 'I want you to use your imagination, travel with me.' Finally, as he sings, brass, woodwinds and strings envelop the listener in a desolate mood of cinematic sugar.

Having propelled soul music into this zone of atmospherics, imaginative visualisation and a sensual indulgence in pain and pleasure, the next step for Hayes was film scoring.

Commissioned to score *Shaft*, he created a sound that would influence action films for the next two decades. Unlike the average jobbing soundtrack specialist, Hayes knew how to cater for the blaxploitation target audience of black youth. The chattering, metallic wah-wah guitar that he foregrounded so effectively in the theme song became a signal of urban drama, and in his opposition of funk drumming against lush flutes and strings, Hayes mapped a noir-ish vision of city life, a nomadic pursuit of sensuality through grime, stress and intoxicating speed.

The success of 'Shaft' as a hit single ensured employment for a tiny number of black stars. In the following year, Curtis Mayfield's score for *Superfly* was more consistent than the *Shaft* score. In the musically liberal milieu of the early 70s, Mayfield had begun to explore extended song forms and unusual arrangements; but unlike Hayes, who was prone to slip into by-the-numbers easy listening, Mayfield stuck close to his songs. During the few years before blaxploitation was displaced by Hong Kong martial arts films (which simply transferred blaxploitation music clichés to a kung fu setting), Hayes scored two more films – *Truck Turner* and *Three Tough Guys* – and artists ranging from Bobby Womack and Marvin Gaye to Donny Hathaway and James Brown were given a brief taste of the film composer's life.

Some of this music, particularly Marvin Gaye's haunted score for *Trouble Man*, could be compared favourably with the more mainstream work of these singers, and the influence of this flawed but enjoyable genre has resurfaced in the 90s. As the first sustained example of black cinema,

From psychedelia onwards, the adventurous end of rock and pop evolved into a kind of film music without film – the dreamscape of the unconscious

blaxploitation has been an inspiration to rapper-actors and hip-hop producers such as Run-D.M.C., Ice-T, Dr Dre and Ice Cube. Films such as *Colors* (1988), ostensibly scored by Herbie Hancock yet dominated by rap tracks, reintegrated the musical flavour of blaxploitation into young black music, and although no single composer has emerged to match Isaac Hayes or Curtis Mayfield, the soundtrack of a film such as *Above the Rim* (1994, supervised by Snoop Doggy Dogg producer Dr Dre) is a comprehensive cross-section of hip-hop and street soul in the mid-90s.

Listened to as a document, rather than a commercial product, the most intriguing album to emerge from the blaxploitation phase of the early 70s was director, composer and vocalist Melvin Van Peebles' soundtrack for his own film, *Sweet Sweetback's Baadasssss Song*. Released on Stax and featuring the music of Brer Soul and Earth Wind and Fire, the album jump-cuts across fragments of gospel, soul and street funk, incorporating snatches of dialogue and sound effects along the way.

From the late 60s, experimentation and fragmentation became endemic in popular music. From psychedelia onwards, the adventurous end of rock and pop evolved into a kind of film music without film – the dreamscape of the unconscious to which much twentieth-century art has aspired. If commercial constraints inhibited this trend, then film scoring offered opportunities to experiment further. As for directors, they could benefit from a star name as well as buying in music which was ambitious enough in its scope to work in the cinema yet non-specific enough to serve narrative. So, early in their career, Pink Floyd contributed to a number of insubstantial feature films, including Antonioni's *Zabriskie Point* (1969) and Barbet Schroeder's 1972 film *La Vallée*, set in Papua New Guinea, as well as releasing one of the earliest examples of the rock-band-in-concert movie distributed to high-street cinemas, *Pink Floyd Live at Pompeii* (1971).

From the mid-70s onwards, musicians as diverse as Brian Eno, Giorgio Moroder, Keith Emerson, The Grateful Dead and Tangerine Dream were exploring musical territory, mostly electronic, which suited both the vision and budget of a new generation of film directors and thus led to soundtrack work. In some cases, a mutual aesthetic emerged. Dario Argento's employment of keyboard showman Keith Emerson in *Inferno* (1980) opened up a world in which visceral horror and the masculine, adolescent infatuation with electronic angst were free to go forth and multiply.

For more serious potential, the Berlin LP collaborations (*Low*, *Heroes* and *Lodger*) between David Bowie and Brian Eno suggested a torrent of visual images which only needed an imaginative director to respond to them. When David Bowie wrote sleevenotes to support the CD release of his music for Hanif Kureishi's BBC2 adaptation of his novel *The Buddha of Suburbia* (1994), he acknowledged the importance of this working relationship: 'I should make it clear that many of my working forms are taken in whole or in part from my collaborations with Brian Eno.' Later, he uses his reflections on writing music for image to state a broader aim: 'My own personal ambition is to create a music form that captures a mixture of sadness and grandeur on the one hand, expectancy and the organisation of chaos on the other.' That, give or take a detail or two, encapsulates the challenge of composing for the big screen.[3]

As the sleevenotes of a Rykodisc album, *The Apocalypse Now Sessions: River Devils Play River Music,* explained, 'In search of the missing percussive underscore for the soundtrack to *Apocalypse Now*, Francis Coppola attended a Grateful Dead concert at the invitation of Bill Graham, and found inspiration in the music of drummers Mickey Hart and Billy Kreutzmann. This meeting of musicians and filmmaker provided the final link for Coppola's musical accompaniment to his cinematic vision of the Apocalypse.'[4] Once again, film gave scope for adventure

Apocalypse Now

John Lone in *The Last Emperor*

to already marginal figures who risked being sidelined into oblivion in an increasingly rationalised music business. The sheer scale and vision of a film such as *Apocalypse Now* demanded a music without constraints. Once the family unit of the rock band was no longer strong enough to support the diversity of available choices, so a move sideways into the visual realm was inevitable. A gift for establishing mood was particularly valuable to directors who were searching for an alternative to the intensive underscoring of more traditional film composers. So, Brian Eno scored films for the late Derek Jarman, contributed to David Lynch's *Dune* and, with his brother Roger Eno and producer Daniel Lanois, created a marvellously strange fusion of ambient electronics and country music for the space-programme documentary *Apollo*. From the glare or shadows of various pop projects, rock stars Peter Gabriel, Eric Clapton, Prince, Mark Knopfler and David Byrne, Police drummer Stewart Copeland, saxophonist John Lurie, electro-boffin Thomas Dolby, session keyboard player Harold Faltermeyer and oddballs such as Tom Waits, Graeme Revell, Enya and Nick Cave stepped into the soundtrack composer role.

Out of all these musicians, Ryuichi Sakamoto, former keyboardist for the Yellow Magic Orchestra (and occasional screen actor), and the Greek keyboardist and composer Vangelis have achieved the most consistent success in scoring for mainstream films. Perhaps the soundtrack is a job for an outsider, an observer, a technocrat, a musician educated in all disciplines, a pragmatist. Yet for Sakamoto, a very real tension existed between his image and his musical ability. Offered an acting role opposite David Bowie in Oshima's *Merry Christmas, Mr Lawrence*, he accepted on condition that he could compose the score. The same line of bargaining was taken when Bernardo Bertolucci wanted to cast him in *The Last Emperor*. In return for playing updated equivalents of Sessue Hayakawa's tormented Japanese officer in *Bridge on the River Kwai*, Sakamoto demanded the opportunity to fill Maurice Jarre's shoes as a purveyor of epic, romantic music for epic, romantic film – a role which led to a difficult, though continuing, partnership with Bertolucci on *The Sheltering Sky* and *Little Buddha*.

As with Graeme Revell, whose music for films such as *Dead Calm* or *No Escape* seems to have come from a different planet from the industrial nausea aesthetic of his old band SPK, there is a sense in which Sakamoto is writing self-consciously for the neo-romantic demands of mainstream cinema at its most conventional. But the transition from his relatively autocratic role of pop producer to becoming an endlessly manipulated functionary within the movie machine has proved problematic. 'Some people say it's too sweet,' he protests when discussing his theme music for *The Sheltering Sky*. 'It is sweet but I didn't choose. I gave Bernardo three or four demos of themes and he chose. It's not my fault.'[5]

Working within the often fraught dynamics of a music group is notoriously hard to sustain; yet compared with the fragmented, pressured task of interlocking into a feature film schedule and acceding to the demands of directors, producers and studios, a career in pop can seem a paradise of simplicity. 'Making films is very, very difficult generally,' says Sakamoto. 'Post-production is very difficult. When I can have simple direction it lets me work much easier, but it's not always like that. We're confused sometimes in our mind.'[6]

Ryuichi Sakamoto

NOTES

1.   John Barry, personal interview with author.

2.   Sleevenotes, *The Graduate* (CBS 70042).

3.   Sleevenotes, *The Buddha of Suburbia* (Arista 74321 170042).

4.   Sleevenotes, *The Apocalypse Now Sessions* (Rykodisc RCD 10109).

5.   Ryuichi Sakamoto, personal interview with author.

6.   Ibid.

access all areas:
the real space of
rock documentary

N ostalgists frequently hark back to a mythical moment in pop – around the height of the punk era – when the prospect genuinely appeared to beckon of a brave new epoch ahead, in which anybody (or nobody) could be a star. What was at stake was something more utopian than the mere fifteen minutes prophesied in a spirit of gnomic cynicism by Andy Warhol. Punk seemed to herald nothing less than a democratisation of the institution of performance – a definitive breaking down of the barriers between performer and audience. To an extent, the club culture of the 80s and 90s has indeed entailed the progressive diminution of the artist's role as creator of a record, and a rising to power of the dancefloor crowd as the force that gives the record meaning.

Jonathan Romney

In the mainstream, however, in which stars are made and marketed, those barriers have remained firmly in place. Live music documentaries above all continue to affirm the myth of the star as glittering repository for the fantasies of fans struggling under the burden of their own supposedly humdrum existence. A recent example, *The Cure Show* (Aubrey Powell/Leroy Bennett, 1993), opens with panoramic shots of the crowd at a Detroit concert decked out in their Goth finery. But, sorry mortals that they are, they are condemned to live out their existence in black and white; their world only explodes into colour when their objects of adoration arrive on stage. (This cruel devaluation of the fan could be called pop's Wizard of Oz complex.)[1]

There is a sacred space in this fantasy scenario which underpins the institution of stardom, and that is Backstage. Backstage may be literally the space behind the stage, or it may more generally be the 'off-screen' of in-concert fantasy – the tour coach, the hotel room, the interview situation in which the stars 'play' themselves off duty. But it always remains a mythical area, uneasy of access but promising fabulous rewards – or horrific humiliations – for the intrepid punter who dares penetrate it. It is the place where, in *Wayne's World* (1992), Wayne and Garth – the very embodiment of uncowed fandom – get to meet their idol Alice Cooper ('We're not worthy!') and hear him hold forth graciously about Milwaukee's municipal history; it is also where, in *Wayne's World 2* (1994), they signally fail to be greeted with open arms by their babe-of-all-babes, Heather Locklear.

'Backstage' is the most potent of all concepts designed to separate performer and fan. It is a space of privacy, a world behind the curtain in which the *real being*, the ineffable precious essence of the performer's self, supposedly lies shielded from sight. (It is as well to remember, though, the function of the curtain at the end of *The Wizard of Oz*, which was precisely to conceal that there is nothing behind the curtain – or even on the stage itself – but a manipulating sound-and-light technician.) The audience is not normally permitted behind the sacred veil, but it is a convention of the music documentary to include scenes which take us backstage and offer us tantalising glimpses of the reality behind the show.

An element of demystification is partly at stake; such footage demonstrates to us how the illusion of on-stage spontaneity is the result of careful planning and struggle against seemingly insuperable odds. The Rolling Stones documentary *Gimme Shelter* (Albert Maysles/David Maysles/Charlotte Zwerin, 1970) includes several sequences in which the band's lawyer attempts to secure the use of the Altamont Speedway for the ill-fated free concert of December 1969. But such demystification only serves to remystify – tour schedules, scribbled set lists and faulty lighting rigs have become as redolent of the ineffable mystique of rock performance as suspended sandbags, trap-doors and pancake slap are of theatre's or grand opera's.[2]

Ronnie Hawkins and Rick Danko in *The Last Waltz*

Backstage moments in film promise not only to initiate us into closely guarded arcana of the music biz in general, but also to reveal the star as he or she really 'is', with the motley off, the dance moves temporarily dropped. They offer us a fantasy 'Access All Areas' pass, one of those areas being the artist's very soul. Above all, they promise access to the truth, for backstage is imagined as a far more 'real' space than the stage on which the artists do their work – which is supposedly to provide a spectacular, ritualised display of their very being. But, in pop more than in most arts, what artists produce – records, shows, videos – is generally insufficient to satisfy their public. Rather, their off-stage existence is expected to be their defining 'authentic' achievement, for a pop star is assumed to be not so much a performer as an elemental force manifesting itself. And whenever a pop star *is* seen openly to be performing, donning different masks, the effect is both troubling and stimulating (hence the importance of David Bowie and Madonna as pop's foremost 'transparent' players; hence too the uncertainty that began to riddle their musical careers as soon as they stretched their brief as performers by taking on acting roles).

Backstage, then, is supposedly where we will see the artist, make-up off and guard down, revealing his or her true self. As such, the pop documentary owes much to the older genre of the backstage musical, and to every film that makes a virtue of displaying performance as a complex, unnatural negotiation, from the Busby Berkeley canon through Chaplin's *Limelight* to *Gypsy*. But the fantasy of the revealed self is bound to disappoint us. Backstage, particularly when cameras are present, is no less a space of display than the stage itself. Artists have every reason to be less at ease there than on the stage. A stage is always a stage, its geography always

Truth and dare: *In Bed With Madonna*

basically the same, the rules of behaviour governing it always determined simply by the presence of a watching audience. Backstage space, however, is always different, contingent. It's potentially hazardous, a space where any unexpected presence – camera crews, well-wishers, rival acts – is potentially disruptive and therefore subject to strict control. The sense of backstage as alien territory is brilliantly captured in a scene from *This is Spinal Tap* (1983), in which the witless metal band attempts to negotiate the labyrinthine backstage corridors of an unfamiliar venue.

For a theatre star, occupying the same dressing room every night, backstage might be imagined as a personal domain. The backstage space of a music tour, changing from night to night, is more like a military camp, subject only to provisional occupation, and thus to be guarded all the more fiercely. That space derives its value only from the artist's presence, and from the potency of whatever executive machinery (road crew, management, security) comes with it – backstage can be 'strong' or 'weak', depending on whether it's occupied by Pink Floyd or this week's up-and-coming indie band. But it can never properly be the artist's space – it can never be 'home'. The very idea of home is inimical to pop myth – traditionally, a pop act occupies a succession of different 'camps', as befits the 'band of gypsies' or 'rock 'n' roll circus' self-aggrandisingly invoked by Hendrix and the Stones respectively.[3] Hence the aptness of the UK title of Madonna's *Truth or Dare* – *In Bed with Madonna*. Quite apart from the sexual intimacy it promises, it announces the way in which the sex goddess's intimate space (in which we dream of seeing her perform) is replaced by a stage, a place of display – part of her live performance in fact comprises a bed routine. It serves above all to underline how implausible it would be to call a film *At Home with Madonna*.

If no one is truly at home backstage, it is all the more necessary for artists to appropriate that space,

to assert their dominance over it and over any visitors or intruders. This may apply to film crews themselves – Martin Scorsese certainly does his subjects a service in the interview sequences of *The Last Waltz* when he allows himself to appear quite so uneasy and awe-stricken in the presence of The Band. And it is significant that the one moment in the flamboyantly 'unguarded' *In Bed* when Madonna appears to draw the line, holding up an imperious hand to deny the camera access to her trailer, appears very near the beginning of the film, as if to establish from the start just who is boss.

D. A. Pennebaker's *Don't Look Back*, a documentary of Bob Dylan's 1965 visit to Britain, established many of the conventions of representing the backstage. Shot in black-and-white, it exemplifies the apparently off-the-cuff hand-held style associated with *vérité* documentary. It certainly *looks* like *vérité* in that it captures, in seemingly uncooked form and with omnivorous receptivity, the apparent randomness of event on the tour. In particular, it proclaims its status as a behind-the-lines report – from the sequence early on when the camera waltzes through British passport control with Dylan's entourage, to the end, when Dylan leaves the Albert Hall by car after his gig. Here, the camera is placed – by necessity, one assumes – somewhere at Dylan's feet looking up at him; it's a definitive closing image of the star as unassailable hero, riding high on the night's success.

Immediately afterwards, however, the credits remind us of the fine distinction between a job from behind the lines and an inside job. *Don't Look Back* is co-produced by Dylan's manager Albert Grossman (who himself 'stars' in more than one sequence). What we see therefore carries, implicitly or explicitly, the family stamp of approval. This is in no way to impugn Pennebaker's integrity as a film-maker. Even in the 60s – an era that now seems relatively innocent about the protocols of star-image manipulation – no performer with any marketing acumen, still less their manager, would readily expose themselves to 'off-duty' scrutiny. Invariably, backstage footage is by necessity shot with the agreement of, if not at the behest of, the artist concerned; in real terms, a film crew cannot even get into a concert venue, much less backstage, without the express permission of the management.[4]

Ultimately, *Don't Look Back*, for all its apparent objectivity, cannot be seen as anything other than a 'promo' for Dylan (even the apparently independent, freewheeling mode of its shooting is closely linked with Dylan's persona – what is Pennebaker's hand-held camera if not the film-maker's equivalent of Dylan's own acoustic guitar?). At the very least, everything Dylan does can be seen as in some sense laid on for the camera.

The film is, indeed, a rich repertoire of backstage clichés-in-the-making. One wonderful sequence offers an almost parodic image of the artist as someone who simply can't stop being creative even off duty – in a hotel room, Dylan sits typing, swaying compulsively as Joan Baez serenades him with a song. On the whole, however, *Don't Look Back* thoroughly disabuses us of the notion that artists, rubbing against each other, naturally strike more illuminating sparks than ordinary mortals. (Again, the cliché of the 'hanging out' scene is joyously debunked in *This is Spinal Tap*, in which our heroes are pointedly snubbed in a hotel lobby by an erstwhile protégé.)

The 'hanging out' scenes in *Don't Look Back* derive a special piquancy from Dylan's status as an American performer, already possessed of something like demigod status, visiting a country whose own American-inspired acts were still working off a bitter cultural insecurity (the mid-60s 'British invasion' of the US pop market notwithstanding). One of Dylan's companions in the film is Alan Price, who introduces him to British mores and explains the rise of Donovan, the putative 'British Dylan'. An uneasy-looking Price seems almost to be apologising for the secondary nature of British pop: regaling Dylan with a Herman's Hermits number, for example, hardly comes across as an act of national pride. On an intimate level, the exchanges are distinctly awkward. 'Aren't you

playing with the Animals no more?' Dylan asks, and Price, who had recently left the band, shuffles and mutters, 'It happens, y'know?'

The dialogue is even less effective with those acts who directly take their lead from Dylan. One eager young crew of hopefuls earnestly explains their intent ('We try to get people to listen to the words') to their indifferent guru. Donovan himself, whose name features as a running gag throughout the film, finally appears in a hotel room, where a taciturn Dylan is playing host to an enclave of

At the very least, everything Dylan does can be seen as in some sense laid on for the camera

haggard British beats; with a heroic lack of self-awareness, Donovan sings one of his songs, a decaffeinated pastiche of 'The Times They Are A-Changin'. Dylan looks implausibly appreciative, but it seems very much a case of Donovan being given enough rope to hang himself. There is only room in this film for one folk superstar, and Donovan is allowed into the frame only in order to be discounted as a chancer.

If other performers fail to register in the Dylan universe, punters and press fare even worse. The film is a thoroughgoing repertoire of the techniques used by an artist to repel criticism or scrutiny while maintaining his own mystique, at the price of aggravating the public entirely. Dylan's technique is to remain silent, answer with gnomic obliqueness, or challenge his interlocutor's right to address him in the first place. His reputation as an inscrutable Zen master originated in scenes like these; but in retrospect, he comes across as a curmudgeonly attention-hog, anxious to silence anyone except himself. We may enjoy his cutting-up of a *Time* journalist with abstract quizzing about the notion of truth; his treatment of a student journalist looks like grandstanding brutality. A backstage interview turns into a furious joust, with Dylan establishing his dominant terrain from the outset, picking insistently at his guitar and meeting questions with questions from behind his shades ('What's your attitude to life?'), wrong-footing his increasingly flustered opponent. We're entirely on the young man's side, until, the pitch of his voice rising, his cool about to blow, he shoots himself in the foot. 'Aren't you an artist?' asks Dylan, and he retorts, proudly defensive, 'I'm a science student!'

The effect of scenes like these is to assert Dylan's cool at the expense of everyone else's. Of course, in austere 1965 Britain, where he seems like a marvellous freak, he's barely challenged; crowds, journalists, hotel officials, no one has any hope of equalling his charisma (the only British exception is the grand Denmark Street hustler Tito Burns, who now looks like an exotic creation of Colin MacInnes). *Don't Look Back* is an object lesson in enhancing the star's status by excluding mortals – or anyone else who may be more interesting than the star. It has its footnote in *Eat the Document* (1972), which Dylan himself, with co-editor Howard Alk, assembled from Pennebaker footage of his 1966 British tour. In one scene, Dylan and Johnny Cash jam a song at the piano, and a man appears at the door to tell Dylan he's wanted on stage; peering in, he retreats mystified, giving a spectacularly confused double-take. It's not clear who he is (Dylan associate, venue dignitary, hapless interloper); he's simply set up as another mystified oaf, the generic Mr Jones of 'Ballad of a Thin Man', who sees that something's going on but he don't know what it is. In fact, the trick of excluding him from the creative intimacy of Dylan and Cash is a cruel effect of editing: shots of the doorway are intercut with the two men at the piano, but there's nothing to assure us that the man is really reacting to what he sees – it's purely the cutting that sends him on his way.

By the late 60s, it had become clear that the audience could no longer be ignored or subjugated in the same way. Michael Wadleigh's *Woodstock* deployed the audience as a lavish spectacle, the panoramic tableau of a supposed 'nation'. The Stones' *Gimme Shelter*, however, presented its crowd as an uncontainable, anarchic rabble of *sans-culottes*, intent on challenging the primacy of the stage. The Altamont stage is continually invaded, the bands' thunder stolen by the terrifyingly authoritative entrance through the crowd of the Hell's Angels on their hogs, and ultimately by the stabbing of audience member Meredith Hunter. The Stones can only retreat to the safety of the film's one real backstage: the Maysles' editing suite, in which the band numbly watch the concert footage, in a framing sequence.

Punk's tentative revolution was itself preceded by the early 70s glam boom, during which audiences took on masquerade as an absolutely serious imperative; in practically any music press report of Bowie or Roxy Music concerts of the period, it is clear that the artists *only just* manage to maintain pride of place. It was in the wake of such changes that Pennebaker, in 1988, seemed almost to be making amends for his deification of Dylan with *Depeche Mode 101*, his film about Depeche Mode's American tour. Here, the cement for the concert footage is a mini-narrative about a group of American fans travelling by coach to see the band play at the Pasadena Rose Bowl (quite simply 'the band', rather than 'their idols': there is no sense of adulation here). The fans dress up, get drunk, debate fashion and indulge in all the traditional on-the-road pastimes, and are imbued with far more charisma than Depeche Mode, whose patina of glamour is skin-deep at best. Between the songs, in which singer Dave Gahan intones dour fantasies of alienation and anomie, we see them as a quartet of personable Basildon boys earning their keep with what seems to have been an intolerably long, monotonous tour. There's no entertainment in hanging around backstage – Gahan frets about whether or not to say 'Good evening, Pasadena', tells a tall story about beating up a cab driver (no one listens), and a solicitous tour manager checks up on the band before the show: 'Anyone got to go to the toilet? Wee-wees?'

In the post-punk climate of tarnished stardom, Madonna's entire career looks like a last-ditch attempt to reinfuse pop fame with the glamour now accorded to an increasingly select class of film stars (but any number of clotheshorses). *In Bed with Madonna* (Alek Keshishian, 1991) is more than anything about the control of audience perceptions, and uses the very unnaturalness of Madonna's public persona (itself largely a composite of ironic 'takes' on earlier figures – Dietrich, Monroe, Mansfield *et al.*) as an ambivalent selling point. Far from 'being herself' in the film's backstage moments – as Dylan at least *appeared* to be himself in *Don't Look Back* – Madonna is seen constantly acting out the implications of her stardom, so that everything that might be assumed to belong to her private life is projected onto the public facade and absorbed into it. Moments that might normally seem revelatory of a star's psychology are here orchestrated as full-blown routines: 'The Star's Relationship with Her Father', 'The Star Mourns for Her Mother', 'The Star's Thirst for the Camera'.

The insight into the private life that we are usually promised is delivered, but to excess – thereby defusing the very idea of a private self. The film's US title, *Truth or Dare,* refers to the scene in which Madonna confesses what are supposedly the ultimate intimacies about herself, naming her ex-husband Sean Penn as the love of her life, then demonstrating her blow-job technique on a

bottle. But what we get is truth *and* dare. Whatever truths Madonna gives away are either unreliable or unilluminating: the film *dares* us to find any psychological depth in them. (Madonna subsequently elaborated on this process in her infamous photo-album *Sex*, in which the unveiling of her body and supposed sexual fantasies simply provided another set of screens, as opaque and resilient as the metal wrap the book was packaged in.)

In Bed with Madonna consists of scenes on-stage and backstage: but once again, backstage *is* a stage. Instead of the star admitting us into her privacy, elements of the private life are exposed and brought under her rigorous control, as performance. From the start, it is clear that this strange production, as much fabulation as documentary, has only one real director: not Alek Keshishian, but the film's subject and executive producer herself. She provides the voice-over commentary, spoken in the muted, confiding tones proper to the recitation of an intimate journal, and she determines what we see (her final words, after the credits, are, 'Cut it, Alek! Cut it, godammit!'). She brings her father on stage for her birthday, and uses his disapproval of her act's sexual tenor as evidence of her seriousness. His voice is heard, with suspect clarity, talking to her on the phone: 'Can you tone it down a bit?' 'No,' she replies, 'because I'd be compromising my artistic

integrity.' The scene in which she visits her mother's grave is edited for effect that is the very opposite of *vérité*: on the soundtrack, Madonna sings, 'Little girl...', while she kneels at the grave and ponders aloud, again unusually audible, 'I wonder what she looks like now...a bunch of dirt.' The sequence is intercut with shots of Madonna on tour, and an archly poignant shot of her staring into space, and ends with her muttered aside by the grave: 'I don't want to stay here any more.' This is the punchline for what is effectively a promo clip for the star's inner life – an MTV of the emotions.

Warren Beatty, Madonna's lover at the time, is used as a distanced, amused commentator on his consort's moods. Intent to display him as her prize accessory (a neat inversion of Beatty's own reputation as inveterate sexual headhunter), she admonishes, 'Warren – don't hide!' as he lurks out of shot. Later, during a throat examination, her doctor asks, 'Do you want to talk off camera?' and Beatty, slouched in the background, remarks, 'She doesn't want to *live* off camera, much less talk! There's nothing to say off camera.' Given the fact that he is on camera as he says it, there is no small irony in this notoriously narcissistic star commenting on his paramour's spotlight-fever. We can only wonder how much of this apparently unstaged, unedited sequence is itself a put-up job – whether he is in collusion with her 'script', or whether she, rather, is using his competitive play for the camera's attention as more fuel for her own primacy as Grand Narcissist. In an earlier scene, certainly, we become aware of 'Warren' as a character of Madonna's invention. She picks up a phone and asks to talk to him; apparently they talk, but his voice is never heard; finally she yells 'Asshole!' and slams down the receiver – then grins conspiratorially at the camera. Who's to say he was there on the other end – that she's not just acting out a 'shouting at Warren' sketch?

Elsewhere it appears that the artist's control of her life and her image is at others' expense (a star's traditional prerogative, after all). Whether or not Madonna really is emotionally exploiting her entourage, her stance consistently looks like an acting out of an archetypal Hollywood-bitch scenario. The scene in which her home-town friend Moira McFarland appears to be deeply upset by her brusqueness – intercut with the star's indiscreet revelations about finger-fucking – is indeterminate; Moira too could be acting, competing with her former protégée. Even if it is a set-up, however, what prevails is the message that for a true star nothing is private, much less sacred.

The film's quintessential backstage scene comes in the ritual pep talk that Madonna gives her dancers before each show – part encounter group, part enactment of the 'Break a leg' moment in movie musicals. It's clear that the dancers' presence is functional to a particular aspect of her role-playing. 'I sort of feel like a momma to them,' she explains. 'I think I've consciously chosen people that are emotionally crippled in some way or who need mothering.' This startling claim is programmatic of Madonna's larger project: traditionally, stardom works by appealing to some emotional lack in the fan, which the star's persona can respond to and fill on a fantasy level. But rather than simply addressing the audience's lack, Madonna needs to be seen addressing a lack in everyone around her.

This relation takes on both a personal and a theological dimension. It is in these scenes that Madonna achieves apotheosis, gets to live up to the full connotations of her name: playing the healing mother, she gives the role a truly ritual significance. Performing her ceremony in the wings, just as the show is about to start, the self-sanctified Holy Mother seals the fusion between the two realms, on-stage and backstage. Ritualistic and deadly serious as her service of benediction is, it shows that there's no longer any distinction between what is and isn't 'heartfelt', or between what is and isn't 'entertainment'. As with all showbiz-ritualised emotion, feeling placed on display may conceivably be real, but it can never be intimate: female Pope that she's become, the thought that Madonna's fans could ever literally or figuratively get in bed with her becomes tantamount to sacrilege.

P.J. Harvey

An exhaustive display of stardom as a perpetual annexation of *any* space that can be appropriated as a stage, *In Bed with Madonna* may well have used up for now all the tropes of pop documentary. After it, the routine celebration of pop fame – as opposed to transcendent stardom – looks like a bathetic response to that film's demystificatory mystification. In the 90s, it may be impossible for any female pop performer not to measure herself against the Madonna archetype, however ironically. One example comes in a work at the other end of the celebrity spectrum. *Reeling With P. J. Harvey* (Maria Mochnacz/Pinko, 1993) records a tour by the up-and-coming British band P. J. Harvey; a video release by the band's record label, it's a routine promotional appendix to their records. The focus is singer Polly Harvey, who to all intents and purposes *is* the band; but instead of celebrating her personality and distance from the audience, the film minimises that distance, as much from embarrassment as from refusal of the institution of stardom. Harvey's resolute ordinariness is not on sale, simply on display, and serves as a foil to the intensity of her stage performance.

Here, in fact, there's absolute separation between stage and backstage – the concert footage directed by Pinko is animated, luridly lit, while the backstage sequences are static and artlessly banal. Mochnacz, Harvey's friend, confidante and photographer, often just places her video camera on a table and lets it roll, capturing desultory pre- and post-gig chat; way beyond Pennebaker, this is the *vérité* of the camcorder age, in which the real can be captured with minimum intervention on the part of the film-maker. Not only is there no event, there is no one behind the camera (who knows whether the next generation of rock documentary won't be shot entirely on venues' surveillance cameras?).

But still, there's an uneasy lip-service to the trappings of stardom, even if they are shown to be trappings and no

more. On stage and in her videos, Harvey dons ironically tawdry tat in a routine parody of glamour – vamp dress, boa, cheap sunglasses. It's not a refusal of narcissism, but its uneasy acceptance: the film's dullness but also its appeal come from the fact that neither star nor director is at ease with Harvey's new celebrity.

There's one scene, however, in which Harvey seems genuinely to be relishing her star status; but suddenly caught in the act, she steps coyly off the pedestal, only too aware of the conventions she's acting out. She is sitting in her hotel room, presumably after a bath, posing for Mochnacz, who is crouched at her feet with a camera; it's the archetypal intimate off-duty star moment, and, conventional as it is, both are making the most of it. Suddenly, the phone rings and the spell is broken. 'I look like Madonna,' she tells her caller. 'You know those bathrobe shots with her hair up and the towel and everything? We're doing some of those now.'

NOTES

1. See review by Louise Gray, *Sight and Sound,* August 1993.

2. A particular sub-genre is the 'Making of' movie which takes promotional video as its subject – far from making an artist's video mystique appear 'merely' constructed, such films (invariably made for video release or TV) celebrate the spectacular nature of that very construction. Perhaps unsurprisingly, the clever deployment of this genre seems to be a Jackson family prerogative: Michael Jackson, *The Making of Thriller;* Janet Jackson, *Janet Jackson's Rhythm Nation 1814.*

3. The absurd, contradictory notion of the rock star 'at home' was recalled in a set of 1967 pictures reprinted in *Mojo* 5, April 1994, pp. 10-11. In them, Jimi Hendrix is seen supposedly relaxing in a swinging London pad. He could barely have looked less at home in a Brentford Nylons showroom.

4. This can, of course, misfire: Robert Frank's Rolling Stones documentary *Cocksucker Blues* is a limit-case of uneasy collusion. Shot at the band's behest, it contained such revealing scenes of bad behaviour among the Stones entourage that the band deemed it virtually unshowable, and it can only be screened with their permission at complete Frank retrospectives. See Adrian Wootton, 'Looking Back, Dropping Out, Making Sense', *Monthly Film Bulletin,* vol. 55, no. 659, December 1988, pp. 355-6.

Glorious mud: Woodstock

93

the do's and don'ts of rock documentaries

Adrian Wootton

David Byrne: *Stop Making Sense*

Rock concert movies and film/television documentaries about famous musicians are perhaps the first and most common form where visual images and popular music meet. From the first footage of Elvis filmed by a TV news crew in 1955 through Woodstock to MTV, rock and roll has been a defining element of popular culture and its trends have been visually documented in every decade since its birth. These products fall into easily recognisable categories: the concert movie, the tour concert movie, and the documentary profile of living or dead stars. Taking into account video song compilations, there are hundreds of films, television programmes and videos constantly in production; but very few of them are made with verve, originality or skill. Many of the obvious technical and aesthetic considerations that would normally go into the production of a documentary product are either ignored or subjugated to crude marketing and promotional

film. Here, then, are some of the key 'don'ts' of rock documentary.

Careful with that Camera, Eugene – Shooting the Performance

Film-makers have a recurrent problem of trying to make a live concert performance translate into something that remains emotionally engaging when recorded, edited and exhibited either in a cinema or on TV. Many film-makers resort to a battery of flashy stylistic tricks in an attempt to pep up the performance impact, and this often results in a more frustrating experience, where a band or artist's charisma is undermined by inappropriate techniques. Some of the most basic recurrent examples are:

a) *Cutting back and forth between stage and audience*
This tactic, inoffensive in itself, has become a staple of

Most interested spectators of a film want to see the band, not the audience

requirements. This is something of a self-defeating strategy, as rock concert films and music videos tend to be relatively unsuccessful commercially. The purpose of this essay, from the point of view of one disaffected consumer, is to describe some obvious examples of bad aesthetic and technical practice in both concert films and documentary biopics, and to outline a possible model for what a more arresting and coherent documentary might be, using as an example one dead rock star's life.

There are of course exceptions to every rule, and the work of Martin Scorsese and D. A. Pennebaker is almost exempt from every aspect of this list of bad habits. Scorsese's *The Last Waltz* and Pennebaker's various films from *Don't Look Back* onwards show an exemplary understanding of how to make rock music come alive on

music documentary for two reasons. First, in the early days of the genre, directors felt that the audiences at concerts were at least as interesting as the performers – this is especially true of *Woodstock* (1970) and *Monterey Pop* (1968), which emphasise the momentous importance of both these festivals to the development of 60s/70s youth culture. Secondly, intercutting between stage and spectator can help establish an emotional identification between the 'real' spectator participating in the atmosphere of a live event and the passive consumer watching the recorded performance. However, in most cases it is unlikely that there will be anything interesting about the audience at a particular event that singles them out from any other. Most interested spectators of a film want to see the band, not the audience, unless the audience is doing something so extraordinary it has to be filmed – as in the Rolling Stones

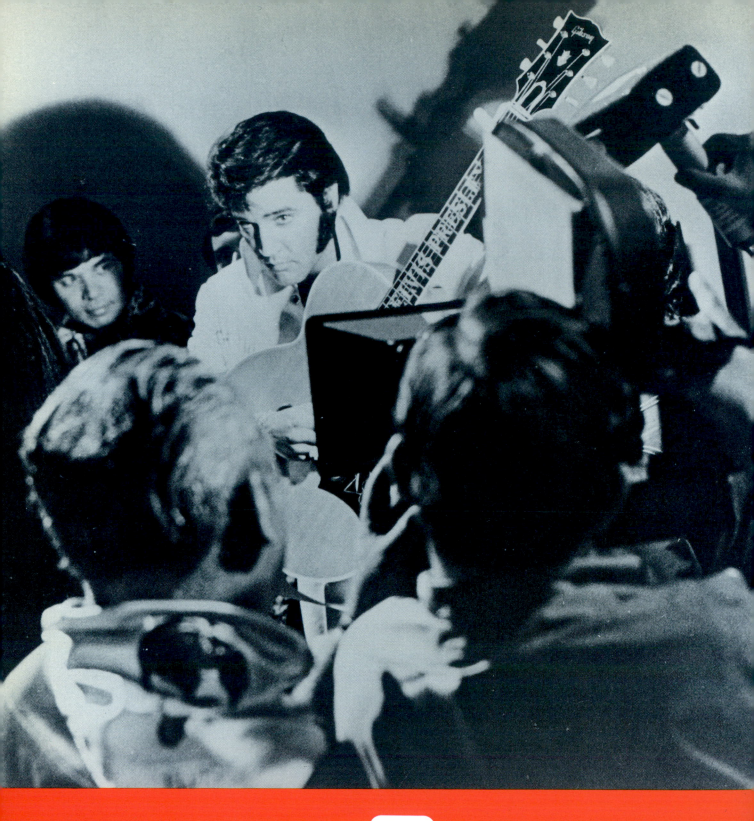

U2: *Rattle and Hum* (photo: Anton Corbijn)

You often find the camera getting a close-up of the singer picking his nose when it should be focusing on the guitarist in mid-solo

film *Gimme Shelter*, in which the real action clearly happens in the crowd. Most viewers watch concert films for one of two reasons: either they were not present at the concert being filmed, and so want to experience it vicariously, or they were and want to relive their memories of the event. Both Scorsese in *The Last Waltz* and Jonathan Demme in *Stop Making Sense* use little or no audience reaction content, because they understand that this attempt to create an artificial link between the spectator at a real event and a passive post-event spectator confuses two very different forms of viewing experience.

b) *Multiple cameras/Camera movement/Rapid editing*
When shooting on stage during a live performance, multiple cameras filming from different positions can be a very good idea, as can the rapid, fluent movements of Steadicam,

which has become common currency in concert documentary since the coverage of 1985's Live Aid concerts. Even so, rapid camera movement, quick-fire montage and split-screen effects can unnecessarily distance the spectator from the sense of a real performance. Triptychs, where the screen is split into three segments, can be extremely annoying, and the split-screen effects of *Woodstock* and *Elvis on Tour* (1973) – even though both were the editing work of Martin Scorsese – still add nothing to the viewer's participation in the spectacle. Instead we get a disorienting lack of focus – who are we meant to be looking at? what image has priority now? – and a sense that we are missing something vital in terms of the performance.

With regard to rapid camera movement, the use of a zoom lens in *Elvis, That's the Way It Is* (1970) – which is shot in and out of close-up supposedly in rhythm both with the music and with Elvis' body swings – is surely one of the worst examples of a film misusing technology and so destroying the performance of a star. Additionally, the constant employment of on-stage cameras, combined with more and more rapid editing – as seen in David Byrne's recent concert film *Between the Teeth* (1993) – was neither innovative nor exciting but simply engendered more confusion.

It is interesting to note that most of the films held up as models of good practice in the rock concert sub-genre restrict themselves to elegant, classically orthodox editing. The camera cannot act as a vicarious spectator, and elaborate camera effects simply make the viewer more aware of the technology used, or make it obvious that the director is bored with the scene depicted and wants to impose a stylistic signature. In fact, it is a mistake that can be usefully compared to the filming techniques of Robert Montgomery's bizarre adaptation of Raymond Chandler's *The Lady in the Lake* in 1946, where, in the attempt to shoot the entire film from the point of view of the main character Philip Marlowe, the audience is simply made aware of the presence of the camera. The same applies to slow-motion photography (unlike sports programmes, rock documentaries don't require action replay), colour washes and reverse negative shooting (clichés used for psychedelic effect in the 60s and early 70s, for example in Tony Palmer's 1968 TV film *All My Loving* and the 1971 *Pink Floyd Live at Pompeii).*

Elvis on Tour

c) *Shooting individual songs*

Although this may seem an obvious point, it is crucial that when an artist is filmed in performance the camera should be in the right place at the key moments of any song. Ignorance of a song, or indeed of a specific style of music, regularly leads to inept close-up and editing work. It is something of a truism that, if a crew or a director is not fully aware of the structure of a song – the position of its instrumental passages, vocal extravaganzas or notable climaxes – then you often find the camera getting a close-up of the singer picking his nose when it should be focusing on the guitarist in mid-solo; or a cut to the pianist just when you should be seeing the singer's finest moment. The problem is one of understanding the codes of musical performance and how these help to define pop stardom in a live context.

Needless to say, directors who have a love and understanding of the music they are recording do anticipate and plan for the essence of a performance. It might be argued that excessive advance planning and filmic choreography of a live event can remove any spontaneity in recording a unique experience. Indeed, some of the best rock movies are notable not because of their technique, but because they have captured a never-to-be-repeated moment. They may not be focused properly, but they were there, and we can be too, albeit in a limited and detached way. There are examples of film-makers not knowing exactly what they are doing but getting something good anyway – a good one being Amos Poe in his 1976 documentary about the New York rock scene, *The Blank Generation* (Poe has since gone on to be an accomplished independent film-maker).

There is a certain romantic appeal in this notion of DIY guerrilla film-making. Unfortunately it does not really hold water in the history of rock documentary. The vast majority of good concert movies have been made by competent movie-makers who spent a lot of time preparing for the limited shooting period they had and then carefully edited it afterwards. They may have got something unexpected, but this is a bonus, not a requirement. The essential purpose is always to record the show, not wait for the riot.

d) *Interviewing the band*

Perhaps because pop and rock musicians are not known for their verbal articulacy and thus are not often exposed to live, filmed television interviews, the general history of interviews in rock documentaries is one of banality and wasted film time. Of course, there are exceptions, notably the filmed press conferences of Bob Dylan in *Don't Look Back* (1967) and Madonna in *In Bed with Madonna* (1991); but the most typical pop musician interview is of the kind found in Phil Joanou's otherwise excellent *U2 Rattle and Hum* (1989). Apart from one relatively sombre scene in Elvis' Graceland home in Memphis, U2 seemed so desperate to preserve their hip but happy-go-lucky mystique that we get nothing but silly and irritating conversational sequences. Some may argue that pop musicians' eloquence is best illustrated on a stage rather than in an interview room, but if one is going to try to do interviews they should contain a degree of information and revelation. Scorsese narrowly avoids disaster with The Band in *The Last Waltz* because he overcomes their innate shyness and elicits some decent on-the-road stories.

If this cannot be achieved, then film-makers should stick to simple fly-on-the-wall *vérité* observation, as Robert Frank does in his Rolling Stones tour film *Cocksucker Blues* (1973); Frank's fascinating naturalistic approach spares us the embarrassment of watching our idols make themselves look stupid to camera. Unfortunately, this is not an aesthetic shared by the producers of MTV. The vast majority of the channel's interviews take the uncritical grab-what-you-can approach, with this week's pop sensation uttering inarticulate banalities as a lead-in to their new promo clip.

Cocksucker Blues

e) *Interviewing the audience*

While there is a certain horrific fascination in witnessing the hysterical/naive/hagiographic/sentimental hero-worshipping ramblings of stoned fans, this is all too often used as an opportunity for lazy film-makers to spice up otherwise dull footage. This is not to suggest that only tediously worthy pop buffs should be allowed to pontificate on screen, but we've seen too much of film crews door-stepping doped-out lads in an effort to emphasise the stupidity of pop audiences. Examples of this particular element are too numerous to list. Suffice it to say, it didn't work for Pennebaker, the Maysles brothers or even Scorsese, so there is no reason to suppose it will work for less luminous talents that have succeeded them.

The above caveats may appear a little puritanical, but if the purpose of a rock film is to convey the essence of performance and the sense of an event, this can be much better achieved by careful

Rock documentaries are mostly made at great speed, with little money, often by people with no film-making experience or musical understanding

structuring rather than by technical tomfoolery. Admittedly there are occasions when a director has little or nothing to work with; if a performance is poor, then anybody is going to struggle. Even so, there is a back-to-basics philosophy which most film-makers fail to adopt. Why then do film-makers keep making the same mistakes? The answer is largely to do with production schedules and finance. Rock documentaries are mostly made at great speed, with little money, often by people with no real film-making experience or understanding of the music they are trying to capture. Still, that is no excuse. The history of fiction film-making is full of gems made on little or no money, and invention and imagination can nearly always overcome logistics.

Filming the life –
Live fast and die young but only if it's on camera

All the mistakes listed above tend to be compounded when film-makers or television editors are commissioned to produce supposedly informative histories of famous, mostly dead, rock and roll stars. Indeed they not only mess up in the same way as directors filming concerts but also have their own checklist of irritating production gaffes.

a) *Don't crash the archive footage*
It is an often broken rule of disc-jockeying that DJs should avoid talking over the beginning and end of records (e.g. crashing the vocal). It is even more important to avoid ruining the impact of rare archive footage by editing it stupidly or having a contributor to talk over it. Time and again, researchers delve into the archives of vintage television shows to find rare pieces of exciting visual material about or featuring a particular act, only for it to be ruined by bad editing.

It's depressing enough if a director has shot some wonderful footage, then cut away from it at a crucial moment in the performance. But it is absolutely criminal to have a rare clip of Marvin Gaye singing 'I Heard it Through the Grapevine' in a television studio in the late 60s and then to plaster onto it a banal voice-over commentary, or to use only a part of the clip, or to cut in and out of it to other material. (This is a real example, taken from an absolutely terrible television documentary on twenty-five years of Motown Records screened all over the world in 1993.) In cases like this, one must insist on the primacy of original material in the hierarchy of what is shown. It should be shown untrimmed and unsegmented, otherwise the producer is removing a vital opportunity for the audience to experience for themselves what it was that made an artist famous in the first place.

b) *Avoid banal interviews with the rich and famous*
It is very useful – not least for promotional purposes – for a documentary to feature famous personalities who admire or have had a musical association with a performer. However, one can easily end up with a film full of glib, soundbite-ridden cameo appearances that add nothing to our understanding of the subject. A particularly bad example of this is to be found in a German TV documentary about Hank Williams, *I Will Never Get Out of This World Alive: The Hank Williams Story* (1994). In an effort to pepper their story with famous faces from the world of Country and Western, the film-makers sneak backstage at a big music festival and doorstep every performer they can find to talk about good ole Hank. The result, almost without exception, is a litany of clichés from many greats of contemporary country music, including the legendary Willie Nelson. The problem lies with the interviewers, who are so in awe of the personalities they meet that they find nothing interesting to ask them. This does a disservice not only to the personalities interviewed but also to the significance of Williams himself.

A similar difficulty is evident in *Hail! Hail! Rock n' Roll!*, Taylor Hackford's 1987 tribute to Chuck Berry. Apart from witty and enjoyably sarcastic comments from Keith Richards, its interviewees offer nothing apart from myth-reinforcing quotes about the living legend. While it would be foolish to underestimate the difficulty of getting famous people to say anything revealing or intelligent on camera, there has to be a way of interviewing potential contributors which assists the story, rather than merely offering diversionary glimpses of yet more individuals anointed by fame. Indeed, one notable exception to this tendency is *The Kids are Alright* (Jeff Stein, 1978) – a marvellously informative, amusing and candid history of The Who. *The Kids are Alright* is a rarity because the band members themselves, Pete Townshend in particular, have a long history of being self-deprecatingly honest in interview, and the film was at least in part their own production.

Dennis Wilson and James Taylor in *Two Lane Blacktop*

c) *Cut the travelogue*

A classic failing of rock documentary is the attempt to translate the codes of the rock 'n' roll road movie into factual form. In a road movie, it is common to have classic songs cut with images of characters driving across awesome landscapes – see *Thelma and Louise*, *Easy Rider* and *Two Lane Blacktop*. Unfortunately, this fictional convention is less than effective when one is cutting either shots of a film-making crew or a bunch of roadies in a trailer truck to the documentary subject's famous songs. Apart from the fact that it seems like an attempt to spice up a boring sequence with a bit of music, it adds nothing to our understanding of the music or the person involved. The use of songs in road movies often has a symbolic significance and can illuminate a key part of the narrative. In rock documentaries, this technique comes across as mere travelogue, and stands a chance of working only in those rare cases where the surrounding landscape or setting has a relevance to the music of the personality being explored. Robert Frank's *Cocksucker Blues* contains some wonderful sequences of the Rolling Stones travelling from gig to gig in the Southern States, cut to some of their songs. The Stones at the time of filming were absorbing and reinterpreting elements of Country and Western and Blues in their own recordings, so it makes perfect sense to see sequences of the band interacting, even if vicariously, with the culture they recycle. Similarly, the sequences of The Band walking around the sites of the bars and clubs they played in their early days in *The Last Waltz* have a fascinating resonance. But it is nonsensical to see a band on the road in Anytown, USA when there appears to be no relationship between music and image.

d) *Be careful with stock footage*

Using film library footage to represent a particular era is a commonplace of historical documentaries. Black-and-white shots of cities by night are a particular cliché that film-makers use when they want to invoke the atmosphere of a specific time where there is no new, more original footage

Bob Dylan and Robbie Robertson in *The Last Waltz*

available to link the subject of the narrative to the place where he or she lives. This is a relatively unusual element in rock documentaries, as few film-makers try to unearth archive footage that associates a personality with the period they lived in. The only instances which spring to mind are from the 60s – both Tony Palmer with Jimi Hendrix in *All My Loving* and Jean-Luc Godard in *One Plus One* (1968), with the Rolling Stones, cut performance footage with newsreels of the Vietnam war. Instead, most film-makers content themselves with shots of a star's birthplace as it looks when the film is made, or simply ignore the possibilities altogether.

It is not that rock documentarists should always try to contextualise their subject into historical reality; but there is a case to be made for thinking about this much more imaginatively. There is, however, one notable minor use of stock footage, pioneered by the long-running BBC Television series *The Old Grey Whistle Test*, in which songs were synched with extracts from unidentified archive fiction films. This device has gone on to become a staple of rock videos, but it has never been properly thought through in the context of documentaries. It is also interesting to note that almost no rock documentary about a band or individual has ever attempted to take clips from a fiction film in which the subject's music has been used, to include as part of the documentary information. Presumably this is because of copyright costs, but you could easily imagine a documentary about Jimi Hendrix using a clip of *Easy Rider* (which featured his song 'If Six Were Nine') to help illustrate the wider cultural impact of his music.

Outlining a new Rock Documentary

Ineptitude is endemic to rock documentary, but does it matter? By and large, rock documentaries are an adjunct of the marketing of music products by a global industry, and if they are not very good, why should anyone care? It could be argued that rock documentaries are little more than a bastardised sub-strand of more significant cultural forms and that it is too much to expect them to be anything other than occasionally diverting. This is a cynical but accurate assessment of music film production. There is never going to be a precise template for creating the 'right' kind of concert movie or documentary, and in view of the restrictions of production schedules and financing, it's naive to believe that all the flaws detailed here will ever be completely eradicated from the form (until, that is, the completely interactive CD-ROM appears and is accessible to everyone). Nevertheless, there have been some good examples of the genre, and working within such limits there have to be methods of continuing to make rock and pop breathe on celluloid.

At the time of writing, things are improving slightly in terms of straight live-performance recording on TV. The successful MTV concert series *Unplugged*, while more interesting musically than visually, at least has the virtue of unobtrusiveness, while the BBC's review show *Later with Jools Holland* has a refreshing simplicity of approach. At the moment, however, most rock documentaries are neither fish nor fowl, neither coming across as great film or television, nor offering real pleasure to the diehard music fan.

Keith Richards: *One Plus One*

Background: *Gimme Shelter*

103

There is never
going to be a
precise template
for creating
the 'right' kind
of concert movie
or documentary

Still, there are clearly new avenues to be explored in creating fresh forms of rock documentary. In fact, for an object lesson of the rock biopic genre, we can look to an instructive example of how a musician's life and work can be stunningly translated onto film – François Girard's *Thirty Two Short Films About Glenn Gould* (1993). This witty, original drama-documentary essay on the elusive and mysterious virtuoso of classical piano takes its structure from Bach's Goldberg Variations. Like Bach's piece, Girard's movie comprises thirty-two vignettes, ranging from dramatised recounting of notable incidents in Gould's life, through interviews with real friends and relatives, to animated sequences and wonderfully visualised lists of the many prescription drugs he consumed.

Clearly, there can be no straightforward equivalence between Gould's life and that of a rock musician; the complexity of the film reflects the complexity of the music, and the complexity of the music provides a platform for exploring the complexity of Gould's personality. Rock stars, by and large, don't have such complicated aesthetic philosophies and very few have written in such a variety of styles that they could provide a structure for a full-length feature film. Nevertheless, Girard's film is inspirational and exceptional in the way it completely interrelates aesthetic considerations of utilising music with the life of a particularly reclusive musician, and as such its rarity value should be noted. Furthermore, Girard has now ventured into the world of rock by directing Peter Gabriel's *Secret World Live* (1994) video in a careful and unsurprisingly proficient fashion.

Bearing this in mind, one could imagine the sort of project based on a deceased rock music personality that might provide new direction for the form. Gram Parsons (1946–1973), a semi-legendary singer/songwriter, who is credited with the creation of Country Rock, would be an ideal case. Parsons had a short but significant career, working with many of the major rock musicians of the late 60s and early 70s, and has recently been credited with influencing a whole new generation both of country performers, such as Dwight Yoakam, and new wave rock musicians, from U2 to The Lemonheads. His life has been extensively documented, there is film and television material featuring him, and his entire recorded output is currently available. It would therefore be eminently possible to undertake a research project which could contextualise Parsons in the history of rock and country music, and also look forward to many of the new performers of today.[1]

For now, one can only hope that new, young film-makers, who are as interested in music as that 60s generation of film-makers like Scorsese, Pennebaker, Coppola and Demme, will come through to help this illegitimate child known as rock documentary to grow. Maybe, when he gets through with rewriting the crime film genre, it's a job for Quentin Tarantino? Or can we hope that François Girard will now do a full-blooded rock 'n' roll movie?

NOTE

1.   Parsons' life is chronicled in Ben Fong-Torres, *Hickory Wind - The Life and Times of Gram Parsons* (London: Omnibus Press, 1984), and Sid Griffin, *Gram Parsons: A Musical Biography* (USA: Sierra Books, 1985).

music as film

Mark Sinker

t's fun to think of the Shangri-Las' 'Leader of the Pack' as a great lost Elvis movie. Better than any he made (it's *meant* to be funny), it's a tragedy-in-a-teacup that sets misunderstood outsider against straight society, locating the pathos as well as the silliness in this situation. But producer George 'Shadow' Morton was part of the Leiber and Stoller stable, and his main dramatic influence was radio: 'Leader of the Pack', for all its economy of means, its instinctive shifts in focal depth, its temporal jumps and flashbacks, is not 'film' at all, but radio-soap for teens. For a hint that the codes of cinema – film soundtrack especially – were by the early 60s deeply enough embedded in pop culture that they were turning up without being commented on, we have to turn to a lesser known Shangri-Las song. 'Past, Present, Future', next to 'Leader of the Pack' and the group's other hits, is as modernist, resignedly beautiful and static as anything made by Antonioni or Resnais (plus some three hours shorter).

In waltz-time, in three chapters, each solemnly announced by the whole group ('Past'; 'Present'; 'Future'), with Beethoven's Moonlight Sonata setting the elegiac, hokey opening-bars mood, it reserves for its climax the most gnomic verse of all: 'Don't try to touch me/Don't try to touch me/Because that will never/happen/again/Shall we dance?', followed by an up-swirling, all-enveloping movie-strings climax. What draws you in is the enjoyment of the – plainly fruitless – effort to script the gaps in the tale that's being backed. You jump to every kind of perverse 'modern' conclusion. *What* will never happen again? 'Was I in love? I called it love...'

The coming of magnetic tape in the late 40s turned the music industry inside out. Tape was cheap and reusable; it made audio-fidelity a reality, and stereo, and echo, and artificial audio space. And, like celluloid before it, it was eminently editable: montage and jump cuts were suddenly possible. Out of tape came the slap-back echo of Sam Phillips' Sun sessions with Elvis, and the intimate fantasy space in which Phillips, the Lee Strasberg of pop production, through take after take coaxed threat, sneer and mania out of the unlikeliest Method Actor material. Out of tape came

the vast whispering canyons of sound and the impossible orchestras of Phil Spector's singles: the Cecil B. DeMille of pop production dealt in the purest romantic subjectivity, and the artificial grandeur of the backdrops allowed listeners to suspend disbelief and enjoy. And out of tape, structured like a film production crew – Morton as writer-director, the Weiss sisters and the Ganser twins as cast, Jeff Barry and Ellie Greenwich as scriptwriters, for the Leiber-Stoller production company – came the rightly celebrated Shangri-Las series of hilarious and poignant melodramas-for-kiddiewinks: 'Remember (Walking in the Sand)', 'Sophisticated Boom Boom', 'I Can Never Go Home Anymore', 'Give Him a Great Big Kiss'.[1] 'Past, Present, Future' is the exception in all this – no less stripped down, it swaps near-parodic melodrama for a plotline so skeletal it's Structuralist Cinema.

Beyond simple association – analogies between technological means (collaborative authorship, jump-cut editing) – pop and rock from the mid-60s became self-conscious enough to work at being filmic. As a history, this essay is necessarily fragmentary. No consensus has been reached on what 'film-like' might mean (how 'like'? which films?). But there are links, and a pattern seems to form, around pop-culture notions of film and what pop or rock can learn from them. The realisation that sound images could be manipulated – taking film's difference from theatre as the model – evolved slowly, and is still evolving.

The Shangri-Las are the last bright glimmer of pre-rock pop. In 1965, when 'Leader of the Pack' was a hit, the rock underground was already beginning to look towards musicians who directed themselves (wrote their own songs, chose their own image). Tape's ease of access – anyone could now afford to set up a studio, while musicians no longer needed to be able to read scores – detonated an explosion. Records – LPs in particular – sold on a scale never before known: record companies gave up trying to groom their charges towards tried and true light entertainment, and let them slouch scruffily in the opposite direction, towards artistic autonomy – that way lay the prize.

Late 50s jazz had seen various suites and unifying projects – from Ellington to Mingus to Miles – aiming to use the expanded space of the 33^{1}/$_{3}$ microgroove long-player. The Beatles' *Sergeant Pepper* (EMI, 1967) and the early Mothers of Invention albums explored other ways to utilise a new freedom, in the context of countercultural aesthetics, allowing the condensed themes of a pop song room to grow, weave together, speak to one another – at least, so it was hear clearly, or to use. *Tommy* is responsible for most of the worst of 70s rock's pretensions to seriousness (taking a long time to say not very much, miscuing what it does say, mistaking scale for significance).

After *Tommy*, the deluge: its success gave the wrong signal. Minor talents seized on all the weakest elements in Beatles, Kinks or Who LPs. Just as movies in the late 50s had bloated into fatuous spectacle (to meet the challenge of TV), Progressive

Tommy is responsible for most of the worst of 70s rock's pretensions to seriousness

hoped. Industry practice had favoured LPs as collections of songs (ballad, rocker, country, novelty, Vaudeville – a mood to suit everyone): the new thing was the 'album', a *unified* art-object. Many of the groups that followed had fairly unexalted aims: with little or no practice in thinking long-form, they could either recycle *Pepper* and Zappa (who had both chosen to subvert the something-for-everyone approach), or else look outside pop altogether.

What better way to unify than devoting a whole record to a single story? The Kinks' Ray Davies turned to music hall, a plausible route for his spiked nostalgia and elegant melodies: the result was 1969's *Arthur (Or The Decline & Fall of The British Empire)* (Reprise/Pye), a critically lauded LP that had begun life as a TV soundtrack. In the same year, The Who delivered *Tommy* (MCA/Track), the first rock opera. As it happens, 'Past, Present, Future' was one of Pete Townshend's favourite songs,[2] but the 'filmic' elements of Brill Building pop seem to have been the ones he found it hardest to

Rock began to churn out recorded equivalents of *Cleopatra*: overextended, structureless monstrosities, pretending to a classicism they hadn't earned.[3]

Tommy is about the machinery and the lures of stardom and the spectacle, about rock's chaotic power and its limitations. As a major element of The Who's stage show it worked; as a record, not really. As a movie – given that the subject ought to make an excellent film – it's even worse. Stretching out on LP was an attempt to bypass pop's entrapment in song-form, or the trivial restrictions of performer identity – the very things that *Tommy* the movie makes a fetish of. Questions about stardom are simply diffused in the film's ragbag of cameos. The problems of the LP are magnified, since nothing was allowed to appear that wasn't in the 'script' (i.e. the lyric sheet). As a result, even when made into a film by Ken Russell, it wasn't very much like a film. Rendered episodic by fidelity to the lyrics, and thus disastrously literal in terms of filmic economy, it was as if a Broadway musical had been reconstituted for celluloid, relying only on the soundtrack LP.[4]

Jean-Luc Godard's use of jump cuts and collage had given the cinema a new aesthetic self-

Pete Townshend and Keith Moon in *Tommy*

consciousness – about classic scenes, iconic poses, the sexiness of the star. Godard's nearest equivalent in pop was David Bowie, who has usually been hymned – or hissed – as the prince of self-conscious 70s inauthenticity. But actually Bowie is a belated Tommy Steele, an all-singing, all-dancing light entertainer destined for a few terrible films, then his own TV show – he is actually part of the very pre-rock vaudeville tradition that other figures in rock (Paul McCartney, Ray Davies) were so keen to raid. It isn't so much that the self-styled 'cracked actor' is a trained mime as that you feel he'd do *tap* if his agent advised him to.

This career course, so out-of-time it *exuded* alien dissociation, went wholly wrong, brilliantly. Unlike Brill Building Pop or UK Light Entertainment, rock orthodoxy didn't acknowledge the unbounded exchangeability of genre; rather, rock was all, everything else a subgenre. Never understanding this, Bowie shot to success. He travelled through poses, donning and shedding images with every successive fiscal year: The Man Who Sold The World, Ziggy Stardust, Aladdin Sane...

The Rise & Fall of Ziggy Stardust & The Spiders from Mars (RCA, 1972) was the first true dissection on record of *Tommy* territory. It has a neatly hermetic structure/content: Bowie acted out the part of a self-destructive rock star, and the 'part' became a star in Bowie's behalf, an implicit comment on celebrity and spectacle (and audience). A suite of songs linked into a narrative, this specific project is not particularly film-like in terms of collectivity or collage (though many of the songs *are* very visual). But Bowie's trajectory was such that the real 'film of *Tommy*' would eventually be made – Nic Roeg's 1976 *The Man Who Fell to Earth* – to coincide, more or less, with the true 'filmification' of Bowie's LP-making.

In 1974, he looked to 1984. *Diamond Dogs* (RCA) opened with a curl of background music – through a murk of phasing and wolf howls, a synthpomp rendition of 'Bewitched, Bothered and Bewildered' – as soundtrack to his scene-setting voice-over: 'ten thousand peoploids split into small tribes', and cut, to rock-show audience screaming and the infamous, enigmatic shout, 'This ain't rock 'n' roll, this is genocide.' George Orwell's estate had refused permission for *Diamond Dogs* to sell itself as *1984* revisited; as a result, there's no lyric-narrative to speak of. We supply the action; which is why it works. Story-wise, perhaps inevitably, *Diamond Dogs* recalls as many apocalypse movies (*The World, the Flesh and the Devil*) as it prefigures (*The Warriors*, *Jubilee*, *Blade Runner*), but a deeper parallel with film arises accidentally, via style cut-up and the highlighting of Bowie as icon. With its sleeve by Guy Peellaert, the pin-up pop artist of *Rock Dreams* fame, *Diamond Dogs* is at last able to set up in an LP the weird, close web of actor/character confusions that a film inherently exploits in its actors and actresses.

Bowie, in other words, 'stars in' *Diamond Dogs*. In early 1977, after a succession of further, less filled-out starring roles (The Young American, The Thin White Duke) and further dissections of public role-play ('Fame'), he arrived at *Low*, mature rock's first return to the chilly European art-house aesthetic of 'Past, Present, Future'. With *Low*, the first of three collaborations with Brian Eno, Bowie broke with the notion of LP-as-star-vehicle and concentrated on the LP as cinematography and soundtrack.

An intense struggle had developed in the late 60s, to inject into rock culture a degree of grown-up reality, of fully rounded intellect and emotion. If books were intrinsically over-cerebral and composed art-music was for effete intellectuals only, film had pop *and* intellectual cachet. By the mid-70s, film-makers like Martin Scorsese were paying handsome tribute to 60s pop (making no distinction between a Spector-group like the Ronettes and the Rolling Stones). Where *Tommy* had unleashed a tiresome flood of rock concerti, rhythmically inept tone poems to nothing more than half-baked virtuosity, the maverick anti-rock rock star Eno put out several limited edition records which extolled their own 'non-musicianship', their background being: *Discreet Music* (1975), *Music for Films* (1978), *Music for Airports* (1979) – translating highly avant-garde notions about 'environmental sound' into off-mainstream pop prophecy.

The hook, with *Low*, is the lack. The sleeve-shot is a still from *The Man Who Fell to Earth*: as if this were a record made by a *fictional* character, an alien in a movie. Eno's ambient backdrops become the foreground; the important content is the decor. By draining colour from the mainman, the Bowie/Eno partnership invented *background music without a foreground*.

Badly wanting to seem adult and evolved, rock 'n' roll in the mid-70s had tended instead to produce work simultaneously trivial and pretentious. Abstraction and allegory had both been disasters: as the music took stock of itself in the mid-70s, music without words was considered suspect. Punk, wise to the failures of its predecessors, was obsessed with self-justification: all art a fraud, mere fun never enough. Rock 'n' roll was dead and rotting. Why make music at all? One common way out – you told the press you were going to be making music for films.

Awareness of film was basic to rock's new adult sense of its small self within a wider world. Some American New Wave groups began writing songs to be featured *in* films.[5] But this in a sense was business as usual, and others chose to go further. From the moment Magazine put the theme from *Goldfinger* on their second B-side, punk and post-punk succumbed to a rush of cross-media would-be legitimation – choosing film titles for themselves, their LPs, their songs, riffing on (or ripping off) ideas worked up elsewhere.[6]

111

The Clash had liked to flourish their film literacy: wised-up homage to James Dean or Montgomery Clift as a badge of emotional authenticity. At some point, they all trooped into some Notting Hill cinema to see Jimmy Cliff's gangster-reggae film *The Harder They Come* (Perry Henzell, 1972), and never really made it back out again. Groups that were serious about themselves but didn't want to be caught *being* serious (such as Public Image Limited) sagely broadcast their intention to make film soundtracks (PiL, typically, made many noises about how much more remarkable their film soundtracks would be than anyone's hitherto – and never in fact made any[7]). Groups that didn't mind so much not being not-serious, such as Talking Heads, flirted with the notion of film as extended art-rock video (David Byrne directed 1986's magic realist quasi-documentary *True Stories*, to a Heads soundtrack).

Whether you're Gary Numan or Laurie Anderson, the function of a film reference is to import emotional and/or intellectual baggage wholecloth, from a pop-culture region as usefully volatile as rock but subject – crucially – to very different rules or geometries of affect. But such importation need not simply operate at a crass quotational level. In 1982, Tom Waits, after years as a minor rock cabaret act, switched out of boozed-up *noir*-narrative jazz rambling into a vaudeville of the same world, with himself as a character in his own songs. The song sequence on the second side of *Swordfishtrombones* (1982) is the signal that film sensibility is being redirected back into live or theatrical performance: after the fragmentary accordion instrumental 'Just Another Sucker on the Vine' fades in and then out like a locating shot, Waits grumbles his way through 'Frank's Wild Years', to a distant jazz organ backing: it isn't a song so much as a shaggy dog story.

Since his appearance, as himself as a barman, in Coppola's 1983 *Rumble Fish* (and his work as soundtrack composer to *One from the Heart*), Waits has been able to play an unfolding game of cross-reference, to underpin and elaborate this character – down-at-heel musician-actor-writer moving through grungy hobo-beatnik nowhere – across a series of records and movies, most importantly Jim Jarmusch's 1986 *Down By Law*. Elements of the persona in one setting bleed over into another, blurring, or elaborating, the uses of role. The song 'Frank's Wild Years' was expanded into a full musical of the same name in the mid-80s, followed by another, 1988's *Big Time*.

Using harmonium, with an agglomeration of faintly weird, carnival-sounding instruments to the fore, as well as guitar swathed in echo and his own guttural voice increasingly draped in estranging distortion and compression, Waits wrote songs for a band that seemed to be acting itself. By turning a music that is background sound into its own performance, he can evade the more degrading, trivialising and stereotyping effects of soundtrack commodification.

Waits' achievement has been to cast jazz as itself in its own situation, which is a small, if attractive, street corner of a much wider world. In the ecology of music as nurtured by film, rock – like jazz, like anything – is simply one flavour among many: one colour in the palette, rather than the whole world. Awareness of this has been liberating for a

David Byrne is in the house: *True Stories* (right)

whole generation of 'rock' musicians, from Elvis Costello to Foetus (for the generation that follows, rap operates in a world which *begins* from such a perspective). While rock has always defined itself in opposition to classical composition and pre-rock popular music, it has rarely had the gumption – and its performers have rarely had the chops – to play around with the borders of such a definition, to create an art out of rejuxtaposition of pre-created slabs of meaning.

One artist who has, however, is producer Hal Willner, who began as music director for *Saturday Night Live* and its short-lived, fondly remembered NBC spin-off *Night Music* (more recently, he was musical director on Robert Altman's *Short Cuts*). His technique of mix-and-match combines Elvis Costello's total command of fifty-odd years of pop and jazz with a cultivation of musicians able to step back from the music they are playing and put it into wider, symbolic (deconstructive?) context. Across a series of LP tributes to great past musicians and music styles – Nino Rota, Thelonious Monk, Kurt Weill, Disney soundtracks, Charles Mingus – Willner set up tracks by 'casting' a variety of musicians from many areas in roles in scenelets. That this links up with Waits' world is undeniable: Willner has extended the method to backing-track work, using a core corps of his (and Waits') favourite New York players (Michael Blair, Ralph Carney, Marc Ribot *et al.*) on spoken-word records by the likes of William Burroughs and Allen Ginsberg, who laid the literary ground for this hobo-beatnik bohemia.[8]

A key co-worker in this re-ordering of perspective is New York composer/improviser John Zorn, who has pulled film music even further out of the shadows. Consider his treatment of Ennio Morricone's music on his Willner-produced tribute album *The Big Gundown*. In Zorn's music, role-casting at the outset is designed to recreate editing in real-time, so that slipping from one 'pastiche' to

113

The best soundtrack music is simultaneously transparent – instantly readable as to mood or reference – and swift in shifting

another at lightning speed is the main skill to be mastered – the next is to keep your head when those around are playing to undermine your last move. Elements of music are deployed like characters in an improvised drama, soliloquising, squabbling, making up: the musicians, picked as a cast, adopt and then throw off these elements like so many roles. Zorn's success has spread to less particular settings, but it has centred round the re-presentation of two influences, two innovative (if unlikely) figures: Morricone the Spaghetti Western man; Carl Stalling, composer to Bugs Bunny *et al.*[9]

More than anything, this has highlighted the way that, in responding to scene changes, the best soundtrack music is simultaneously transparent – instantly readable as to mood or

reference – and swift in shifting (Stalling is an extreme example, since none of his compositions exceeds five minutes, and scenes that exceed five seconds therein are very rare). The point is less 'mickey-mousing' – the trade jargon for music that sonically *describes* the action – than music that reads, subconsciously, in such a way as to pinpoint, flavour or otherwise render comic whatever might be happening, at that instant, on screen.

If this trend towards borrowed form was in the early 70s driven by a sense of inadequacy, by the mid-90s it has resulted in a useful non-mainstream category: a sub-genre that allowed for the development of instrumental music which can bask in its own purposefulness. In the mid-80s, the eclectic Belgian label Crammed Discs set up a sub-label – Made to Measure – explicitly dedicated to music for films that didn't yet exist: as they put it, 'atmospheric to abstract, postcard to post-modern, a collection of aural garments that have or could have been commissioned as soundtracks'. Figures of greater or lesser obscurity – among them, Colin Newman of Wire, John Lurie, Hector Zazou, Karl Biscuit, Seigen Ono – put out records of greater or lesser worth, some highly entertaining, some fairly dreary: whatever else they achieve, they provide a forum for wide-ranging genre-wandering, pastiche, rootless mutation, exploration and professional tourism.

Holger Czukay, bass player of the German group Can – a band whose soundtrack explorations since the late 60s really deserve a whole chapter to themselves – had long professed a taste for found-sound, tuning during the band's live sets into exotic music on short-wave radio: his 1980 solo LP *Movies* is built round this, becoming the first ambient quilt-pop masterpiece. Its successors through the 80s lock ever closer into mainstream movie-soundtracking, until the two can't really be distinguished (as Vangelis' *Blade Runner* score[10] demonstrates): continuity is layered from small surprises, while music as furniture folds into SFX as music. It has become the cliché style of the 90s: just as cut-and-splice methods in sound recording suggested an intriguing technological link with film in the 60s, the exact equivalence of digital 'composing' programmes like Q-Base and video-editing programmes like AVID placed the two disciplines within morphologically similar techno-grids. In both cases, the praxis is the same – bunch of folks in an airless city room staring at a screen.

Film's link with dance music and sampling subculture is also unavoidable. Critic Jon Savage has long argued that rap, from its highly referential outset with 1981's 'Grandmaster Flash on the Wheels of Steel', with its bite-size clips from Queen, Chic and everything between, is in this sense filmic. The ever greater involvement of its stars in roles in movies based on rap subculture and rap subjects, seems to confirm this. Run-D.M.C. appeared in 1988's *Tougher Than Leather*, Kid'n'Play in 1990's *House Party*, and Ice-T and Ice Cube in a whole series of gangsta-ish movies – Dennis Hopper's *Colors*, Mario Van Peebles' *New Jack City*, John Singleton's *Boyz N the Hood* – as 'themselves', bearing in mind that their performance personas are already more 'character' than not. Clearly the popularity of gangsta-rap – as kicked off by Niggaz With Attitude in 1988's huge-selling *Straight Outta Compton* (4th & Broadway) – led to Hollywood's decision to press forward with what would have seemed incendiary and impossible material five years before. (Spike Lee's decision to make Public Enemy's 'Fight the Power', the totemic song of his 1989 *Do the Right Thing*, gave the trend more momentum.)

The black relationship to film, however, is often very different from its white cousin: certainly the sense of formal inadequacy that 70s rock felt

Do the Right Thing (Spike Lee, right)
Background: *Boyz N the Hood*

In digital composing and video-editing programmes, the praxis is the same – bunch of folks in an airless room staring at a screen

never applied. When rap artists like Ice-T reach out to the blaxploitation canon, it's not because they feel rap is in need of legitimation (if anything, precisely the reverse). In a sense, records *are* African-American film. As Tricia Rose has written, Public Enemy's 'Night of the Living Baseheads' is 'one of rap music's most extravagant displays of the tension between post-modern ruptures and the continuities of oppression. The video for "Baseheads" is an elaborate collage of stories, many of which move in and around the lyrical narratives, all of which address a variety of oppressive conditions and offer stinging media critique and political statements.'[11] PE's music is not an embrace of celluloid imagery with soundtrack on the side, but a refusal of all such mediated settlements; the whirl of visual pastiche in a PE video is an accompaniment to the words, a series of clues as to translation, for the outsider. If anything, rap has turned to black film to attack established white media outlets, especially television newscasting, as fabulous, ludicrous, irresponsible cultural fantasy.

White dance-culture cut-up merchants – such as Steinski or the UK-based Coldcut – have brought film-like jump-cut precision to their constructions as a kind of audience-collusive wit. But once producer-DJs Hank Shocklee and Terminator X start mixing and scratching for Public Enemy, the emphasis is on intensity rather than playfulness, on rough-hewn mesmerism rather than cultured PopCult reference. The layers of music and noise that propel hip-hop set up a charged field for the rapper to act out in: often no more than an ambient space. Filmish sound FX – sirens, helicopters, crowd noise – are as likely to be looped into the beats as Coltrane sax-licks; but they are also made to know their place. Unlike most pop and rock, which is nervous about its own lasting worth, hip-hop recognises no cultural hierarchy which does not have hip-hop at its summit – film is just one form to be appropriated, fragmented and reconstituted towards this goal. Film is a way to disrupt 'organic' modalities of music production, perceived by rappers as one more showbiz trap.

'With *Delusion*,' Barry Adamson has said of his only film soundtrack proper to be released as a LP to date, 'I mickey-moused a bit, believing that's what you did.'[12] With *Soul Murder* (Mute, 1992), ex-Magazine and Bad Seeds bassist Adamson, who began his solo career with a 12" cover of Elmer Bernstein's film theme 'The Man with the Golden Arm', dispensed with mickey-mousing, if not with the overspill of filmish puns – and put together a record which slipped as easily as Zorn from style to style, as purposefully (and politically) as any gangsta rap producer. Laid out as if it were not a film, but the original soundtrack record to that film – with snatches of dialogue, sound effects, songs that resemble themes, or background excitement-heightening throb – *Soul Murder* is a brilliantly original refocusing of all facets of the original notion.

At the beginning, ranting found-sound from a religious-criminal maniac fades into a lumbering, drunken Wagner overture, cycling over and over itself – to be interrupted by a knock on the dressing room door, and a briskly courteous 'Sorry to disturb you, Mr Adamson – there are two gentlemen here to see you from the Police Department.' Cue low and distant kettledrum, and then a cruising jazz bass, while the hero introduces himself in hard-boiled mock-Marlowe monologue. And so on through the record: repetitive instrumental themes for echo-laden twangy guitar are overlaid with hiss and muted radio chatter; newscasts about race hatred and lynchings dissolve into techno-bleep loops, then canyons of ambient whispering; '007 – A Fantasy Bond Theme' relocates James Bond to the culture his creator Ian Fleming lived in and never noticed, the Caribbean.

'Was I in love? I called it love…' Compressing the anomie and indeterminacy of the European art movie into three minutes, 'Past, Present, Future' is able to function, against the simplistic grain of the Shangri-Las' parent genre, as a figure for gay romance, pre-Stonewall. Adamson is working, in more complex times, towards more complex revelations: he's a private detective on the hunt for twentieth-century racial identity. The gumshoe pulp thriller constitutes a secret history of hint and denial, about the roots of crime in class and desire. *Film noir* in particular set such stories in a psychic forest of shadows, backlit with the subversive intensities of iconic glamour (where beauty often *was* the beast: the moral easy to read but hard to grasp). Adamson, toying with the means to rebuild – or, at least, to rescore – such clichés, works to turn such manipulations on themselves. The narrative that would make clear who is to be hero, who love-object, who villain, never materialises: instead we're left with a surge of contradictory fragments, some soothing, some chilling, some joking. If ever you as spectator jump in, to fashion from the sound montage a story of your choosing, you'll find the next bit of music seems to be accusing you of the crime.[13]

NOTES

1.   Mwah!

2.   So it says in the sleeve-notes to my *Golden Hits of the Shangri-Las* (Phillips/Mercury), and they're written by Phil Spector biographer Richard Williams, so it must be true.

3.   Oddly enough, *Tommy* is a real opera: that's to say, its problems are the problems of classical opera – it has to tell a story, in songs, without allowing the songs to puncture the unity of musical developmental logic, or let this unity muffle the drama. Plus it has a stupid plot. See Joseph Kerman's *Opera as Drama* (London: Faber, 1989) and the relevant chapters in Carl Dahlhaus's *19th Century Music* (University of California Press, 1989).

4.   The Who's biographer Dave Marsh is convinced that Russell set out deliberately to *sabotage* – rather than recreate – Townshend's intentions, implying that the rock band were first too naive to realise this, and ultimately too compromised to counter it. *Before I Get Old: The Story of the Who* (London: Plexus, 1983).

5.   For example, The Ramones in 1979's *Rock 'n' Roll High School* and Blondie's theme-tune/hit single 'Union City Blue' (Chrysalis) for 1979's *Union City*, starring Deborah Harry.

6.   The worst culprits – or most entertainingly cheeky, depending on your viewpoint – being Billy Idol (*Valley of the Dolls, Kiss Me Deadly,* 'Eyes Without a Face', all Chrysalis); and Kirk Brandon ('Westworld'), with Theatre of Hate for Burning Rome Records, 'Grapes of Wrath', 'One-Eyed Jacks', with Spear of Destiny for Burning Rome/Epic).

7.   PiL were to have been involved at an early stage on Michael Wadleigh's 1981 *Wolfen*, but the mix of sarcastic punker indolence and Hollywoodstock inertia seems not to have been conducive to satisfactory follow-through.

8.   Willner productions include *Amarcord Nino Rota/I Remember Nino Rota* (A&M); *That's the Way I Feel Now – A Tribute to Thelonious Monk* (A&M); *Lost in the Stars – A Tribute to Kurt Weill* (A&M); *Stay Awake* (A&M); *Weird Nightmare – Meditations on Mingus* (Columbia); William Burroughs, *Dead City Radio* (Antilles), *Spare Ass Annie and Other Tales* (4th and Broadway); Allen Ginsberg, *The Lion for Real* (Antilles).

9.   *The Carl Stalling Project* (Warners).

10.   *Blade Runner – Original Soundtrack* (EastWest).

11.   Tricia Rose, *Black Noise* (Wesleyan/New England, 1994), p. 115.

12.   *Delusion* (Mute, 1991).

13.   A longer version of this history will appear in my book *The Electric Storm*, a cultural history of technology's effects on music (to be published by Quartet Books).

The Shangri-Las go quadraphonic

interviews

In this section, we talk to a number of film-makers and musicians – plus one music co-ordinator – whose work illustrates some of the particular appeals and challenges of the encounter between film and pop. Each interview was conducted separately – in most cases face to face, occasionally by phone – but all the interviewees were asked roughly the same series of questions, designed to cover the range of their careers, influences, obsessions and critical opinions. Because of space limitations and the desire to construct something like a coherent debate out of a mass of diverse argument and anecdote, we've condensed all the interview material into a mosaic of opinions, to allow the interviewees' contributions to chime with each other. Rather than manipulate the answers to illustrate our own points of view, we've juxtaposed them in order to raise questions, set up chords and strike some discords.

The section is ordered question by question; each interviewee is identified in the margin at a point where he or she is involved in the debate.

Allison Anders

trained at UCLA, then made several short films which used pop music, before becoming a production assistant on Wim Wenders' *Paris, Texas*. Her debut feature *Border Radio* (1987), the fictional story of a rock band, used much contemporary LA rock and featured a variety of musicians in cameo acting roles. Since then Anders has made *Gas Food Lodging* , with music by J. Mascis of US indie band Dinosaur Jr, and British musician Barry Adamson. *Mi Vida Loca* , about Chicano gang girls, features a soundtrack by John Taylor of Duran Duran. Anders is currently working on *Grace of the Heart*, to be produced by Martin Scorsese, about a female songwriter in the New York song factory The Brill Building, and directing a segment for the portmanteau movie *Four Rooms*.

The Unholy Alliance

These days, it's largely taken for granted that pop music and cinema have a tight-knit relationship, but beyond the fact that they both belong to popular culture, we rarely examine the reasons. What are the affinities that film-makers feel with pop, and why do musicians learn to make themselves at home in the visual field?

Allison Anders: It's just the basis for communication in our culture. I think that we can have a common reference, a common sort of 'Where was I when I heard this song?' It's so evocative and coded so deeply in our psyche, it's a whole world culture. I remember Wim Wenders talking about doing *The Scarlet Letter*, and he said, 'It was just a drag – there were no juke-boxes, no pinball machines – I couldn't do it.' I totally understand that – when I read something, I go, 'OK, now where can I put in the popular songs?' I have this dream for a period piece, I want to do a Thomas Hardy movie. I think the most successful thing was *Far from the Madding Crowd*, where they took the really cool folk singers from England at that period and had them do old folk songs. I think I could do that 'cause then I could use cool folk singers from now and create a sort of now-and-then situation.

But popular music is the only cultural reference we hold in common any more. We are not all the same religion, we don't hold the same views on whether we eat meat or we don't eat meat, whether we are monogamous or we're not. There's no common ground except for pop culture, so in a way it's what's holding it all together, it's the new myth. And when songs can live on, it's such an amazing thing, considering that they're not created for that. They're marketed in a capitalistic way to not survive, and be replaced by the next new thing. So when they live on, it's so amazing, it's more powerful than anything, that creative spark in a two to five-minute song.

Alan Rudolph: You can make an argument that music is the soul of the film. In movies it's like a flavouriser – it heightens, it sharpens, and it's contradictory presentation of action and emotion. Sometimes the best things that work in film are things that are undercurrents and other meanings, and music allows you to do that more than almost anything because you don't have to explain anything. It instantly becomes an emotional event.

An audience will trust music before they will trust narrative, before they will trust actors. When they hear music it's something they're comfortable with. I think we are starting to think in soundtracks. People think in soundtracks before they think in films. With movies you are sort of trusting something else, but with music it's yours. It's the people's art and it makes everyone more dynamic.

Michael Mann: From the very start I always wanted to mix my love for rock with film-making, and my first major short in the late 60s has that in it.

Isaac Julien: Music always plays a central role in my films – that's to do with the generation I'm from, the post-punk generation, and also to do with the influences of advertising, MTV, etc. They've all become central preoccupations in thinking about images.

Wim Wenders: I woke up when I heard rock and roll and it has accompanied me and it has helped me a lot. I work with it and I travel with it. I feel I would have probably turned into someone else if it wasn't for Dylan or the Kinks or Van Morrison, because it woke up something in me and it made me get in touch with what I was able to do. Rock and roll and movies really have something in common. They are both contemporary at the same time, more than other forms of expression or languages. They are both able to really feel the pulse of the time.

Bob Last: At the time of *Rock Around the Clock*, it wasn't part of people's memories. Now you've got this whole generation of film-makers who've been surrounded by popular music from their youth, and it's therefore very resonant for them. It's such a condensed form, you can very efficiently bring a lot into something. As it's become part of that memory, it's become possible to use it in a way that doesn't undermine the music you're using, doesn't make a fool out of it. And because it's part of everybody, there are textures – a certain type of guitar or whatever – that is a universal language. You can introduce those genre textures and use them.

Penelope Spheeris: Given the fact that it seems to be impossible to be creative with rock music, it's probably difficult to be creative with rock music in a film. What's surprising is that a lot of directors and studios will allow real kind of cutting-edge music to take a prominent place in big movies. Like for example, *Terminator 2* – didn't they have Guns 'N' Roses as their title song? Whereas in the days when Axl and Slash were hanging out on the street up there at the Whisky a Go Go, you would never have thought that they'd be affiliated with $60 million movies.

Ry Cooder: See, you just have to begin to understand where music is in a film – it's sub-textual and it's an interior sound. When Jack Nitzsche started doing that on films in the 60s, the engineers didn't like it, the producers didn't like it, everybody said, 'This guy's nuts. He's crackers, what do you want him for? He's gonna ruin your film.' But quickly that changed and the people who made the films got younger all of a sudden and they expected to hear something from their own experience in there. And if their own experience wasn't necessarily a German, compositionally

Michael Mann

trained at the London International Film School before entering the American television industry, where he directed episodes of numerous successful shows including *Starsky and Hutch*. In 1979 he directed his first feature, *The Jericho Mile,* and has since made *The Keep, Thief* (scored by Tangerine Dream), *Manhunter* and *The Last of the Mohicans*. In addition, he created the seminal TV series *Miami Vice* (1984-87) and *Crime Story* (1986-88) as well as producing several other TV programmes.

Ry Cooder

is a guitarist, composer, arranger and producer who performed with Captain Beefheart's Magic Band and The Rising Sons (with Taj Mahal), before embarking on a solo career that took in such albums as *Boomer's Story*, *Into the Purple Valley*, *Bop Til You Drop* and *Borderline*. He has also collaborated on records with John Hiatt and Nick Lowe (in the group Little Village) and the Malian guitarist Ali Farka Toure. He has had a long association with director Walter Hill, scoring films like *The Long Riders*, *Streets of Fire*, *Johnny Handsome*, *Crossroads*, *Trespass* and *Geronimo: An American Legend*. He also scored Wim Wenders' *Paris, Texas*, Michelle Manning's *Blue City*, Louis Malle's *Alamo Bay* and Tony Richardson's *The Border*, and contributed to *Candy*, *Performance* and Paul Schrader's *Blue Collar*.

trained disciple of Wagner, why then, they were having other thoughts. Michael Mann, for instance.

I found that I could think in images, because I didn't care about stories at all, I just wanted to see something start to happen in terms of visual rhythm, the look of light, faces, to let your mind wander.

But I don't know about rock and roll in films. Personally I don't have much use for it. Only because it's so one-way all the time. I like rock and roll all right once in a while, but to me it's a narrow path that you're going on because it has more to do with performance than some kind of style and some progression. Jack Nitzsche had a lot of trouble because every time somebody played an electric guitar on one of those scores it'd stop the show like that. I could never understand that. We'd look at these things, and I was pretty young, and I didn't know anything at all. I had no idea what was going on except that I could see these goddamn electric guitars fucking up this imagery, and I couldn't figure that out. Now I do believe I understand that. Finally Jack figured, 'Hey, the cymbals, it's the cymbals', and I said, 'Yeah, but why?' Then of course you learn if it sounds like a song it's no good in a movie, unless it's *Miami Vice* or you want somebody to sing a song and then that can be great to suddenly have a song. But I don't know about rock and roll as score because it's so predictable – like, how many things *are* there?

When they start putting these pop songs into films, to me it just stops the film. It crashes, everything goes crash unless the film is about pop song. I've worked on some films that have pop songs and they weren't good, they hurt the film even though they were thematic.

The trouble with rock and roll is it's so much about that phoney heroism. I really mistrust that. In a film you don't want that, you don't want to send the message 'We're winning with our bad trip and our guns and our shit.' Let them work on TV. The bad guy wins, then the good guy wins, then the bad guy wins, then the good guy wins. But that's not a movie, that's a TV show.

Hearing Pictures, Seeing Music

It's not just since the advent of pop video that people have been hearing music as movies in their head. Musicians have constantly referred to the ideal pop single as a 'three-minute movie', while film-makers give music its due as the stimulus that sets off the train of mental images.

Amos Poe: Almost literally the first movie I made was – I took the Beatles' *White Album* and made movies, like narratives, for every song. Some of them were literal renderings of the lyrics, and some of them were just things that I had got off on if I had smoked a joint. Obviously Dylan's songs are very visual – Dylan was probably the nexus between visuals and music for me. Neil Young as well, and I think some of the longer Led Zeppelin songs, like 'Dazed and Confused'. If you can only afford one song for a movie, get 'Dazed and Confused', because it's so long you can use bits of it in several places.

Cameron Crowe: Led Zeppelin's 'Immigrant Song', which I've never been able to use, but I remember hearing that and thinking, 'It's a movie, man!' It's so sad, so many oldies are getting used in commercials now – you can have your favourite tucked away in the background and think, one day it would be so good to put this into a movie, and you turn on your TV and it's a Bubbleicious ad.

Penelope Spheeris: When I did my student films I kept putting bands like Traffic to the picture. I did this film years ago called *Hands Up for Hollywood* and I had Traffic up there, 'The Low Spark of High Heeled Boys'. I think I decided to be a film-maker the moment that I put a piece of music to film. The light came down from the heaven and just went zap. It was the moment – I was making that movie and put that Traffic record to some shots of Hollywood Boulevard at night. I went 'Wow – this is what I'd like to make my life about.'

Isaac Julien: I do think of a lot of house music as music I'd want to visualise cinematically, but it has a lot to do with ambience – with being in New York, in the centre of a specific urban black queer culture. In *Looking for Langston*, 'Can You Party' by Royal House was one such song.

Quentin Tarantino: Phil Spector is totally like that. 'River Deep Mountain High' completely fills that bill, and also in that girl group vein, in particular the records of the Shangri-Las that Shadow Morton produced. They were totally little movies. And then you get those cool story records like Marty Robbins' 'El Paso' or Don McLean's 'American Pie'. Bob Dylan totally told little movies. The songs on *Blood on the*

Amos Poe

co-directed (with Ivan Kral) *The Blank Generation* (1976), a documentary about the original New York New Wave bands such as Television, the Heartbreakers and the Patti Smith Group. His subsequent films include *Alphabet City, Unmade Beds, Subway Riders* and *Triple Bogey on a Par Five Hole*. He has also written scripts for Daniel Petrie's *Rocket Gibraltar*, starring Burt Lancaster and Macaulay Culkin, and has directed videos for Run-D.M.C. and Anthrax, among others. His latest feature is *Dead Weekend*.

Tracks, 'Tangled Up in Blue', 'Lily, Rosemary and the Jack of Hearts' – that's a movie with a beginning, a middle and an end and sub-plots and everything.

Allison Anders: I think for me the two things went completely hand in hand. I had a really shitty childhood and to escape I bought records and went to movies. That was it. And I had a huge fantasy life and a lot of it involved Paul McCartney. In fact, I feel like I learned to write great female characters from Paul McCartney. He continues to write really amazing female characters, like woman-centred songs, that are melodramas really. So for me it was really he who influenced my films. His song 'For No One', instead of being about him, when his girlfriend's leaving, it's about her. Amazing!

Julien Temple

has made music promos for a number of acts, including the Rolling Stones, Neil Young, Janet Jackson and ABC, the latter as a short feature, _Mantrap_. His first feature, _The Great Rock 'n' Roll Swindle_, was a fictionalised version of the Sex Pistols story, and his follow-up, _Absolute Beginners_, was an attempt to reinvent British pop history, using a vast array of artists including Ray Davies, Sade, David Bowie and Gil Evans. He has also made _Earth Girls Are Easy_ and _At the Max_, a live Rolling Stones concert movie in IMAX format.

Favourite Pop Movies

A fairly self-explanatory question about favourites and influences, this produced some surprising answers, but even more surprisingly, revealed a degree of implicit consensus about which films were the most important in defining the relationship between popular music and cinema.

Julien Temple: To me, _The Girl Can't Help It_ is probably the best film because it was right at the beginning and so a lot of the actual music was fresh. But I think it was also directed by someone [Frank Tashlin, 1956] who wasn't in awe of the thing or wasn't particularly trying to be part of it. It had a wonderful ironic distance but it was also celebrating the energy of the beginning of it in a wonderful way, and visually it's extraordinary. I love _Performance_ – it's not strictly a music movie but it tells me a lot about London.

Alan Rudolph: I wouldn't vouch for _Tommy_ all the way because I'm sure there's too much kitsch in there, Ken Russell threw in kitsch and the kitchen sink. But I think you'll see things in it that make you go, 'Oh man! How did they know that?' Nic Roeg, in a more severe way, is also someone whose work almost articulates the power of rock and roll. Without those kind of visuals, people wouldn't have anything to define what they are listening to. I remember being very influenced by _A Hard Day's Night_, which is probably the most influential rock film. Richard Lester – how can you not consider him a major part of the whole evolution? The best of those rock movies was _Quadrophenia_ somehow, because it _wasn't_ a rock movie and I don't think any of the people involved have ever done anything as good.

Cameron Crowe: To me, *Quadrophenia* is one of the great movies and that had a real rock spirit to it. I felt, sitting in the theatre watching it, that I had gone through that experience, and was trashed and in that club and high on amphetamines and everything, that was a movie I felt was very successful giving you that feeling – not unlike what Scorsese gives you in that Harry Nilsson 'Jump into the Fire' sequence in *GoodFellas*, where you just feel physically moved. *Quadrophenia* is thought to be an unsuccessful film, but it's one of my favourite movies of all time in terms of capturing music.

A Hard Day's Night... Jonathan Kaplan's *Over the Edge*, that was a big influence on me. It was a real contemporary use of music – Cheap Trick actually worked in that one! I really love movies about rock that capture the spirit too – that's why *A Hard Day's Night* really holds up, and in a way the Led Zeppelin concert film *The Song Remains the Same* holds up, because it has all that imagery, like the songs, and it's basically incomprehensible on a certain level, but it's just so perfect for Zeppelin – it's just such a midnight movie classic. And Penelope Spheeris' movies are great.

Amos Poe: *A Hard Day's Night*.

Allison Anders: The very first intoxicated experience of music and movies working together was, needless to say, *A Hard Day's Night*. When I saw that, it was hard to distinguish you were watching a movie. I was in our massive theatre in our home town, for one thing. I waited just like it was a concert. I was 9 years old and I stayed home one weekend because I wanted to wait for *A Hard Day's Night* – I was so 'I can't wait'. It was just like torturing myself, for the great gratification. Needless to say, when I went to see the movie, I didn't see the movie itself until I saw it for maybe the tenth time because we were screaming through the whole thing. So it was like seeing a concert with all the little girls, like – 'aargh!'

When I started out making shorts, I was hugely influenced by Wim Wenders and Martin Scorsese. I was so amazed at how they had both used pop. Before them, when you heard a song from the past it was only to be a part of the period to signify the period. Whereas *they* said, 'I'm in 1977 and I love the Ronettes' – they were the first people to do that. Then of course Fassbinder blew this all away by putting pop music from the future in the past of a period film in *Berlin Alexanderplatz*. So I have always been pretty obsessed by the relationship of people to their pop culture icons and their records.

Penelope Spheeris: *The Kids Are Alright* is a great rock and roll movie and I think *The Commitments* is as well. The ones with the real strong story and not a lot of bluff I think are great. All the Pennebaker documentaries are great and *Monterey Pop*

Cameron Crowe

began his career as a rock journalist on *Rolling Stone* before writing the novel *Fast Times at Ridgemont High*, which he subsequently adapted for Amy Heckerling's 1982 film version. He followed it with his own films *Say Anything*, and *Singles,* set in Seattle and with a soundtrack featuring many mainstays of that city's grunge scene.

Penelope Spheeris

made some of the early rock promos in the mid-70s, for bands such as Fleetwood Mac and the Doobie Brothers, before working as a director on *Saturday Night Live*. She made two documentaries about the L.A. rock scene, *The Decline of Western Civilization* and *The Decline of Western Civilization Part Two: The Metal Years,* about the West Coast punk and heavy metal scenes respectively. Her other films include *Suburbia*, *The Boys Next Door, Dudes, Little Rascals* and *Wayne's World*, for which she directed the Grammy-nominated 'Bohemian Rhapsody' video.

was great. I'm not a real fan of these festivals. *Woodstock* is too chopped up and weird for me, too long. But *Monterey Pop* was great.

Isaac Julien: *Do the Right Thing* was a film I thought a lot about while doing *Young Soul Rebels*. *Boyz N the Hood* had a fantastic soundtrack. The use of music can be really exciting, but it can also be embarrassing. I'm thinking of *Something Wild* – a black person walks into frame and there's reggae. Independent films tend to do that more, to make it groovy.

What is a pop movie, anyway?

More of a Zen riddle than this might appear, this question produced some unexpected responses. It's clear that pop culture implies a wider field than simply pop music alone. But many of our interviewees felt there was such a thing as a pop movie as such – and that to have one, there didn't need to be an electric guitar or a greased quiff in sight.

David Byrne: It's very apparent that the movies that encapsulate the attitude are often movies that don't feature a lot of music. There are films that feature a lot of music, or are about music, ones that purport to be about rock and roll, about a band or whatever. And yet the ones that express the kind of contemporary attitudes are films like *Reservoir Dogs*, which have older music, but express one aspect of contemporary attitude more than a music film would.

Cameron Crowe: Somebody said *Reservoir Dogs* was the ultimate Generation X movie, and I agree. That is a movie that really captures a spirit, even if it's not about this generation, that are 20, 22 years right now. But there are a lot of movies that are roughly the equivalent of the John Hughes movies of the 80s – almost like *Pretty in Pink* for Lemonheads fans.

Quentin Tarantino: A lot of movies about bands – in particular when they try to do a movie about a rock figure – don't work, they're trying too hard. Either the musicians can't act well enough or the actors will never sell you that they're musicians, or they just carry too much baggage, of having to be the last word on rock or whatever. For me, the use of music in movies is one of the most cinematic things you can do. That way you can really take your movie in and just, like, *rock 'n' roll* – you get, like, a really cool song, you put it on your stereo and you blast it, or you're driving down the street and a song that you really love kicks on the radio, makes you drive a little faster and just catches your adrenaline, catches something in you, all right. And the same way you can have the right kind of scene in a movie, whether taking rock and roll music and applying it to a scene and getting that effect or like in a movie like *Terminator 2* or something that has that big truck chasing a kid on the motorbike – that action scene is the equivalent of rock and roll. It opens your pores up, it gets you all cut up and you're just into the excitement and the emotion of it all. I'm not a big heavy metal fan, but action movies are to movies what heavy metal is to rock. They're not very respectable, but they totally give you just pulsating thrills, they are completely euphoric...

Amos Poe: *A Clockwork Orange* is a rock and roll movie as far as I'm concerned.

Wim Wenders

was born in Düsseldorf in 1945. While still a film student in Munich he began making short films, including *Three American LPs* (1968) and *Alabama 2000 Light Years from Home* (1969), cut to songs by 60s rock acts such as the Kinks and the Rolling Stones. From his first feature, *Summer in the City* (1970), through the Palme d'Or winner *Paris, Texas*, to his 1993 feature *Faraway, So Close!*, Wenders has used popular music as an integral element in his film-making and has maintained a close working relationship with musicians such as Can, Ry Cooder, Nick Cave and U2 (for whom he shot a video as part of the *Red Hot and Blue* AIDS charity project). Wenders also acted as executive producer on Chris Petit's influential post-punk road movie *Radio On* (1979).

Film-makers on Musicians

Film-makers often choose to work with the musicians who have inspired them and fuelled their own visual music in the head. But from the film-maker's point of view, too, getting the right sound can be a complex process.

Wim Wenders: It is one of the biggest pleasures in the movie-making process that you produce certain images and then you get to the editing table and you actually ask these people whose music you listened to while you were shooting the film if they couldn't help you finish it. And the biggest kick in the whole process for me is not shooting and not preparing and not finishing the film, but the moment when the tape arrives with the songs. It's really the most fantastic moment. Like the moment that Ry Cooder started with the first note of the song we had chosen, at the front of the screen, and for the first time playing the subject of *Paris, Texas*. It was like he was really cranking the film once more, but on his guitar not on the camera. I remember that moment. I had a shiver on my back. And it is still one of the most exciting things I feel.

Allison Anders: For me it's just another exciting interpretation – somebody else interpreting the movie you're making, helping you to make the movie you're trying to make. It's no different from trying source cues and them not working. The composer writes some stuff and you're, like, 'That doesn't work', or, 'Oh, my God, I can't believe...' – the exciting thing is, like, 'Oh, my God, that's exactly it, I can't believe what you added here, how much that process brought the movie out!'

J. Mascis' score for *Gas Food Lodging* did exactly what the score is supposed to do. It brought out the emotions without knocking people over the head – which I think rock musicians can do so much better than guys who are used to working on

Quentin Tarantino

moved from being a video clerk to highly
acclaimed writer/director with the release of
his debut film *Reservoir Dogs* (1992), notable
among other things for its bubblegum pop
soundtrack. Since then he has seen a number
of his old scripts filmed by other directors –
Tony Scott's *True Romance* (1993) and Oliver
Stone's *Natural Born Killers* (1994) – while
also completing his second feature *Pulp
Fiction*, which won the Palme d'Or at the 1994
Cannes Film Festival. Tarantino has also
made a cameo appearance in Rory Kelly's
Sleep with Me, was executive producer on
Roger Avary's *Killing Zoe* and has recently
been filming his section of the portmanteau
movie *Four Rooms*.

TV and all that stuff. When they are used to being composers for film or TV they tend
to be far more heavy-handed and not go with the feel of the piece as much.

Quentin Tarantino: I'm a little nervous about the idea of working with a composer
because I don't like giving up that much control. Like, what if he goes off and writes
a score and I don't like it? I don't like using new music that much because I want to
pick what I know. *Dogs* wouldn't have benefited from having a score, it would have
broken the real-time aspect of it. *Pulp Fiction* has score but again I didn't work with
a composer. We used surf music a lot as score.

Bob Last: There are two reasons why it doesn't work. One, for pop musicians,
making the transition to score is a very loaded moment in terms of their own
perceptions. They always see it as something where they should be seen to be
composing in a way they would never burden themselves with if they were doing a
song. From the other side, the whole structure of post-production is still based on
applying sound to silent pictures. Nobody really is making audio-visual material. It
means you lock off the picture and you have your composer come and do it. It
absolutely militates against taking advantage of what pop musicians are good at,
which is improvisation. The reason it's good pop music is because pop genres are
so tightly defined that where you do break them, you can be completely wild and
uncontrolled in a way that classical composition will never allow. If you took a film
composer and told them to do a pop record, they'd never be able to do it.

Michael Mann: I used Tangerine Dream for *Thief* because although the film was
set in Chicago, my home town where I grew up in the 60s listening to Muddy Waters
and Howling Wolf at Curly's Place (a famous neighbourhood bar), the thematic
values of *Thief* as a high-tech political metaphor needed more abstract form and the
specificity of ethnic music wouldn't work. Hence the need for an electronic score. I
had known about the interesting origins of Edgar Froese as an early 60s blues
guitarist, which gave a blues composition base to Tangerine Dream's work. So there
was a link between the sound I needed and the film's Chicago setting. I started off
by selecting from their earlier work material I liked prior to shooting and it was that,
with some variations, we subsequently recorded in Berlin.

Cameron Crowe: It's hard when you're a huge fan of your scoring artist and
you're both kind of on a journey together. You'll be in the studio one night with Paul
Westerberg – who scored *Singles* – and he plays one of the great instrumental
passages, and you as a fan love it, but you as the guy who made the movie know
it's not right. It's hard to say, 'Paul, that's not quite right – but can you put it on a
tape so I can have it myself?' Which I did do so many times that I think by the end
he felt he was doing a tape collection and not a score.

Alan Rudolph: I work completely unconventionally with Mark Isham. He will give me all the elements and then sometimes I'll ask him to redo something or to look and listen and maybe make a cleaner version. But you just *discover* with music, and that's really the key to it. Mark is a very, very gifted musician and composer, but without his horn he would lose an edge for me.

For *Return Engagement*, I worked with this guitarist Adrian Belew. I got him on the phone and I said, 'Listen, we made a documentary, are you interested in doing the music?' I said, 'Come to this garage where we are working in New York and I'll teach you everything you need to know about putting music to movies.' 'Oh, OK.' So we had this one scene on the editing machine and we watched it and put on this piece of music of his and we played this scene. It was great, it was kind of a bouncy thing and it played against what was going on. Then we put on a ballad, one of those spacy kind of things, and played the same scene. And he says, 'Oh, my God – that's all you need to know about music and movies.'

Penelope Spheeris: For me there are obvious places when I'm working on a film which ask very specifically for a song. And then there are obvious places which ask specifically for score, so for me there's never a question as to which I would use. If I show a film to a composer and I say, 'There needs to be a source cue here', and he says, 'But I could write some great score', I say, 'OK, then go ahead and write it and then we'll put them both up next to each other and we'll decide.' And sometimes I'll test it one way and the other. But I normally shoot montage sequences so that I can have places to put source music.

Alan Rudolph

worked as assistant director to Robert Altman and as co-writer of his film *Buffalo Bill and the Indians* before going on to direct his own features, including *Welcome to L.A.*, *Remember My Name*, *Trouble in Mind*, *Equinox*, the rock comedy *Roadie*, starring Meat Loaf, *Made in Heaven* – with cameos by Neil Young, Ric Ocasek and Tom Petty – and *Mrs Parker and the Vicious Circle*. He also worked on the Alice Cooper promo film *Welcome to My Nightmare*. He has had a long association with composer and trumpeter Mark Isham.

Musicians on Directors

Where pop musicians tend to be autonomous in the studio, working to a director's requirements involves a whole new range of pressures and conflicts. Here, David Byrne and Ry Cooder talk about the pleasures and pains of yoking sound to vision.

David Byrne: Jonathan Demme had shot most of *Something Wild*, and was doing some fine trimming in the editing. Usually it gets to about that point and then directors and producers all of a sudden say, 'We need some music.' He said, 'Could you do a song for this?' I sort of tried to get out of it and made what I thought was an impossible request. I said, 'I'd really love to do it as a duet with Celia Cruz. If you can arrange that, I'll do it.' They came back of course within a couple of days and said, 'She agreed to do it.' So I had to get hard at work. And that was real straightforward – he had a video clip, a three-quarter inch of the title sequence, and we talked

David Byrne

was the founder of Talking Heads, with whom he recorded several albums, including *Talking Heads 1977, More Songs About Buildings and Food, Remain in Light* and *Naked.* The band appeared in two films, Jonathan Demme's record of their live show *Stop Making Sense,* and *True Stories,* directed by Byrne himself. He has recorded a number of solo albums, including *Rei Momo* and *David Byrne,* and collaborated with Brian Eno on *My Life in the Bush of Ghosts.* As well as directing two films, *Ile Aiye* – on the Brazilian *candomble* religion – and his own concert film, *Between the Teeth* (with David Wild), he has co-written the soundtrack of Bernardo Bertolucci's *The Last Emperor* (with Ryuichi Sakamoto) and contributed songs to Jonathan Demme's *Something Wild* and *Philadelphia.* He is also the founder of the Luaka Bop record label.

through it. He wanted to emphasise that Manhattan was an island; he was shooting all of it from a boat while using Manhattan, so I made it seem like a tropical island.

For Bertolucci's *The Last Emperor*, I think they decided to assign different scenes to Ryuichi Sakamoto and me, based on what they thought we could do. There was no overlap at all. We met and passed in a studio but that was about it. I didn't know that I could make everything I was asked to do work, but I'd had enough experience doing dance scores, or writing to something else, so I knew that I could do that up to a point. I listened to a lot of Chinese music that they brought back, that was different from what was commercially available here, and it seemed to run this complete spectrum from almost like Western rock to real percussive things to things that sounded like Bartok meets John Cage. Really bizarre harmonic kind of stuff, it didn't sound like what we imagined as traditional Chinese music, so I thought that almost anything you did would fit the definition of twentieth-century Chinese music and as long as you stayed away from too many gongs and things then anything applied. At the same time Bernardo wanted a little bit of music to some extent to evoke the place and time. He didn't want it to be totally contemporary-sounding, so I tried to walk that line.

Ry Cooder: My experience is, from most of the musicians that I know and from scoring films, that most musicians are not oriented visually too much. Because you're working with your own emotions and your own focus, and 'my sound' this, and 'I wrote' that. So to look into another person's image bank is not the typical day in the life of a typical musician in a creative sense.

I begin to think how I do things. I have to imagine I can hear it, but who the hell's going to play it? I have to play a lot of the stuff 'cause I can't talk to anybody about it, I have to do it myself. So I have to find instruments to do it and learn to play those instruments or make them. There are people who invent weird instruments, and I ask them, 'Do you have anything that goes "Weeeouuuu", only fifty times lower than that?' And they say, 'Oh sure.'

I was told years ago, if a director doesn't want you, don't do the work. If the studio's pushing you, don't do the work. Which turned out to be very good advice. I did a picture once where the director didn't want me around and hated it; it was a great score. But I realised I was not what the director wanted and no matter what I did, it could be Jesus walking on water, he wouldn't like it. You have to understand how these things operate. The structure of a movie is so Byzantine, it's people and money and egos and everything. Frankly, I don't relate to it at all. On the other hand, if somebody hires you and you want to do work, you gotta say, 'Well, I'm gonna try and fit into the scheme somehow. Try to make myself a part of this and be a team player.'

I've noticed that directors sort of fear music as an area that they don't necessarily control. Wim Wenders was paranoid to get involved. He had made *Paris, Texas* a delicate, fragile thing. But the music could murder this film. So he paced the floor and climbed the walls and I said, 'Just calm down. This is easy, there's going to be no problem. Let me do a couple of cues and show you what's happening.' And he said, 'Oh, thank God, he's got it.' I feel at ease with Walter Hill. I'm not scared of his aesthetics, because I see some films and they scare me. I think, 'I'm so afraid of this director's aesthetic. I'm going to be pinned to the wall like a bug.' Me and Walter have all the systems, and when he starts a film he shows me the script, which I don't like to read, and I know that I can't visualise it from the printed page and he'll change it anyhow. And then by and by you go out to the set or you look at some footage and then you say, 'Oh, I see', and I'll know where this thing's going to go and how it'll work.

Finished films, they mix them like records – mix in whatever you got. I like them before they're cut. I never like those street versions, man, give me the four-hour weird version that the studio doesn't like 'cause that's got all the strange little inside stuff. Fascinating little bits. But the process is enjoyable and you really can push. I have pushed myself into doing things, I can tell you, that are quite insane.

The Celluloid Jukebox

Whether it's a director programming his or her personal Top 10 into a film, or trying to get the right tracks to fit a place, a time or a subculture, there's an infinite repertoire of music available on CD and vinyl to be plundered – as well as the possibility of having music specially written. How do those difficult choices get made?

Quentin Tarantino: I started realising how much I liked pop music and how much I listened to it. I'd hear music and I would imagine a scene for it – this would be a great opening credit sequence in a movie. One of the things that I do as a film-maker now is if I start to seriously consider the idea of doing a movie, I immediately try to find out what would be the right song to be the opening credit sequence even before I write the script. When I find the right one, it's like OK, boom, OK, I got that. It's not that the personality of the movie is in that song, but it really gives me a good handle on it. I did the opening credit sequence for *Reservoir Dogs* and I think it's one of the best scenes of the entire movie, just all those guys walking out in their black suits with 'Little Green Bag' on the soundtrack. Does 'Little Green Bag' have anything to do with the movie? No. But it's just the right sound, and the right feel.

If a song in a movie is used really well, as far as I'm concerned, that movie owns that song, it can never be used again. And if it *is* used again... You know, they used 'Be My Baby' in *Dirty Dancing* and it's like, that's *Mean Streets*' song, how *dare* you use 'Be My Baby'. If you use a song in a movie and it's right, then, you know, you've got a marriage. Every time you hear that song you'll think of that movie.

I've seen movies where they put music all the way through and it's worked very well. Phil Kaufman did it great in *The Wanderers*, he had music all the way through and it was clever. But the problem is that nowadays you're trying to sell soundtracks and what they'll do is just pay for a movie with music all the way through it. So basically the record company is just trying to put music in wherever they can: 'Is there a reason why we can't have music playing in this scene?' What happens is it tends to dull the effect. Unless the intention is to throw you back into another time – Richard Linklater's *Dazed and Confused* has music all the way through it from the beginning to the end but that's perfect. It takes you all the way back to '76 and all the different songs playing there and they're very cleverly used. He never has a sequence built around a song, necessarily – a lot of it is just hearing Bob Dylan sing 'Hurricane' or something out of the corner of your ear. But it's cool. The movie does what it's supposed to do. You see the opening credits and you walk out of the movie singing 'Sweet Emotion' by Aerosmith.

Isaac Julien: My approach to music has a lot to do with memory. My memories are usually to do with past chart hits. In *Young Soul Rebels*, songs are used to evoke memory, but it's more than that. We're talking about the signifying practices of black popular culture – if you have no representations of your own as you're growing up, then obviously black popular culture has a pivotal link for you with American culture. So using 'One Nation Under a Groove' was a pun on the 1977 Silver Jubilee; the nation Funkadelic are talking about is the black nation, of a particular kind. But with reference to the Silver Jubilee, it's another nation, the British nation, the Commonwealth, the Empire. So it's an example of music being used to read against the grain of the hegemony.

Bob Last: There are structural reasons why it's almost impossible not to deal with the repertoire. But you use it for the associations it brings with it. In that sense the repertoire, even if it's very recent, is twice as efficient as anything that's completely new. It's because of the resonance of pop and its presence in everyone's life that you're now able to use it in movies in a particular kind of way.

If you're using popular music, part of its meaning is that it's popular. Pop music that isn't popular is no longer pop music, it's something else. So you're forced to make that jump – you've got to say, we'll make those calculations for a UK market, or we'll make them for a US market. It's easier to make them for a US market because it moves at a rate that's comparable with that of film-making; you can't make them for a British market.

It's no good just gluing a piece of music on at the end, saying, 'There's a radio on in this scene, we'll put it in here.' The most interesting example of that was *Touch of Evil*, where 90 per cent of it is done with source, it's all on jukeboxes. Obviously there was that excitement at the time about jukeboxes and the radio – Mancini did endless fake jukebox tracks and it's fantastic.

Cameron Crowe: The best part of the process for me is when you finally get the film back and there are pieces of scenes and you get to try the music that always worked in your head. Very rarely is that the music that ends up working.

Alan Rudolph: One thing I learned is that anything that has ever been produced on CD, I don't care who, a Malian guitarist or whoever, is owned by some big company. If it got to a CD, believe me, Island or EMI or somebody is behind it. I go to the International section of these esoteric record stores in any city I go to, I find these albums, and I take a chance on them like you do with pop albums. I came to my producer David Blocker with about ten songs and I said, 'OK, here's what I'm interested in.' And he said, 'Wow, what *is* this – Bulgarian, guitars from Timbuktu, Norwegian?', and I said, 'Well, it's, it's ... you'll love it.'

Allison Anders: Making *Mi Vida Loca* was pretty wild. These Chicano gang kids have this whole repertoire of music that they listen to, and they have their own standards, from the 50s up until now. They continue to add music on to their subculture, so they'll like 50s stuff and Motown, then James Brown, then in the 80s they're into disco, and Rick James and Zapp and stuff like that. Then with the new stuff, they're actually reluctant to take something on – they were the last kids to come around to rap. I have this sense that because when it is taken on in the subculture, it is taken on forever, it has to prove itself to be really good – it's just gonna stick around for another four, five generations.

John Taylor from Duran Duran wrote the score – he was perfect, because he could do the melodic stuff, but he could also do the total street, like Chic sort of street stuff, and dance rhythms. In fact, he turned me on to the song that becomes sort of the theme of the movie, 'Girls It Ain't Easy' by the Honeycombs, and he sampled it for one piece that he wrote for the film. I also gave him the tapes that the kids had made for me. He just thought that the soundtrack that the kids had basically dictated was just great, so he totally understood where to go for sources to sample.

Isaac Julien

was a member of the London-based Sankofa film collective, and worked on a number of projects including *Black and White in Colour*, *Territories* and *This is Not an AIDS Film*. His shorts include *The Attendant* and *Looking for Langston*, a film about the poet Langston Hughes and the 1920s Harlem Renaissance. His feature *Young Soul Rebels*, which used a 70s funk soundtrack, looked at the 1977 Jubilee Year from the British soul scene perspective.

I think the soundtrack album itself is a bit disappointing because it doesn't have the whole texture of the subculture on it. The exciting thing is maybe we have added back on to the subculture, and that maybe Tony! Toni! Toné!'s song will be one of those ballads that kids will dedicate to each other for years to come.

Packaging the Soundtrack

The work of putting music to film can be considerably complicated – or occasionally facilitated – when record companies take a hand. Striking that lucrative soundtrack deal can be decisive in ensuring a film's box-office success – or even in getting it made at all. Here, though, is where matters get complicated for the film-maker, whose own sound agenda might not match the requirements of the record company with their eye on promoting their own catalogue...

Cameron Crowe: A lot of times, music in movies is the poor stepchild of the film process. People slap it on at the last minute, and directors who don't know what 'hit music' is phone up a music supervisor at the last minute and say, 'Let's jam on these soundtrack hits. OK, why don't we just have two seconds of it while the cop's coming out of the car?'

On *Say Anything*, they told me at the last minute that if I didn't have hit music on the soundtrack then it wouldn't be marketed, so we were running with extra money from 20th Century-Fox, trying to find hits. It was such an odd thing to be throwing money at Cheap Trick for a B-side, but that was what the marketing department wanted, and it gave me such a bad taste in my mouth that it did create a situation in *Singles* where it was all unheard music. I think because of the success of *Singles* that they're going to leave me alone musically.

The quest is always to get your video on MTV and to get a hit single out there in the marketplace before your movie comes out. It creates a situation where you have a middle-level artist who has rough cuts of every movie in town! They're basically shoving videos into their VCR and going, 'Coppola's *Frankenstein* – that looks pretty good, maybe we should do a song:' That's so off the mark when you think of music that really mattered in a movie – Scorsese put the Rolling Stones in *Mean Streets* and we know that was a choice that came from the heart, not from somebody at the last minute saying, 'Let's get a Rolling Stones song, Marty.'

Bob Last: It seems unfortunate that film-makers who may have an interesting strategy like that resist it because it's so much associated with the crassest form of packaging in the States. The financial dynamic is, we haven't got a music budget, we'll scam a couple of hundred thousand dollars off the label, the label says, 'We'll give you the money but we're going to put in who we want.' So film-makers who may have an interesting strategy tend to back off from relying on source in any kind of intelligent way.

Penelope Spheeris: When I was hired for *Wayne's World*, I was just told it was going to be a Warner Bros album, so I never questioned it. Then I met the Warner Bros people and they were sort of vaguely interested in the movie and then when we had our first preview and our scores came up in the 90s they took this incredible interest, to the point of forcing me to use the music that I really didn't want to use, and that's when it got tricky. I think Eric Clapton is a cool guy and everything but I thought his music got really soft of recent years and I didn't find it to be appropriate head-banging music, so I didn't really want to put it in the film. But that was it, that's the way it happens and I've got my platinum record at home from the sales and, you know, my job is a series of compromises, what can I tell ya?

Ry Cooder: It happens a lot. The executives would like to see some marketing in place. They like to see some soundtrack but you get a hit like *The Bodyguard* or *Sleepless in Seattle*, they go mad. The feeding frenzy is on – they want some of the goddamn money and they want it now. So you come in and say, 'Well, I'm gonna do this cute little job and I'll do my thing', and they say, 'Oh, Christ. He's gonna do another *Paris, Texas* – silly-sounding guitars with rusty strings, we can't use that. We want hits, we want the big orchestra.' Well, why didn't you say that? You insult me. Had one on *Geronimo*: 'What's he gonna do, one of those *Paris, Texas* scores?' Now why would I... You know, a cavalry charge and two hundred Indians and I'm gonna go 'Weeooougghh'? I resent that, you know, I really do.

Allison Anders: In my film *Border Radio*, we used the underground punk scene in LA. We got John Doe from X, Dave Alvin from the Blasters did our score, with Steve Berlin. We had songs by Green on Red, Los Lobos, Lazy Cowgirls, I mean, just everybody. In fact, our soundtrack was what gave us money to finish the film. We went to Enigma Records and they gave us money to finish, because they could get songs by John Doe and Dave Alvin that they could never possibly afford otherwise – they couldn't get those guys. They gave us finishing funds to finish the film, plus took care of all the licensing and everything for us. So the soundtrack was the only thing that we had.

Bob Last

has worked as music co-ordinator on David Hayman's *Silent Scream,* two Terence Davies films, *Distant Voices, Still Lives* and *The Long Day Closes,* Sally Potter's *Orlando,* and Iain Softley's *Backbeat.* He was the founder of the record label Fast Product, which first released records by the Human League, the Gang of Four and the Fire Engines, and directed his own short film, *Compellance.* He is currently Executive Series Producer for BFI TV.

On *Mi Vida Loca*, it was hilarious, because Mercury Records would start pitching me on somebody and it is such a sexist thing, because they would send me some rapper, or some guy with no teeth, some ugly motherfucker, and they would go, 'This guy is really great.' And then, instead of sending me the tapes of the girl singers, they would send me the pictures first – they would say, 'These girls are really cute.' But they would do these heavy pitches, and I said, 'The bottom line is, the kids in the neighbourhood in the movie are the music consultants.'

Quentin Tarantino: We needed a record deal to pay for the rights to the songs to *Reservoir Dogs*. We had different screenings of the movie for record executives and they all said, 'There's not a soundtrack here', and they all turned us down. Then we had one more screening and three labels were very interested. Then Kathy Nelson at MCA stepped up to the plate and said, 'We'll do it if you put in one of our artists, so we can have something to push.' Bedlam were a group that MCA signed; they actually disbanded soon afterwards. But what happened was, MCA had them and they wanted to do the album, but we had picked all the songs already and they were, like, 'We could do a remake of "Stuck in the Middle With You"', and I was, like, 'Oh, no ...' So MCA go, 'We'd like to have something to promote, how about these guys – if you'd be interested, maybe we'll do the album.' So they played me their CD, and I thought, 'These guys ain't so bad.' They wanted to do 'Magic Carpet Ride' and I thought, fine. But unfortunately their group disbanded a little bit after that.

Isaac Julien: Obviously the music was part of the packaging for *Young Soul Rebels*. If you want to attract different audiences, it's good if one of your tracks is released by Mica Paris – for a film appealing to the club audience, that's important. In some instances, the music can be better than the film. But songs from Hollywood films going to No. 1 in the pop charts, I'm sure that's been an encouragement for record companies to get interested in collaborating with film-makers.

Composers – In the Tradition

Although some film-makers have developed firm alliances with particular soundtrack composers, others are deeply suspicious of the artistic compromises entailed in letting another artist 'hear' their film for them. At the same time, many of our interviewees, however sceptical about traditional film scoring, paid homage to some of their favourite composers, sometimes revealing unexpected affinities.

Amos Poe: The worst sin you can do with music and movies is where the music says exactly what is happening on the screen. You know, it's a love song when they're making love. Sergio Leone is very good at avoiding that. There's a violent scene, he has this pretty little music going on. But the tendency usually is to use music that's just like what's going on – the Joel Silver approach, which is to underline it, underline it, underline it.

David Byrne: I remember in the early 70s becoming familiar with the Fellini movies and Nino Rota scores. That kind of thing, where you notice the music, whereas in a lot of other films, the music may have been an essential part but you didn't notice it. It remained kind of an invisible support. Then there are the obvious soundtrack ones – Morricone, and new composers like Steve Reich or Phil Glass, Robert Ashley. Lots of very quiet music I tended to be attracted to, things that really had a strong mood attached as opposed to music that was dramatic and oriented towards cues. After I'd done music for a little bit of film here and there, I started to notice, say in Spielberg films, that some of those were wall-to-wall music. Like in *Indiana Jones,* music started at the opening credit and didn't stop till the last credit, maybe one little bit of silence for a reel change or whatever but that was about it. And it was almost all cued for hits in the action, punches and explosions.

Quentin Tarantino: Of course Morricone, that goes without saying. If I were seriously considering doing a movie with a composer, I would consider Joe Jackson. His score for *Tucker* was really good. And I guess Jerry Goldsmith and Elmer Bernstein, they're great. They do probably too many movies, but if I could get Jerry Goldsmith and know he was going to do a score as good as he did for *Under Fire,* which I think is one of the most beautiful scores ever in the history of film, I would say, 'Yeah, wow.' I talked with John Cale at one point to do the score for *Dogs.* I thought he did a good job of the *Caged Heat* score.

Ry Cooder: I always loved Georges Delerue, for what he did in those Truffaut pictures. They've got beautiful melodies in them. For me, melodies are the thing. It may be considered schmaltzy by the post-modern era but I like melodies pretty good.

Romantic melodies, I like them. And Morricone's great at that, he's got this funny sense of humour – so cool. Fearless guy, just totally fearless. But he was also coming from a place of real high understanding. He's not so rustic that he uses a bad accordion because that's all he knows. He uses a bad accordion or crackly electric guitar because it makes the difference. And Mancini is just awesome. He's maybe my favourite of all. Anyone who writes 'Peter Gunn' is a goddamn genius of the highest sort.

I used to really like French movies and Japanese movies but I'm not so sure any more. Everything's gotten homogenised, it's not what it was. That sense of regional style is missing. I like Buñuel a whole lot, but I'm a retro guy, you know, I like Robert Aldrich. I'd like to have scored *Kiss Me Deadly*. Tremendously deep sound, like they have one open mike or something, and you feel the room that the instruments are in. But that kind of stuff is of no consequence now, nobody makes films like that. And those post-war Italian films, De Sica and all those guys, they could make films with a sense of that hyper-reality thing.

Cameron Crowe: I've noticed that a real hack syndrome has developed among a lot of these guys. They come in to meet you and they say, 'I'll give you whatever you want – what do you want?' It's like they're selling you music by the yard. A lot of it isn't very inspired – I know it's a tough job, you have to please directors who change their minds all the time, but I was surprised when I met traditional scoring guys how little soul they put into it.

Allison Anders: I think there is little place any more for the classic film scores. Film has become so coded now that you don't need as much for the emotions to come through. Sometimes you have to work with rock musicians, in terms of pacing and stuff like that because I find that they understand the feelings a whole lot better. Theirs is a kind of innocence that doesn't crowd, they don't add on so much that you are distanced from the feelings. I think that's what an overblown score would do now. Somebody who used it really well, who could work with great composers, was Douglas Sirk; he even used pop songs – in *There's Always Tomorrow* the score is variations on the song 'Blue Moon', which is very important to both of the characters and their past hopes.

Pop Video

Although we've chosen not to treat music video as a major theme of the book, many of our interviewees have made promo clips, or featured in them, or are acutely aware that video presents a challenge – one that these days simply can't be ignored – to the whole language of film, and to conceptions of film's relation to music.

Penelope Spheeris: I personally was never really comfortable doing videos. I did videos to pay my house payments. It's not a form which I understand, it's not a form which I enjoy. And it's not a form in which I can successfully deal with all the political people that you have to deal with. It's awful. The last video I did was 'Bohemian Rhapsody'.

David Byrne: My thought was, here's an opportunity to make short, somewhat experimental films to music and have an outlet. You can have them seen, if you're lucky, within a couple of months of making them. I realised at the very beginning, it wasn't as clear that it was a selling tool. It was more just this ancillary thing. There were some that were obviously selling tools – you know, just get a beautiful girl in there and whatever. But there was a little window to play around some more and do things that weren't obviously connected to the music, that aren't a literal interpretation of the music. Going back to feature films, there are numerous features that have attempted to capture music, to be about bands or rock and roll, and I think it generally fails.

Julien Temple: For all the bad videos there are, there are some wonderful pieces that push the language of film further and I've always felt that it is a laboratory, particularly for young film-makers. You can always cut to the drummer – there's a safety net because you have the characters of the band playing instruments, that gives it a skeleton if you need it. There's no other outlet that reaches the audience that allows that degree of experimentation. It's a far more director-driven form of film-making than anything, other than personal movies. It's also very hard film-making, in a sense – the conventions and the rules of video are that you need a lot of different shots because it has to keep firing that interest up, so you have to get a bigger number of shots in a day than on a movie or commercial. So the actual pace of it has to be driven very hard by the director. It's clearly influenced cinema – it's provided a far more visually vigilant mass audience for cinema.

MTV Moments

With film-goers becoming as literate about the shorthand language of pop video as they are about more traditional movie language, cinema has come to cater increasingly to the new tastes which that shift has nurtured. Many films now contain – some are even composed predominantly of – song-anchored sequences that are effectively videos-within-the-film, in which narrative needs are subjugated to the rhythms and iconography of the hit. Our interviewees tended to be deeply suspicious of this tendency – but we found it has its defenders as well.

Bob Last: There are a lot of mainstream movies where you can see the MTV moment coming up, and the worst are those that pretend not to – it's better just to go for it. How do you tell it's coming up? There are subtle cues in the pacing of a movie. If I was looking in a rough assembly and thinking about source, I would spot it a mile off. There's a change in the pace, it adjusts itself, sometimes very subtly. 'OK, this is our MTV moment, we need to go through the chorus twice or else they won't notice it.' Directors should take much more account of the underlying rhythm of music. You can cut pictures to even unheard musical rhythms, but that's not the same thing as your MTV moment, when it clearly just changes gear for this external 'actor'. An audience can spot it a mile off. But if you're completely blunt, you can have a musical moment, and then it becomes more like a musical. Real MTV moments are fine by me.

Leslie Harris: Music just has to be a part of the film. When you do dialogue, it's very important – but music is just as important. Film is image, but it's also sound – you pick your images carefully, you should pick your music just as carefully. You can really choose music to take advantage of the *tone* of the film, and I don't think you can go wrong. It's when you try to fit a square peg into a round hole, it can backfire. A lot of music in today's films tends to do that.

Quentin Tarantino: It's like, 'Let's put a familiar song in – let's put "Pretty Woman" on the soundtrack or some old ditty that everyone knows and then build a little montage around that song...' It's mostly lazy film-making – unless you're doing it for a specific reason, I don't think you should do it. After Scorsese working with music brilliantly his entire career, I didn't like his use of music in *GoodFellas* at all. I waited my whole life for someone to use 'Layla' in a movie and then you barely even notice that he does. Scorsese is probably the best that there is at the use of music in movies, and it's interesting that the movie he wallpapered with music is the one that is the least effective. But my editor Sally Menke completely disagrees with me, she loves the use of music in that movie.

Miami Vice

Although it might seem surprising that any one TV show should merit a section of its own, the fact that Michael Mann's influential cop series cropped up so often in conversation testifies to its importance as a template for new ways of working song into narrative...

Ry Cooder: Michael Mann's the perfect example. He would think up stuff with this kind of emotional level in mind, like his *Miami Vice*. That is an extended video, it's an environment put up there. I'm sure he thought, 'How will I reflect the aesthetic values in this music that we have?' He conjures up this little scenario involving cars, clothes, guns – 'Bring me a car, I don't like it, send it back, get me another.' 'The gun doesn't look right, I want a blue one... I want a purple one... The hat, the suit' – and then the neon and all that stuff. So for him that worked, the music and the whole thing, and at that time it was perfect.

Quentin Tarantino: *Miami Vice* used music very well. To this day I'll get some of those songs from the 80s, which I don't like, or retain that much from, but from time to time I'll hear a song that I remember seeing on *Miami Vice* and I see Don Johnson driving around. That image. That Phil Collins song, 'In the Air Tonight' – whenever I hear that song I see them driving at night, getting ready to blow somebody away.

Michael Mann: The intention in *Miami Vice* was to achieve the organic interaction of music and content. Sometimes an episode would be written around a song, as was the case with 'Smuggler's Blues', where Glenn Frey wrote the song and it acted as a libretto for the episode. Sometimes songs would be sought after the fact. We had complete autonomy and never had any problem getting music at all because after the pilot made a success out of Phil Collins' 'In the Air Tonight', record companies constantly offered us anything and everything. As producer, I controlled the music selection with all the directors. The intent was not to achieve complementariness. The objective was to achieve the excitement and integration of the weight of the immediately previous story, the dramatic urgency, the themes and visual thrust into an experience that, when it worked, was magic. An example was the use of 'In the Air Tonight' – Crockett and Tubbs are driving to a confrontation which they may not survive and Crockett stops to ask his ex-wife about their history. 'When we were together, what we had, it was real, wasn't it?' and she answers, 'Sure it was, Sonny. Are you OK?' Yeah, he's fine and he hangs up. He gets back in the black Daytona and drives the wet streets with Phil Collins singing, 'I can feel it...coming in the air tonight...'

Leslie Harris

wrote and directed *Just Another Girl on the I.R.T.,* a New York drama featuring a rap soundtrack by Bomb Squad/Public Enemy producer Eric Sadler. She has also directed *Bessie Coleman: Dream to Fly,* a TV film about the African-American pioneer aviator Bessie Coleman, and is currently working on *Royalties, Rhythm and Blues,* a thriller set in the record industry.

Musicians as Performers, and vice versa

Since pop movies began, musicians and actors alike have looked for career opportunites in jumping between careers – to vastly differing effects. This turned out to be the most controversial topic. Some of our interviewees welcomed the idea of pop performers acting, others felt the two roles should be kept separate at all costs.

Alan Rudolph: I think people who establish themselves in music first, they have got the range, I think most of them have an instinct and they rely on it. That's why I think people like Willie Nelson especially, he plays Willie. I don't care, he's Willie. And I don't think he'd ever say, 'I'm an actor'. To me, it's boring to have rock stars play rock stars. And they usually play good/bad guys, but bad guys are kind of easy.

Amos Poe: The point with an actor is to draw the audience to you. Madonna plays the audience, she manipulates the audience most of the time, which is why it doesn't really work because you can't do that on film. Elvis Presley actually, if you look at some of his films, there's some sort of comedy going on there, it's like a hick backward guy playing Hollywood – you know, *Viva Las Vegas*. But it's kitsch, it's pop, and you're selling the album for that moment, it's not for posterity.

Quentin Tarantino: Sometimes it works and sometimes it doesn't. I always thought Elvis Presley was a pretty good actor. All right, he put himself in some pretty bad movies but the first six or seven movies that he did were really fucking terrific. He's the biggest tragedy of all the rock stars, because it was conceivable that he could have been a better actor than he was. He was a great singer but he could have been a truly terrific actor if he had worked with a lot of other real actors. When you look at *Blue Hawaii* and those movies, you really see talent just being mind-stripped away. If ever I see Tennessee Williams' play *Orpheus Descending*, I think Elvis would have been the best person to play that part.

To tell you the truth, rock stars have actually come across better than actors trying to play rock stars. There's just something about when actors do it, you just don't believe they're a musician. When you do, it's a big deal – you buy Gary Busey as a musician in *The Buddy Holly Story*. You believe he could have come up with those songs. The only one recently that really pulled it off is Val Kilmer as Jim Morrison in *The Doors*.

Unless they're just naturally in tune with acting, the problem with rock stars acting is the same problem when you put any non-professional actor in a movie – they can offer a couple of gems you wouldn't normally see but there's a certain undramatic drive, a lack of intensity. Non-professionals just don't have the drama about them. Rock stars seem unapproachable and the minute you see David Bowie in a movie playing second banana to Jeff Goldblum, it does kind of knock it down a bit.

Cameron Crowe: The easiest thing to say would be they're out of their element, but I think it's probably like stage actors translating to film actors, they're used to a different sort of power. They're used to projecting so much that to make it small for a camera, a lot of times you see their struggle to make it smaller. Like Bruce Springsteen in the 'I'm on Fire' video – you know the guy's been Mr Bombastic for three days straight on the road and then he comes to do the video and he's just struggling so hard to keep it small. You can see the struggle going on, and it does diminish the aura. But it's funny how middle-level rock stars have been able to do it. I thought David Essex was good in *Stardust*. A lot of times, musicians in movies are window dressing anyway.

Julien Temple: Well, I don't think they're the world's greatest actors. I don't think being a good musician makes you a good actor in any shape or form. I think there are the exceptions. The one guy I think could be a great actor is Neil Young, who I find very subtle and who seems to understand film acting. I think Mick Jagger's great in *Performance*, but he's playing himself. To an extent I think Bowie was best in *The Man Who Fell to Earth*, where he's playing some weird version of himself or at least an image that he had of himself at the time.

Allison Anders: For me it really works because I have a real naturalistic style and with melodrama it tends to work because you can have an overblown atmosphere. Musicians tend to have a persona and if you are trying to get a performance you are not going to get that. But if you are just gonna go, 'OK, I'll take this person's persona in this either small or major role', then I think you've got something really great. You can't lose. You have a kind of freshness because they don't particularly have that training and when something breaks out of the persona it's really interesting. I know Quentin [Tarantino] is, like, 'actors are actors and musicians are musicians' – he really has this thing about it. But you know, I'll use skaters, I'll use anybody.

Biopics

As Michael Atkinson's article shows, the pop-star biopic has been one of the most consistent strands in the history of the pop movie, yet it is also the one that has possibly provided the most disappointments.

Quentin Tarantino: To me that's like the most deplorable genre. They're the same and they're just not very interesting and they offer you up an opportunity to have a groupie performance. *Great Balls of Fire!* totally did it. Jim McBride completely captured that rockabilly time, the one time that white guys were as cool as black guys, 50s Memphis, Tennessee with those big old houndstooth coats and those big pompadours and everything. It was real but also had a movie-movie feeling about it too, and I really thought it was terrific. Another movie that did that was Karel Reisz's *Sweet Dreams*. It really plugged into the music that Patsy Cline was singing.

Rise-and-fall movies are very boring because the rise is always a lot of fun and the fall is a fucking bummer. To me the trick is – and *The Hours and Times* did it perfectly – not to tell the person's life story. Who gives a fuck? Who cares? Take an artist and take three days out of their life, three days out of the end, three days at the very beginning before they've even done anything... You want to take three days of Bob Dylan on his *Don't Look Back* tour. You can have an urgency. If I was going to do an Elvis movie or a movie about rockabilly, I would do a movie about the Million Dollar Quartet, the day that they all showed up at Sun Records and just did their jam session, that would be an interesting movie. Carl Perkins and Jerry Lee Lewis and Elvis there – they just, all with their varying degrees of fortune at that time, happened to show up that day at Sun Records and fuck around.

Bob Last: Using musical copyists of the early Beatles was never an option for *Backbeat*. Everybody understood right from the start that if you attempted to copy, however accurate, you'd fall flat on your face. The whole strategy from the start was to try to find what the attitude was. By saying we'd look at the attitude, using contemporary musicians, we were immediately integrating the music into the storytelling, we were subjecting the music to the requirements of the story. That's why ultimately the film got away with it.

Penelope Spheeris: I wanted to do the Janis Joplin story and then I wanted to do the Jimi Hendrix story and then the Tina Turner film didn't perform as well as everybody wanted. And then I remembered something – when music is involved and all that male ego is involved it becomes a struggle, and I thought, would I want to get into that struggle again? Because it would be, you know, it really would be a big struggle. It has a lot to do with dick size! It has a lot to do with guys saying, [*deep voice*] 'Do it this way, do it this way.' It's so exhausting to fight over it, you know, and I think I'm kinda worn out dealing with it.

Right Place, Right Time

For many film-makers, as for many musicians, finding their voice has been very much a result of connecting with a particular milieu in which new ideas and energies were in the air. With many directors, it's hard to think of their careers without thinking of the particular scenes and moments they've recorded or drawn inspiration from – for Amos Poe, the New York New Wave of 1976; for Julien Temple, the British punk surge of that same year; for Penelope Spheeris, two consecutive LA phases in *The Decline of Western Civilization*...

Leslie Harris: When I start the whole concept of a film, I get an idea and I start hearing the dialogue in my head, and the music too. Rap music and hip-hop were very important in *Just Another Girl on the I.R.T.* – I wanted to get the emotions of the girl in the film. She falls in love, she's very vivacious, very ambitious and driven, but also very unsure about things. So rap and hip-hop projected a lot of what young people go through today. It's just a constant – not being free, wanting to be understood. It's a type of expression of what they're feeling in the inner city – the *here and now*.

Amos Poe: *The Blank Generation* was the film that turned from film as a hobby to actually my first movie. What happened was, I was just there, I had my camera, Ivan Kral kept saying, 'Bring your camera tonight, it will be good.' It was weird – I was shooting bands without sound, and I was using a sound camera, I was using a Bolex with no sound and shooting bands. There was no light there, I wasn't getting a proper exposure, and I was telling people, 'Would you please move your shoulder that way so I can focus, and move your shoulder over, OK', then focusing on David Byrne. A number of people promised us money, but if we had waited, that time would have been over. The excitement was there – for eight months, it was all happening in one place every night, you couldn't miss it. When we started it was the beginning of CBGBs, so nobody was going there, and by the time we said 'all right', it was the very end.

The Talking Heads had an art school background, so they knew where we were coming from. And Blondie always had a pop background.... The hardest person to convince was Patti Smith, because she already wanted to pose for Robert Mapplethorpe. It was like, 'Who the fuck are you?' It was attitude. That was fine, the more attitude she gave me, the better I liked it, because she was doing it for the camera.

Julien Temple: I felt when I started making movies that music was a way of making British movies work worldwide because it was that thing at that time that fascinated the rest of the world about England. That was another interest into it, and then coming across the Sex Pistols again by chance when I did, I saw their first gig and so on, and I was just shocked by how relevant they were. I think *The Great Rock 'n' Roll Swindle* is a pretty vivid document of that time, actually. It was about Malcolm McLaren's whole manipulation of things and about how something as pure as punk could get fucked up in many ways. Not just the band getting fucked up but also Malcolm getting fucked up. It didn't work in the end but it was a wonderful attempt at doing something. It effected a lot of change, which is good, and it empowered the audience in a way that very few things have done.

Penelope Spheeris: I certainly didn't do *The Decline* to make money. I had the strangest compulsion to do it because I felt that it had to be documented for historical reasons, because it was the weirdest thing in the world that I had ever seen. I just did it because I felt that people a hundred years from now should be able to see what a drastic change music had taken. I used to go around the clubs, and I would see people with amateur cameras, and I was so obsessed by this whole idea of *me* being the one that was going to do this film that I would walk up to them and say, 'You can't shoot here, sorry', and pretend to be part of the management so nobody else would shoot it.

I called *The Metal Years 'Part 2'* because I just noticed that I felt inspired to do another film about the music that I'd seen on the street. In the first *Decline*, I was hanging around these people that had this magazine called *Slash,* and seeing these bands like Fear and The Germs, and seeing these people in these clubs that looked like they'd just moved out from the moon. And then, eight or nine years later on Sunset Strip there was not the same kind of feeling but there were as many people involved and they were as adamant about the music. So I said, 'Well, I think I'll just do another one, just because there seems to be so much fervour.' Then as I got to know more about it I found that the part that interested me more than the music was just that social element of 'I want to make it.' All these kids just wanted to be rich and famous. That was the thing that I found to be a contributing factor to the decline of Western civilisation, and that's why I named it that. Since then I've been asked if I'll do *The Decline Part 3: The Rap Years.* But I've said no every time. I'm not a rap fan and someone else could do the film much better than me. I *would* like to do a *Decline Part 3* – I probably would have done 'The Grunge Years' or whatever, but now, that's over with – you know, shotgun to the head and it's over with.

Cameron Crowe: The interesting thing about *Singles* was that while it was released in the heyday of Seattle music, it was a movie that was very hard to get made. It was still the late 80s, it was a movie that I was fighting for that would allow me to work in town, use music that was not commercial, and I would swear there would be no soundtrack album. But in the end we made the movie in early '91, the whole scene exploded later, and there was such a lackadaisical attitude towards the movie at Warner Bros, it took the explosion of Seattle to get the release of the film. The final irony is that the soundtrack that I never intended to be an album became an album, and was huge.

Finally...

You can theorise endlessly about the complex decisions that result in a particular piece of music finding its way into a film. But it's worthwhile noting that there can also be a wonderful randomness about matters – as Cameron Crowe points out, reminiscing about his film _Say Anything_.

Cameron Crowe: This illustrates the situation where artists that have made some personal and moving music get inundated with offers to use that song in a movie. In _Say Anything_, the pivotal scene is where John Cusack is holding up a boom box and you hear Peter Gabriel's 'In Your Eyes'. But it was written to be Billy Idol, 'To Be a Lover', which I loved for about a minute when I was writing the script. We tried 'To Be a Lover', with this guy making a defiant stand outside his girlfriend's window, and it really was bad. Cusack was in love with the band Fishbone at the time, and he wanted to play 'Party at Ground Zero', so we did it again and that was actually what was used in the movie... But when we showed the movie, it was like a crazed Fishbone fan was serenading outside the window, and it destroyed the meaning of the movie. So I had a tape that I made for my wedding, and by now I was so desperate that I was just rummaging through my car – let's try anything, anything! Nothing worked except 'In Your Eyes', which was on this wedding tape, and it was so perfect it even told the story of the movie. It matched everything about the shot, it was great.

We tried to get it, the word that came back is, 'This is a very personal song to Peter Gabriel, it's about his wife, it's a sad situation for him, he will not sell it.' We tried to go back – 'OK, he'll watch a tape of your movie, and maybe he'll think about it.' So we sent a rough cut to Germany or wherever he was recording. A few days went by and they set up a phone call with Peter Gabriel. He comes on the phone and he says, 'I've seen your film, and I'm afraid the song is too powerful, too important to me, I can't let you have it, I really didn't think it worked at the time when he took the overdose.' _Overdose_? Nobody dies in my movie! And he goes, 'This isn't the John Belushi film?' No, no, this is the love-crossed teenagers film. 'Oh, oh, right. I haven't seen that movie.' So he watched the film and we worked it out and everything was great. But I'm haunted by this image of Peter Gabriel in Germany watching John Belushi overdose to 'In Your Eyes', and how close I came to never getting that song.

ABBA The Movie
Lasse Hallström, Sweden/Australia 1977. Cast: ABBA (Anni Frid Lyngstad, Benny Andersson, Björn Ulvaeus, Agnetha Fältskog), Robert Hughes. Music: Benny Andersson, Björn Ulvaeus; performed by: ABBA.

Above the Rim
Jeff Pollack, USA 1994. Cast: Duane Martin, Leon, Tupac Shakur, Tonya Pinkins. Music: Marcus Miller. S/track includes: Lord G., Tha Dogg Pound, SWV, Allen Gordon Jnr (aka All-star), Joe, H-Town, Snoopy Doggy Dogg, Lil' Malik (aka Lil Hershey Loc), CPO-Boss Hog, Terron Brooks, Al B. Sure!, O.F.T.B., Tha Dogg Pound Gangstas, Dat Nigga Daz, Kurupt the Kingpin, 2nd II None, The Pharcyde, Akinyele, Sweet Sable, YZ, The Lady of Rage, Big Pimpin' Delemond, Naughty By Nature, Live Squad, The Beastie Boys, Thug Life, 2Pac Shakur, The Georgetown University Pep Band, Nate Dogg, Warren G.

Absolute Beginners
Julien Temple, GB 1986. Cast: Patsy Kensit, Eddie O'Connell, David Bowie, James Fox, Ray Davies. Music arranged by: Gil Evans. Music performed by: David Bowie, Ray Davies, Eighth Wonder, Slim Gaillard, Sade, Smiley Culture, Tenpole Tudor, Jonas Hurst. S/track includes: Ekow Abban, Laurel Aitken, Jerry Dammers, Wee Willie Harris, The Jet Streams, The Paragons, Bertice Reading, The Scorpions, The Style Council, Working Week, Clive Langer and The Perils of Plastic, Tom Morley, Gary Barnacle.

Across 110th Street
Barry Shear, USA 1972. Cast: Anthony Quinn, Yaphet Kotto, Anthony Franciosa, Paul Benjamin, Ed Bernard. Music: J.J. Johnson. S/track includes: Bobby Womack.

After Cease to Exist (short)
GB 1976. Cast: Cosey Fanni Tutti, Sooo Lucas, Chris Carter, Throbbing Gristle. Music: Throbbing Gristle.

After Hours
Martin Scorsese, USA 1985. Cast: Griffin Dunne, Rosanna Arquette, Verna Bloom, Thomas Chong, Cheech Marin. Music: Howard Shore. S/track includes: Manitas de Plata, Robert and Johnnie, Rosie and the Originals, The Monkees, Joni Mitchell, Johnnie and Joe, The Danleers, The Bad Brains, Peggy Lee.

Alabama: 2000 Light Years (short)
Wim Wenders, West Germany 1969. Cast: Werner Schroeter, Christian Friedel, King Ampaw, Paul Lys, Schrat, Muriel Werner. S/track includes: The Rolling Stones, Jimi Hendrix, Bob Dylan, John Coltrane.

Alamo Bay
Louis Malle, USA 1985. Cast: Amy Madigan, Ed Harris, Ho Nguyen, Donald Moffat, Truyen V. Tran. Music: Ry Cooder. S/track includes: John Hiatt, Jim Dickinson, Jim Keltner, Jorge Calderon.

Alice Doesn't Live Here Anymore
Martin Scorsese, USA 1974. Cast: Ellen Burstyn, Kris Kristofferson, Billy Green Bush, Diane Ladd, Lelia Goldoni. S/track includes: Mott the Hoople, Leon Russell, Elton John, T. Rex, Betty Grable, Alice Faye.

Alice in the Cities (Alice in den Städten)
Wim Wenders, West Germany 1974. Cast: Rüdiger Vogler, Yella Rottländer, Lisa Kreuzer, Edda Köchl, Didi Petrikat. Music: Can. S/track includes: Chuck Berry, Canned Heat, Deep Purple, Count Five, Stories, Gustav Mahler.

Alice's Restaurant
Arthur Penn, USA 1969. Cast: Arlo Guthrie, Pat Quinn, James Broderick, Michael McClanathan, Geoff Outlaw, Pete Seeger. Music: Arlo Guthrie. S/track includes: Joni Mitchell, Woody Guthrie.

Alphabet City
Amos Poe, USA 1984. Cast: Vincent Spano, Michael Winslow, Kate Vernon, Jami Gertz, Zohra Lampert. Music: Nile Rodgers.

American Friend, The (Der Amerikanische Freund)
Wim Wenders, West Germany/France 1977. Cast: Bruno Ganz, Dennis Hopper, Lisa Kreuzer, Gérard Blain, Nicholas Ray. Music: Jürgen Knieper. S/track includes: Kinks.

American Graffiti
George Lucas, USA 1973. Cast: Richard Dreyfuss, Ronny Howard, Paul Le Mat, Cindy Williams, Wolfman Jack. Music performed by: Flash Cadillac and the Continental Kids. S/track includes: The Heartbeats, The Regents, Buster Brown, The Cleftones, The Flamingos, Joey Dee and the Starlighters, The Tempos, Frankie Lymon, Lee Dorsey, The Big Bopper, The Platters, The Diamonds, Chuck Berry, The Monotones, The Spaniels, Fats Domino, The Fleetwoods, The Clovers, Johnny Burnette, Buddy Holly, Bill Haley and His Comets, The Beach Boys, The Silhouettes, The Five Satins, Sonny Till and The Orioles, Bobby Freeman, Booker T. and the MGs, Del Shannon, The Skyliners, The Del-Vikings, The Crests, The Crows, Mark Dinning.

American Hot Wax
Floyd Mutrux, USA 1977. Cast: Tim McIntire, Fran Drescher, Jay Leno, Laraine Newman, Cameron Crowe. Music performed by: Professor La Plano & The Planotones, The Delights, Chuck Berry, The Chesterfields, Screamin' Jay Hawkins, Timmy and The Tangerines, Jerry Lee Lewis, Frankie Ford. S/track includes: Big Beat Band, Clark Otis, Jackie Wilson, The Moonglows, The Drifters, The Mystics, Buddy Holly, Maurice Williams & The Zodiacs, Little Richard, The Cadillacs, The Turbans, Bobby Darin, The Spaniels, The Elegants, Del Vikings, Sam Turner, The Coasters, Johnny Otis, Richie Valens, The Heartbeats, The Everly Brothers, Bill Doggett, The Dominoes, Tommy Edwards, The Diamonds, Bobby Freeman, Eddie Cochran.

Annie Oakley
Michael Lindsay-Hogg, USA 1985. Cast: Jamie Lee Curtis, Cliff De Young, Brian Dennehy, Joyce Van Patten. Music: Ry Cooder.

Apocalypse Now
Francis Coppola, USA 1979. Cast: Marlon Brando, Robert Duvall, Martin Sheen, Frederic Forrest, Sam Bottoms. Music: Carmine Coppola, Francis Coppola. Music performed by: Patrick Gleeson, Richard Beggs, Bernard L. Krause, Don Preston, Shirley Walker, Nyle Steiner, Randy Hansen, Mickey Hart, Airto Moreira, Michael Hinton, The Rhythm Devils, Jordan Amarantha, Greg Errico, Zakir Hussain, Billy Kreutzmann, Phil Lesh, Jim Loveless. S/track includes: The Doors, The Rolling Stones, Flash Cadillac.

Aria
Nicolas Roeg, Charles Sturridge, Jean-Luc Godard, Julien Temple, Bruce Beresford, Robert Altman, Franc Roddam, Ken Russell, Derek Jarman, Bill Bryden, GB 1987. Julien Temple sequence: Cast: Buck Henry, Anita Morris, Beverly D'Angelo, Gary Kasper, John Hostetter. Music: Ralph Mace. S/track includes: Robert Merrill, Alfredo Krauss, Anna Moffo, RCA Italiana Opera Orchestra and Chorus.

Attack of the Phantoms: see **KISS Meets the Phantom of the Park**

Attendant, The (short)
Isaac Julien, GB 1993. Cast: Thomas Baptiste, Cleo Sylvestre, John Wilson, Paul Bernstock, Roy Brown. Music: Gary Butcher, Jimmy Somerville.

At the Max
Christine Strand, USA 1991. Creative consultant/location dir: Julien Temple. Music performed by: The Rolling Stones, Bobby Keys, The Uptown Horns.

Backbeat
Iain Softley, GB 1993. Cast: Sheryl Lee, Stephen Dorff, Ian Hart, Gary Bakewell, Chris O'Neill. Music: Don Was. Songs performed by: The Backbeat Band - Greg Dulli, Dave Pirner, Don Fleming, Thurston Moore, Dave Grohl, Mike Mills. S/track includes: Howling Wolf, Edith Piaf, Jimmy Reed, Marcelle Duprey.

Back to the Future
Robert Zemeckis, USA 1985. Cast: Michael J. Fox, Christopher Lloyd, Lea Thompson, Crispin Glover, Thomas F. Wilson. Music: Alan Silvestri. S/track includes: Huey Lewis and the News, Eric Clapton, Lindsey Buckingham, The Four Aces, Etta James, Marvin Berry and the Starlighters.

Bamba, La
Luis Valdez, USA 1986. Cast: Lou Diamond Phillips, Esai Morales, Rosana De Soto, Danielle von Zerneck, Joe Pantoliano. Music: Carlos Santana, Miles Goodman. Music performed by: Marshall Crenshaw, Howard Huntsberry, Brian Setzer, Daniel Valdez. S/track includes: Los Lobos, Bob Diddley, Santo & Johnny, Carlos Santana, Jerry Butler and the Impressions, Little Richard, Huey Smith and the Clowns, The Skyliners, The Big Bopper, Chuck Berry, La Vern Baker, The Platters, Johnnie & Joe.

Batman
Tim Burton, USA 1989. Cast: Michael Keaton, Jack Nicholson, Kim Basinger, Robert Wuhl, Pat Hingle. Music: Danny Elfman. S/track includes: Prince, Percy Faith and his Orchestra, Hill Bowen & Orchestra.

"Beat" Girl
Edmond T. Gréville, GB 1959. Cast: David Farrar, Noelle Adam, Christopher Lee, Gillian Hills, Adam Faith. Music: John Barry; performed by: The John Barry Seven, Adam Faith.

Be My Guest
Lance Comfort, GB 1965. Cast: David Hemmings, Steve Marriott, John Pike, Andrea Monet, Ivor Salter. Music: Malcolm Lockyer. Songs performed by: Jerry Lee Lewis, The Nashville Teens, The Zephyrs, Kenny and the Wranglers, The Niteshades.

Benny Goodman Story, The
Valentine Davies, USA 1955. Cast: Steve Allen, Donna Reed, Berta Gersten, Herbert Anderson, Sammy Davis Snr. Music: Henry Mancini. Music performed by: Harry James, Martha Tilton, Gene Krupa, Ziggy Elman, Ben Pollack, Teddy Wilson, Edward 'Kid' Ory.

Berlin Alexanderplatz
Rainer Werner Fassbinder, West Germany 1980. Cast: Günter Lamprecht, Hanna Schygulla, Barbara Sukowa, Gottfried John, Franz Buchrieser. Music: Peer Raben.

Between the Teeth
David Byrne, David Wild, USA 1993. Cast: David Byrne, Bobby Allende, Johnathan Best, Angel Fernandez, Ten Car Pileup. Music: David Byrne, Ten Car Pileup Band.

Beverly Hills Cop
Martin Brest, USA 1984. Cast: Eddie Murphy, Judge Reinhold, John Ashton, Lisa Eilbacher, Ronny Cox. Music: Harold Faltermeyer. S/track includes: Glenn Frey, Pointer Sisters, Patti Labelle, Junior, Vanity 6.

Big Time
Chris Blum, USA 1988. Music: Tom Waits; performed by: Tom Waits, Michael Blair, Ralph Carney, Greg Cohen, Marc Ribot, Willy Schwarz.

Bird
Clint Eastwood, USA 1988. Cast: Forest Whitaker, Diane Venora, Michael Zelniker, Samuel E. Wright, Keith David. Music: Lennie Niehaus. S/track includes: Lennie Niehaus, Charlie Parker, Monty Alexander, Ray Brown, John Guerin, James Rivers, Red Rodney, Pete Jolly, Chuck Berghofer, Ronny Lang, Gary Foster, Bob Cooper, Pete Christlieb, Chuck Findley, Conte Candoli, Rick Baptist, Dick Nash, Bill Watrous, Barry Harris, Charles McPherson, Jon Faddis, Walter Davis Jnr., Ron Carter, Mike Lang, Chuck Domanico, Charlie Shoemake, King Pleasure, John Lewis, Percy Heath, Kenny Clarke.

Blackboard Jungle, The
Richard Brooks, USA 1955. Cast: Glenn Ford, Anne Francis, Louis Calhern, Margaret Hayes, John Hoyt. S/track includes: Bill Haley and His Comets.

Black Caesar
Larry Cohen, USA 1973. Cast: Fred Williamson, D'Urville Martin, Gloria Hendry, Art Lund, Val Avery. Music: James Brown, Barry De Vorzon. S/track includes: James Brown. (British release title: **The Godfather of Harlem**)

Blade Runner
Ridley Scott, USA 1982. Cast: Harrison Ford, Rutger Hauer, Sean Young, Edward James Olmos, Daryl Hannah. Music: Vangelis.

Blank Generation, The
Amos Poe, Ivan Kral, USA 1976. Music performed by: Patti Smith Group, Television, Ramones, Talking Heads, Tuff Darts (featuring Robert Gordon), Wayne County, Blondie, Harry Toledo, Marbles, Miamis, Shirts, The Dolls, The Heartbreakers.

Blow-Up
Michelangelo Antonioni, GB/Italy 1966. Cast: David Hemmings, Vanessa Redgrave, Peter Bowles, Sarah Miles, Jane Birkin, Gillian Hills. Music: Herbie Hancock. Song performed by: The Yardbirds.

Blue City
Michelle Manning, USA 1985. Cast: Judd Nelson, Ally Sheedy, David Caruso, Paul Winfield, Scott Wilson. Music: Ry Cooder. S/track includes: Bobby King, Terry Evans, True Believers, The Textones.

Blue Collar
Paul Schrader, USA 1978. Cast: Richard Pryor, Harvey Keitel, Yaphet Kotto, Ed Begley Jnr., Harry Bellaver. Music: Jack Nitzsche, Ry Cooder. S/track includes: Captain Beefheart.

Blue Hawaii
Norman Taurog, USA 1961. Cast: Elvis Presley, Joan Blackman, Angela Lansbury, Nancy Walters, Roland Winters. Music: Joseph J. Lilley. Various songs performed by Elvis Presley including songs written by: Robin, Rainger; Wise, Weisman: Robertson, Blair; Peretti, Creatore, Wise; Wise, Weisman, Fuller; Dee, Weisman; Peretti, Creatore, Weiss; Tepper, Bennett; King, Hoffman, Manning.

Blues Brothers, The
John Landis, USA 1980. Cast: John Belushi, Dan Aykroyd, Kathleen Freeman, James Brown, Henry Gibson. Music: Elmer Bernstein. Music performed by: Cab Calloway, James Brown, Steve Cropper, Donald 'Duck' Dunn, Aretha Franklin, Matt Murphy, Chaka Khan, John Lee Hooker, Walter Horton, 'Pinetop' Perkins, Willie 'Big Eyes' Smith, Luther 'Guitar Jnr' Johnson, Calvin 'Fuzz' Jones. S/track includes: Sam and Dave, Elmore James, Kitty Wells, Ezio Pinza, Fats Domino, Louis Jordan.

Bodyguard, The
Mick Jackson, USA 1992. Cast: Kevin Costner, Whitney Houston, Gary Kemp, Bill Cobbs, Ralph Waite. Music: Alan Silvestri. Songs performed by: Whitney Houston. S/track includes: S.O.U.L. S.Y.S.T.E.M., Kenny G., John Doe, Lisa Stansfield, Curtis Stigers, Joe Cocker, Sass Jordan, Aaron Neville, The Allman Brothers, The Left Banke.

Body of Evidence
Uli Edel, USA 1992. Cast: Madonna, Willem Dafoe, Joe Mantegna, Anne Archer, Julianne Moore. Music: Graeme Revell, Eberhard Weber.

Book of Love
Robert Shaye, USA 1990. Cast: Chris Young, Keith Coogan, Aeryk Egan, Josie Bissett, Tricia Leigh Fisher. Music: Stanley Clarke. S/track includes: The Monotones, Ben E. King, Bo Diddley, John Lee Hooker, Sanford Clark, The Cardinals, Jackie Brenston and His Delta Kings, The Moonglows, The Fontane Sisters, Chuck Berry, The Diamonds, Little Richard, The Teenagers, The Four Freshmen, Gene Vincent, Donnie Elbert, The Penguins, The Platters, Shirley and Lee, Big Daddy, Marty 'The K' Kaniger, Donny 'D' Raymond, John 'Spazz' Hatton, Bob 'Guido' Sandman, 'Rock-a' Billy Block, The Sonny Paxson Quartet, The Drifters.

Boomerang
Reginald Hudlin, USA 1992. Cast: Eddie Murphy, Robin Givens, Halle Berry, David Alan Grier, Martin Lawrence, Grace Jones, Eartha Kitt. Music: Marcus Miller. S/track includes: Keith Washington, George Clinton, Boyz II Men, Aaron Hall featuring Charlie Wilson, Rebirth Brass Band, Kenny Vaughan and the Art of Love, The LaFace Cartel, James Brown, Shanice Wilson, Toni Braxton, Johnny Gill, Arrested Development, P.M. Dawn, Babyface.

Border, The
Tony Richardson, USA 1981. Cast: Jack Nicholson, Harvey Keitel, Valerie Perrine, Warren Oates, Elpidia Carrillo. Music: Ry Cooder. S/track includes: Freddie Fender, John Hiatt, Sam Samudio, Jim Dickinson, Brenda Patterson.

Border Radio
Allison Anders, Dean Lent, Kurt Voss, USA 1987. Cast: Chris D., John Doe, Luanna Anders, Chris Shearer. Music: Dave Alvin, Steve Berlin, Bill Bateman, John Bazz, DJ Bonebrake, John Doe. S/track includes: Green on Red, Tony Kinman, The Flesheaters, Billy Wisdom and the Hee-Shees, Los Lobos, The Lazy Cowgirls, Divine Horsemen, Chris D., John Doe.

Born Losers
T.C. Frank [Tom Laughlin], USA 1967. Cast: Tom Laughlin, Elizabeth James, Jane Russell, Jeremy Slate, William Wellman Jnr. Music: Mike Curb.

Bound for Glory
Hal Ashby, USA 1976. Cast: David Carradine, Ronny Cox, Melinda Dillon, Gail Strickland, John Lehne. Songs performed by: Woody Guthrie, David Carradine, Ronny Cox, Melinda Dillon, Kip Addotta. S/track includes: Cara Corren, Susan Barnes, Odetta, Arlo Guthrie, The Weavers, Country Joe McDonald, Judy Collins.

Boxcar Bertha
Martin Scorsese, USA 1972. Cast: Barbara Hershey, David Carradine, Barry Primus, Bernie Casey, John Carradine. Music: Gib Guilbeau, Thad Maxwell.

Boys Next Door, The
Penelope Spheeris, USA 1984. Cast: Maxwell Caulfield, Charlie Sheen, Patti D'Arbanville, Christopher McDonald. Music: George S. Clinton. S/track includes: Code Blue, The Cramps, Great White, Chequered Past, Tex and the Horseheads, Iggy Pop.

Boyz N the Hood
John Singleton, USA 1991. Cast: Ice Cube, Cuba Gooding Jnr., Morris Chestnut, Larry Fishburne, Nia Long. Music: Stanley Clarke. S/track includes: Newcleus, Dr Buzzard's Original Savannah Band, Zapp, Run-D.M.C., The Five Stairsteps, Monie Love, Hi-Five, Yo-Yo, 2 Live Crew, Tevin Campbell, Tony! Toni! Toné!, Force One Network, Too Short, Compton's Most Wanted, KAM, Main Source, Quincy Jones, Take 6, Sarah Vaughan, Kool Moe Dee, Ice Cube.

Bram Stoker's Dracula
Francis Ford Coppola, USA 1992. Cast: Gary Oldman, Winona Ryder, Anthony Hopkins, Keanu Reeves, Richard E. Grant, Tom Waits. Music: Wojciech Kilar. S/track includes: Annie Lennox, Diamanda Galás.

Breakfast Club, The
John Hughes, USA 1985. Cast: Emilio Estevez, Anthony Michael Hall, Judd Nelson, Molly Ringwald, Ally Sheedy. Music: Keith Forsey, Gary Chang. S/track includes: Gary Chang, Simple Minds, Elizabeth Daily, Wang Chung, Karla DeVito, Jesse Johnson, Stephanie Spruill, Laurie Forsey.

Breaking Glass
Brian Gibson, GB 1980. Cast: Phil Daniels, Hazel O'Connor, Jon Finch, Jonathan Pryce, Peter-Hugo Daly, Zoot Money, Paul McCartney, Rod Stewart. Songs by and performed by: Hazel O'Connor.

Brewster's Millions
Walter Hill, USA 1985. Cast: Richard Pryor, John Candy, Lonette McKee, Stephen Collins, Jerry Orbach. Music: Ry Cooder. S/track includes: Patti Labelle.

Bring on the Night
Michael Apted, USA 1985. Music: Sting, Pete Smith, Billy Youdelman. Songs performed by: Sting, Omar Hakim, Darryl Jones, Kenny Kirkland, Branford Marsalis, Dolette McDonald, Janice Pendarvis.

Broken English: Three Songs by Marianne Faithfull (short)
Derek Jarman, GB 1979. Music: Mark Miller Mundy. Songs performed by: Marianne Faithfull.

Buddy Holly Story, The
Steve Rash, USA 1978. Cast: Gary Busey, Don Stroud, Charles Martin Smith, Conrad Janis. Music: Joe Renzetti. Songs performed by: Gary Busey, Don Stroud, Charles Martin Smith, Gailard Sartain, Jerry Zaremba. S/track includes: Sam Cooke.

Buster
David Green, GB 1988. Cast: Phil Collins, Julie Walters, Larry Lamb, Stephanie Lawrence. Music: Anne Dudley. S/track includes: Phil Collins, The Four Tops, The Spencer Davis Group, Ruby and the Romantics, The Shadows, The Searchers, The Everly Brothers, Gerry & The Pacemakers, The Hollies, Dusty Springfield, Sonny & Cher.

Caged Heat
Jonathan Demme, USA 1974. Cast: Juanita Brown, Roberta Collins, Erica Gavin, Ella Reid, Lynda Gold. Music: John Cale.

Car Wash
Michael Schultz, USA 1976. Cast: Franklyn Ajaye, Antonio Fargas, Richard Pryor, Ivan Dixon, Sully Boyar, George Carlin, The Pointer Sisters. Music: Norman Whitfield. Songs performed by: Rose Royce, The Pointer Sisters.

Catch Us If You Can
John Boorman, GB 1965. Cast: The Dave Clark Five, Barbara Ferris, David Lodge, Robin Bailey, Yootha Joyce. Music: Dave Clark; performed by: The Dave Clark Five.

CB4
Tamra Davis, USA 1993. Cast: Chris Rock, Allen Payne, Deezer D, Chris Elliott, Ice-T, Ice Cube, Flavor Flav, Eazy E. Music: John Barnes, Daddy-O. S/track includes: Public Enemy, Boogie Down Productions, MC Ren, Hurricane featuring the Beastie Boys, Fu-Schnickens, Parental Advisory, P.M. Dawn, Blackstreet featuring Teddy Riley, Traci Spencer, CB4 (Daddy-O, Hi-C and Kool Moe Dee).

Chariots of Fire
Hugh Hudson, GB 1981. Cast: Ben Cross, Ian Charleson, Nigel Havers, Nicholas Farrell. Music: Vangelis.

Choose Me
Alan Rudolph, USA 1984. Cast: Genevieve Bujold, Keith Carradine, Lesley Ann Warren, Patrick Bauchau, Rae Dawn Chong. S/track includes: Luther Vandross, Teddy Pendergrass, Augustus Pablo, The Phil Woods Quartet, Archie Shepp, Horace Parlan.

Christine
John Carpenter, USA 1983. Cast: Keith Gordon, John Stockwell, Alexandra Paul, Robert Prosky, Harry Dean Stanton. Music: John Carpenter, Alan Howarth. S/track includes: George Thorogood and the Destroyers, The Rolling Stones, Richie Valens, Dion & the Belmonts, Thurston Harris, Johnny Ace, Danny & the Juniors, Larry Williams, The Viscounts, Little Richard, Buddy Holly, Tanya Tucker, Bonnie Raitt, Abba, Robert & Johnny.

Chuck Berry Hail! Hail! Rock n' Roll; see Hail! Hail! Rock n' Roll

Cisco Pike
Bill L. Norton, USA 1971. Cast: Kris Kristofferson, Karen Black, Gene Hackman, Harry Dean Stanton, Viva. Songs performed by: Kris Kristofferson. S/track includes: Sonny Terry, Sir Douglas Quintet, Lee Montgomery.

City of Lost Souls (Stadt der verlorenen Seelen)
Rosa von Praunheim, West Germany 1983. Cast: Angie Stardust, Jayne County, Lorraine Muthke. Music: Alexander Kraut, Jayne County, Angie Stardust, Holger Münzer; performed by: Jayne County, Angie Stardust, Joaquin La Habana.

Clambake
Arthur H. Nadel, USA 1967. Cast: Elvis Presley, Shelley Fabares, Will Hutchins, Bill Bixby. Music: Jeff Alexander. Various songs performed by Elvis Presley including songs written by: Hubbard; Weisman, Wayne; Starr; Tepper, Bennett; Byers; Walker, Arnold; Smith, Dixon; Owens, Solberg; Griffin.

Clerks
Kevin Smith, USA 1994. Cast: Brian O'Halloran, Jeff Anderson, Marilyn GhiglIotti, Lisa Spoonauer, Jason Mewes. Music: Scott Angley. S/track includes: Love Among Freaks, Girls Against Boys, Alice in Chains, Bash & Pop, Supernova, The Jesus Lizard, Golden Smog, Bad Religion, Stabbing Westward, Corrosion of Conformity, Seaweed, Soul Asylum.

Coal Miner's Daughter
Michael Apted, USA 1980. Cast: Sissy Spacek, Tommy Lee Jones, Levon Helm, Ernest Tubb. Music Supervisor: Owen Bradley; songs performed by: Sissy Spacek, Beverly D'Angelo, Ernest Tubb, Levon Helm. S/track includes: Kitty Wells, Red Foley, The Jordanaires.

Cocksucker Blues
Robert Frank, Daniel Seymour, USA 1973. Music performed by: The Rolling Stones. (Also released as **CS Blues**)

Cocktail
Roger Donaldson, USA 1988. Cast: Tom Cruise, Bryan Brown, Elisabeth Shue, Lisa Banes, Laurence Luckinbill. Music: J. Peter Robinson. S/track includes: Ry Cooder, David Wilcox, Robert Palmer, The Fabulous Thunderbirds, Think Out Loud, Bobby McFerrin, Jimmy Cliff, Robbie Nevil, Wayne Roland Brown, Little Richard, The Georgia Satellites, Starship, The Beach Boys, Preston Smith, John Cougar Mellencamp, The Everly Brothers, Michael Lanning, Rick Bell.

Color of Money, The
Martin Scorsese, USA 1986. Cast: Paul Newman, Tom Cruise, Mary Elizabeth Mastrantonio, Helen Shaver, John Turturro. Music: Robbie Robertson, Willie Dixon. S/track includes: Charlie Parker, The Del Lords, Jimmy Smith, Muddy Waters, Robert Palmer, Bo Diddley, Eric Clapton and the Big Town Playboys, Don Henley, Mark Knopfler, Willie Dixon, B.B. King, Phil Collins, Bodeans, Warren Zevon, Percy Sledge.

Colors
Dennis Hopper, USA 1988. Cast: Sean Penn, Robert Duvall, Maria Conchita Alonso, Randy Brooks, Grand Bush. Music: Herbie Hancock, Ice-T & Afrika Islam, Jeff Bova, Bob Musso, Charlie Drayton, Tony Meilandt. S/track includes: Ice-T, Los Lobos, Big Daddy Kane, Roxanne Shante, Kool G. Rap, Rosie & The Originals, War, Jaynetts, Dr. John, Willie Nelson, Cannibal & The Headhunters, M.C. Shan, Maly y Su Playa Azul, Manu Dibango, John Cougar Mellencamp, Sly & Robbie, Decadent Dub Team, Rick James, The Penguins, 7A3, Brenton Wood, Salt-N-Pepa, Eric B. & Rakim.

Commitments, The
Alan Parker, USA 1991. Cast: Robert Arkins, Michael Aherne, Angeline Ball, Maria Doyle, Dave Finnegan, Andrew Strong. Music performed by: The Commitments. S/track includes: Benedict Fox, Aidan O'Halloran, Cahir O'Doherty, And And! And, Niamh Kavanagh, The Proclaimers, Anne-Marie Scannell, Conor Malone, Jezz Bell, Colm Mac Con Iomaire, Emily Dawson, Dave Kane, Kristel Harris, Maria Place, Daragh McCarthy, Brian Mac Aodha, Tricia Smith, Canice William, Patrick Foy, Alan Murray, Jody Campbell, Philomena Kavanagh, Eamon O'Connor, James Brown with the Famous Flames, Robert Arkins, Angeline Ball, Maria Doyle, Bronagh Gallagher, Michael Aherne, Dave Finnegan, Maura O'Malley, Isaac Hayes, Avant-Garde-A-Clue, Andrew Strong.

Confessions of a Pop Performer
Norman Cohen, GB 1975. Cast: Robin Askwith, Anthony Booth, Bill Maynard, Doris Hare, Sheila White. Songs by Dominic Bugatti, Frank Musker.

Cool World
Ralph Bakshi, USA 1992. Cast: Kim Basinger, Gabriel Byrne, Brad Pitt, Michele Abrams. Music: Mark Isham, John Dickson. S/track includes: Thompson Twins, Ministry, Brian Eno, My Life with the Thrill Kill Kult, Moby, The Cult, Da Juke, The Future Sound of London, Tom Bailey, Mindless, Frank Sinatra Jnr., Electronic, David Bowie.

Cotton Club, The
Francis Coppola, USA 1984. Cast: Richard Gere, Gregory Hines, Diane Lane, Lonette McKee, Bob Hoskins, Tom Waits. Music: John Barry. Songs performed by: Richard Gere, Larry Marshall. S/track includes: Priscilla Baskerville, Ethel Beatty, Sydney Goldsmith.

Cotton Comes to Harlem
Ossie Davis, USA 1970. Cast: Godfrey Cambridge, Raymond St. Jacques, Calvin Lockhart, Judy Pace, Redd Foxx. Music: Galt MacDermot.

Crossroads
Walter Hill, USA 1986. Cast: Ralph Macchio, Joe Seneca, Jami Gertz, Joe Morton, Robert Judd. Music: Ry Cooder. S/track includes: Terry Evans, Amy Madigan, The Wonders, Joe Seneca, John 'Juke' Logan, Steve Vai, Sonny Terry.

Cure Show, The
Aubrey Powell with Leroy Bennett, GB 1993. Music performed by: The Cure.

Cut-Ups, The (short)
Antony Balch, GB 1967. Cast: William Burroughs, Brion Gysin.

Damned, The
Joseph Losey, GB 1961. Cast: Macdonald Carey, Shirley Ann Field, Viveca Lindfors, Alexander Knox, Oliver Reed. Music: James Bernard.

Dandy
Peter Sempel, Germany 1988. Cast: Blixa Bargeld, Nick Cave, Dieter Meier, Kazuo Ohno, Lene Lovich.

Dark Half, The
George A. Romero, USA 1991. Cast: Timothy Hutton, Amy Madigan, Michael Rooker, Julie Harris, Robert Joy. Music: Christopher Young. S/track includes: Elvis Presley.

Dateline Diamonds
Jeremy Summers, GB 1965. Cast: William Lucas, Kenneth Cope, George Mikell, Conrad Phillips, Patsy Rowlands. Music: Johnny Douglas. Songs performed by: The Small Faces, The Chantelles, Kiki Dee, Mark Richardson.

Dazed and Confused
Richard Linklater, USA 1993. Cast: Jason London, Joey Lauren Adams, Milla Jovovich, Shawn Andrews, Rory Cochrane. Music: Harry Garfield. S/track includes: Aerosmith, Alice Cooper, War, Edgar Winter, Peter Frampton, Bob Dylan, Nazareth, Sweet, ZZ Top, Foghat, Deep Purple, Black Oak Arkansas, Ted Nugent, Black Sabbath, Head East, Rick Derringer, Dr John, Seals & Crofts, Kiss, Steve Miller, The Runaways, Lynyrd Skynyrd, Thin Lizzy.

Death Becomes Her
Robert Zemeckis, USA 1992. Cast: Meryl Streep, Bruce Willis, Goldie Hawn, Isabella Rossellini, Ian Ogilvy. Music: Alan Silvestri.

Decline of Western Civilization, The
Penelope Spheeris, USA 1980. Music performed by: Black Flag, Germs, Catholic Discipline, X, Circle Jerks, Alice Rag Band, Fear.

Decline of Western Civilization Part II: The Metal Years, The
Penelope Spheeris, USA 1988. Music performed by: Alice Cooper and Axl, Slash and Izzy of Guns 'N' Roses, Megadeth, Odin, Trikk Toyzz, Queensryche, London, Seduce, Faster Pussycat, Armored Saint, Lizzy Borden, Metal Church, Motorhead.

Deep Cover
Bill Duke, USA 1992. Cast: Larry Fishburne, Jeff Goldblum, Victoria Dillard, Charles Martin Smith, Jonathan Scott, Bilal Bashir. Music: Michel Colombier. S/track includes: Dr Dre, Snoop Doggy Dogg, Jewel, Marcos Loya, Calloway, The Deele, Times 3, Paradise, Po' Broke and Lonely, Ragtime, 101 Strings, Ko Kane, Nate Philips, Shabba Ranks, Chevelle Franklin.

Delinquents, The
Chris Thomson, Australia 1989. Cast: Kylie Minogue, Charlie Schlatter, Angela Punch, Bruno Lawrence, Todd Boyce. Music: Miles Goodman. S/track includes: Gene Vincent and his Blue Caps, Eddie Cochran, Jerry Lee Lewis, Patti Page, Little Richard, Little Walter, Johnny Diesel & the Injectors, Fats Domino, The Platters, Dinah Shore, Jonny O'Keefe, Kylie Minogue.

Depeche Mode 101
D.A. Pennebaker, Chris Hegedus, David Dawkins, GB 1989. Music performed by: Depeche Mode.

Desperately Seeking Susan
Susan Seidelman, USA 1985. Cast: Rosanna Arquette, Madonna, Aidan Quinn, Mark Blum, Robert Joy. Music: Thomas Newman. S/track includes: Madonna, Junior Walker, Betty Everett, Iggy Pop, Run-D.M.C., Dee Dee Sharp, The Fixx, Carly Simon, Aretha Franklin, Marshall Crenshaw.

Devil's Angels
Daniel Haller, USA 1967. Cast: John Cassavetes, Beverly Adams, Mimsy Farmer, Maurice McEndree, Salli Sachse. Music: Mike Curb.

Dick Tracy
Warren Beatty, USA 1990. Cast: Warren Beatty, Madonna, Al Pacino, Charlie Korsmo. Music: Danny Elfman. Songs by: Stephen Sondheim. S/track includes: Madonna, Mandy Patinkin, Mel Tormé, Janis Siegel, Cheryl Bentyne, Lorraine Feather, Marvelee Cariaga, Michael Gallup, Jeff Vincent, Andy Paley, Brenda Lee, Al Jarreau, k.d. lang, Take 6, Tommy Page, Jerry Lee Lewis, Erasure (Vince Clarke, Andy Bell).

Dirty Dancing
Emile Ardolino, USA 1987. Cast: Jennifer Grey, Patrick Swayze, Jerry Orbach, Cynthia Rhodes, Jack Weston. Music: John Morris. S/track includes: The Ronettes, Frankie Valli and the Four Seasons, Tom Johnston, The Contours, Otis Redding, Maurice Williams and the Zodiacs, The Surfaris, Eric Carmen, Zappacosta, Bruce Channel, Melon, The Drifters, Solomon Burke, The Shirelles, Mickey & Sylvia, The Blow Monkeys, Merry Clayton, The Five Satins, Bill Medley, Jennifer Warnes.

Dr. No
Terence Young, GB 1962. Cast: Sean Connery, Ursula Andress, Joseph Wiseman, Jack Lord. Music: Monty Norman; theme performed by: John Barry Orchestra.

Dogs in Space
Richard Lowenstein, Australia 1986. Cast: Michael Hutchence, Saskia Post, Nique Needles, Deanna Bond. Music: Ollie Olsen. S/track includes: Iggy Pop, Whirlywirld, The Marching Girls, Boys Next Door, The Birthday Party.

Don't Knock The Rock
Fred F. Sears, USA 1956. Cast: Alan Dale, Alan Freed, Patricia Hardy, Fay Baker, Jana Lund. Songs performed by: Bill Haley and His Comets, The Treniers, Little Richard, Dave Appell and His Applejacks.

Don't Look Back
D.A. Pennebaker, USA 1967. Music performed by: Bob Dylan, Joan Baez, Donovan, Alan Price.

Doors, The
Oliver Stone, USA 1991. Cast: Val Kilmer, Frank Whaley, Kevin Dillon, Meg Ryan, Kyle MacLachlan, Billy Idol, Eric Burdon. Songs performed by: The Doors.

Do the Right Thing
Spike Lee, USA 1989. Cast: Danny Aiello, Ossie Davis, Ruby Dee, Richard Edson, Spike Lee. Music: Bill Lee. S/track includes: The Natural Spiritual Orchestra (with Branford Marsalis), Public Enemy, Take 6, Steel Pulse, Ruben Blades, Keith John, Lorri Perry, Gerald Alston, EU, Perri, Teddy Riley featuring Guy, Al Jarreau.

Down by Law
Jim Jarmusch, USA 1986. Cast: Tom Waits, John Lurie, Roberto Benigni, Nicoletta Braschi, Ellen Barkin. Music: John Lurie. S/track includes: Arto Lindsay, Nana Vasconcelos, Marc Ribot, Curtis Fowlkes, Doug Bowne, E.J. Rodriguez, Tony Garnier, Eugene Moye, Tom Waits, Irma Thomas.

Drum Crazy - The Gene Krupa Story; see Gene Krupa Story, The

Dudes
Penelope Spheeris, USA 1987. Cast: Jon Cryer, Catherine Mary Stewart, Daniel Roebuck, Lee Ving, Flea. Music: Charles Bernstein. S/track includes: The Vandals, Faster Pussycat, The Little Kings, The Tail Gators, The Leather Nun, Four Big Guitars from Texas, Jane's Addiction, W.A.S.P., Simon Steele and The Claw, Keel, Robert Gordon, Chris Spedding, Ernest Tubb, Legal Weapon, Ned Sublette, Steve Vai.

Duke Wore Jeans, The
Gerald Thomas, GB 1958. Cast: Tommy Steele, June Laverick, Michael Medwin, Eric Pohlmann, Alan Wheatley. Songs: Lionel Bart, Michael Pratt. Songs performed by: Tommy Steele.

Earth Girls Are Easy
Julien Temple, USA 1988. Cast: Geena Davis, Jeff Goldblum, Jim Carrey, Damon Wayans, Julie Brown. Music: Nile Rodgers. S/track includes: Julie Brown, The B-52's, Stewart Copeland, Depeche Mode, Meri D., Luis Restaurant's World, The Landler Band, Angelyne, Carole Davis.

Easy Rider
Dennis Hopper, USA 1969. Cast: Peter Fonda, Dennis Hopper, Phil Spector, Jack Nicholson, Antonio Mendoza. S/track includes: Steppenwolf, The Byrds, The Band, The Holy Modal Rounders, Fraternity of Man, The Jimi Hendrix Experience, Little Eva, The Electric Prunes, The Electric Flag, Roger McGuinn.

Eat the Document
D.A. Pennebaker, Bob Dylan, USA 1972. Music performed by: Bob Dylan, The Hawks (aka The Band).

Eddie and the Cruisers
Martin Davidson, USA 1983. Cast: Tom Berenger, Michael Paré, Joe Pantoliano, Matthew Laurance, Helen Schneider. Music: John Cafferty, Kenny Vance; performed by: Michael 'Tunes' Antunes, Gary Gramolini, Kenny Jo Silva, Robert Nicholas Cotoia, Pat Lupo.

Elvis
John Carpenter, USA 1979. Cast: Kurt Russell, Shelley Winters, Bing Russell, Robert Gray, Season Hubley. Music: Joe Renzetti. S/track includes: Ronnie McDowell, The Jordanaires.

Elvis and Me
Larry Peerce, USA 1988. Cast: Dale Midkiff, Susan Walters, Billy 'Green' Bush, Linda Miller, Jon Cypher. Music: Richard Stone, Ronnie McDowell.

Elvis and the Beauty Queen
Gus Trikonis, USA 1981. Cast: Stephanie Zimbalist, Don Johnson, Ann Dusenberry. Music: Allyn Ferguson.

Elvis on Tour
Pierre Adidge, Robert Abel, USA 1972. Montage supervisor: Martin Scorsese. Music performed by: Elvis Presley, The Sweet Inspirations, J.D. Sumner and the Stamps Quartet.

Elvis - That's the Way It Is
Denis Sanders, USA 1970. Music performed by: Elvis Presley, Millie Kirkham, The Sweet Inspirations, The Imperials.

Endangered Species
Alan Rudolph, USA 1982. Cast: Robert Urich, JoBeth Williams, Paul Dooley, Hoyt Axton, Peter Coyote. Music: Gary Wright.

Equinox
Alan Rudolph, USA 1992. Cast: Matthew Modine, Lara Flynn Boyle, Fred Ward, Tyra Ferrell, Marisa Tomei. S/track includes: Roger Eno, Ivo Papasov and His Orchestra, Astor Piazzolla, Archie Shepp and Dollar Brand, Terje Rypdal and The Chasers, David Darling, Miroslav Vitous, Jack De Johnette, The Tango Project, Ali Farka Toure.

Every Day's a Holiday
James Hill, GB 1964. Cast: John Leyton, Mike Sarne, Freddie and the Dreamers, Ron Moody, Liz Fraser. Music: Tony Osborne. Songs performed by: Freddie and the Dreamers, The Mojos, John Leyton, Mike Sarne, The Leroys.

Exorcist, The
William Friedkin, USA 1973. Cast: Ellen Burstyn, Max von Sydow, Lee J. Cobb, Kitty Winn, Jack MacGowran. S/track includes: Jack Nitzsche, Mike Oldfield, George Crumb, Krzysztof Penderecki, Anton Webern, Hans Werner Henze.

Expresso Bongo
Val Guest, GB 1959. Cast: Laurence Harvey, Sylvia Syms, Yolande Donlan, Cliff Richard, Meier Tzelniker. Music: Robert Farnon, Val Guest, Norrie Paramor, Bunny Lewis, Paddy Roberts, Julian More, Monty Norman, David Henneker. Songs performed by: Cliff Richard.

Faraway, So Close! (In weiter Ferne, so nah!)
Wim Wenders, Germany 1993. Cast: Otto Sander, Peter Falk, Horst Buchholz, Nastassja Kinski, Heinz Rühmann, Lou Reed. Music: Laurent Petitgand. S/track includes: Nick Cave, U2, Lou Reed, Herbert Gronemeyer, Simon Bonney, J.D. Foster, Johnny Cash, Jane Siberry, The House of Love, Laurie Anderson.

Fast Times at Ridgemont High
Amy Heckerling, USA 1982. Screenplay: Cameron Crowe. Cast: Sean Penn, Jennifer Jason Leigh, Judge Reinhold, Phoebe Cates. S/track includes: Ravyns, Don Henley, Don Felder, Oingo Boingo, Billy Squier, The Go Gos, Graham Nash, Jimmy Buffett, Poco, Tom Petty, Jackson Browne, Joe Walsh, Timothy B. Schmit, Louise Goffin, Stevie Nicks, Gerard McMahon, Quarterflash, Sammy Hagar, The Cars, Darlene Love, Reeves Nevo & the Cinch, Led Zeppelin.

Fear of a Black Hat
Rusty Cundieff, USA 1992. Cast: Mark Christopher Lawrence, Larry B. Scott, Rusty Cundieff, Kasi Lemmons, Howie Gold, Moon Jones, Faizon, Deezer D. Music: Jim Manzie, Larry Robinson.

Flame
Richard Loncraine, GB 1974. Cast: Slade (Noddy Holder, Jim Lea, Dave Hill, Don Powell), Tom Conti. Music performed by: Slade.

Flashdance
Adrian Lyne, USA 1983. Cast: Jennifer Beals, Michael Nouri, Lilia Skala, Sunny Johnson. Music: Giorgio Moroder. S/track includes: Laura Branigan, Irene Cara, Kim Carnes, Cycle V, Joe Esposito, Karen Kamon, Helen St. John, Michael Sembello, Shandi, Donna Summer, Jimmy Castor & The Jimmy Castor Bunch, Joan Jett & the Blackhearts.

Footloose
Herbert Ross, USA 1984. Cast: Kevin Bacon, Lori Singer, John Lithgow, Dianne Wiest, Christopher Penn. S/track includes: Kenny Loggins, Sammy Hagar, Shalamar, Bonnie Tyler, Moving Pictures, Karla Bonoff, Deniece Williams, John Cougar Mellencamp.

Forrest Gump
Robert Zemeckis, USA 1994. Cast: Tom Hanks, Robin Wright, Gary Sinise, Mykelti Williamson, Sally Field. S/track includes: Hank Williams, Duane Eddy, Clarence 'Frogman' Henry, The Rooftop Singers, Jimmy Glimer and the Fireballs, Dresden Philharmonic, Tommy James & the Shondells, Creedence Clearwater Revival, The Four Tops, Aretha Franklin, Bob Dylan, The Beach Boys, The Mamas and the Papas, Buffalo Springfield, Jackie De Shannon, The Doors, Simon & Garfunkel, Jefferson Airplane, The Jimi Hendrix Experience, The Youngbloods, Scott McKenzie, The Byrds, The Fifth Dimension, Three Dog Night, Harry Nilsson, The Supremes, Canned Heat, B.J. Thomas, Tony Orlando and Dawn, Donny Gerrad, Randy Newman, KC & the Sunshine Band, Oren Waters, Lynyrd Skynyrd, Jackson Browne, The Doobie Brothers, Gladys Knight & the Pips, Fleetwood Mac, Willie Nelson, Bob Seger & the Silver Bullet Band.

For the Boys
Mark Rydell, USA 1991. Cast: Bette Midler, James Caan, George Segal, Patrick O'Neal, Christopher Rydell. Music: Dave Grusin. S/track includes: Aina, Beat Goes Bang, Tamaki Kawkubo, Gary LeMel, Cream.

Four Weddings and a Funeral
Mike Newell, GB 1994. Cast: Hugh Grant, Andie MacDowell, Kristin Scott Thomas, James Fleet, Simon Callow. Music: Richard Rodney Bennett. S/track includes: Wet Wet Wet, Elton John, Ira Newborn, Bill Black.

Freejack
Geoff Murphy, USA 1992. Cast: Emilio Estevez, Mick Jagger, Rene Russo, Anthony Hopkins, Jonathan Banks. Music: Trevor Jones, Artie Kane. S/track includes: Scorpions, Jesus Jones, Eleven, 2 Die 4, Little Feat, Ministry, Jesus & Mary Chain, Jane Child.

Gas Food Lodging
Allison Anders, USA 1992. Cast: Brooke Adams, Ione Skye, Fairuza Balk, James Brolin, Robert Knepper. Music: J. Mascis, Barry Adamson. S/track includes: Mark Fosson, Karen Tobin, The Mitch Green Experience, Japan, Antagonist, Renegade Soundwave, Nick Cave and the Bad Seeds, Louise Tollson, Crime and the City Solution, Easy, The Velvet Monkeys, Mr Boyd Rice, Victoria Williams.

Geek Maggot Bingo
Nick Zedd, USA 1983. Cast: Robert Andrews, Brenda Bergman, Richard Hell, Donna Death, Zacherle.

Gene Krupa Story, The
Don Weis, USA 1959. Cast: Sal Mineo, Susan Kohner, James Darren, Susan Oliver, Yvonne Craig, Red Nichols, Anita O'Day, Shelly Manne, Buddy Lester. Music: Leith Stevens, Heinie Beau. Songs performed by: Anita O'Day, Red Nichols, Buddy Lester, Ruby Lane. S/track includes: Krupa Orchestra. (British release title: **Drum Crazy - The Gene Krupa Story**)

Geronimo: An American Legend
Walter Hill, USA 1993. Cast: Jason Patric, Gene Hackman, Robert Duvall, Wes Studi. Music: Ry Cooder, The Americus Brass Band.

Ghostbusters
Ivan Reitman, USA 1984. Cast: Bill Murray, Dan Aykroyd, Sigourney Weaver, Harold Ramis. Music: Elmer Bernstein. S/track includes: Ray Parker Jnr., Alessi, Laura Branigan, The Trammps, The Bus Boys, Thompson Twins, Air Supply, Mick Smiley.

Ghost Goes Gear, The
Hugh Gladwish, GB 1966. Cast: The Spencer Davis Group (Spencer Davis, Stevie Winwood, Muff Winwood, Peter York), Nicholas Parsons. Music: Joan Shakespeare, John Shakespeare. Music performed by: The Spencer Davis Group, Acker Bilk and the Paramount Jazz Band, Lorne Gibson Trio, The M.6, St. Louis Union, Dave Berry, The Three Bells.

Ghosts... of the Civil Dead
John Hillcoat, Australia 1988. Cast: Dave Field, Mike Bishop, Chris De Rose, Nick Cave, Freddo Dierck. Music: Nick Cave, Mick Harvey, Blixa Bargeld. S/track includes: Anita Lane, Keith Glass and the Honky Tonk Band, The Slaughtermen, The Black Sun, Elizabeth Scott, Southern Lightning, Billy Jack Band, Darkside, Olive Bice, Black Dog, U-Boys, Mosquito Coils, Dirty Rats.

G.I. Blues
Norman Taurog, USA 1960. Cast: Elvis Presley, Juliet Prowse, Robert Ivers, Leticia Roman, James Douglas. Music: Joseph J. Lilley. Songs performed by: Elvis Presley.

Gimme Shelter
David Maysles, Albert Maysles, Charlotte Zwerin, USA 1970. Music performed by: The Rolling Stones, Ike and Tina Turner, Jefferson Airplane, Flying Burrito Brothers.

Girl Can't Help It, The
Frank Tashlin, USA 1956. Cast: Tom Ewell, Jayne Mansfield, Edmond O'Brien, Henry Jones, John Emery. Songs performed by: Julie London, Ray Anthony, Barry Gordon, Fats Domino, The Platters, Little Richard and his Band, Gene Vincent and the Blue Caps, The Treniers, Eddie Fontaine, Abbey Lincoln, The Chuckles, Johnny Olenn, Nino Tempo, Eddie Cochran.

Give My Regards to Broad Street
Peter Webb, GB 1984. Cast: Paul McCartney, Bryan Brown, Ringo Starr, Barbara Bach, Linda McCartney. Music: George Martin, Paul McCartney. S/track includes: Paul McCartney, Ringo Starr, The Philip Jones Brass Ensemble, Linda McCartney, Dave Edmunds, Chris Spedding, John Paul Jones, David Gilmour, Herbie Flowers.

Glastonbury Fayre
Peter Neal, GB 1973. Music performed by: Terry Reid, Linda Lewis, Fairport Convention, Magic Michael, Family, Melanie, Arthur Brown and Kingdom Come, Quintessence, David Allen and Gong, Traffic.

Glenn Miller Story, The
Anthony Mann, USA 1953. Cast: James Stewart, June Allyson, Henry Morgan, Frances Langford. Music performed by: Louis Armstrong, Gene Krupa.

Glitterbug
Derek Jarman, David Lewis, GB 1994. Music: Brian Eno.

Goalkeeper's Fear of the Penalty, The (Die Angst des Tormanns beim Elfmeter)
Wim Wenders, West Germany/Austria 1971. Cast: Arthur Brauss, Erika Pluhar, Kai Fischer, Libgart Schwarz, Rüdiger Vogler. Music: Jürgen Knieper. S/track includes: Johnny and the Hurricanes, Roy Orbison, the Tokens, the Ventures.

Godfather, The
Francis Ford Coppola, USA 1972. Cast: Marlon Brando, Al Pacino, James Caan, Richard Castellano, Robert Duvall. Music: Nino Rota.

Godfather of Harlem, The: see **Black Caesar**

Golden Disc, The
Don Sharp, GB 1958. Cast: Lee Patterson, Mary Steele, Terry Dene, Linda Gray, Ronald Adam. Music performed by: Terry Dene, Dennis Lotis, Nancy Whiskey, Sheila Buxton, Phil Seamon Jazz Group, Sonny Stewart and his Skiffle Kings, Terry Kennedy Group, Don Rendell's Six.

Goldfinger
Guy Hamilton, GB 1964. Cast: Sean Connery, Honor Blackman, Gert Fröbe, Shirley Eaton. Music: John Barry. S/track includes: Shirley Bassey.

Gonks Go Beat
Robert Hartford-Davis, GB 1965. Cast: Kenneth Connor, Frank Thornton, Barbara Brown, Iain Gregory, Terry Scott. Music: Robert Richards. Songs performed by: The Long and The Short, The Nashville Teens, Lulu and The Luvvers, Ray Lewis and The Trekkers, The Vacqueros, The Graham Bond Organisation, Elaine and Derek, Alan David.

GoodFellas
Martin Scorsese, USA 1990. Cast: Robert De Niro, Ray Liotta, Joe Pesci, Lorraine Bracco, Paul Sorvino. S/track includes: Tony Bennett, The Cleftones, Otis Williams and the Charms, The Moonglows, The Cadillacs, Billy Ward and his Dominoes, The Marvellettes, Johnny Mathis, Betty Curtis, The Crystals, The Chantels, Bob Vinton, The Harptones, The Shangri-Las, Dean Martin, The Crystals, Donovan, Jerry Vale, Aretha Franklin, Bobby Darin, The Rolling Stones, Jack Jones, The Ronettes, Darlene Love, The Drifters, Vito and the Salutations, Cream, Derek and the Dominos, Harry Nilsson, The Who, George Harrison, Muddy Waters, Steve Jones.

Good Morning, Vietnam
Barry Levinson, USA 1987. Cast: Robin Williams, Forest Whitaker, Tung Thanh Tran, Chintara Sukapatana, Bruno Kirby. Music: Alex North. S/track includes: Lawrence Welk, Them, The Grass Roots, Frankie Avalon, Annette Funicello, The Rivieras, Sounds Orchestral, Marvelettes, Perry Como, The Vogues, Wayne Fontana & the Mindbenders, The Beach Boys, James Brown, Wilson Pickett, Adam Faith, The Castaways, Herb Alpert and the Tijuana Brass, Jack Jones, Martha Reeves & the Vandellas, Ray Conniff, The Searchers, Louis Armstrong, Georgie Fame & the Blue Flames.

Good Times
William Friedkin, USA 1967. Cast: Sonny and Cher, George Sanders, Norman Alden, Larry Duran, Kelly Thordsen. Music: Sonny Bono. Songs performed by: Sonny and Cher.

Graduate, The
Mike Nichols, USA 1967. Cast: Anne Bancroft, Dustin Hoffman, Katharine Ross, William Daniels, Murray Hamilton. Songs: Paul Simon. Music: David Grusin. S/track includes: Simon and Garfunkel.

Grease
Randal Kleiser, USA 1978. Cast: John Travolta, Olivia Newton-John, Stockard Channing, Jeff Conaway, Barry Pearl. Songs performed by: John Travolta, Olivia Newton-John, Frankie Avalon, Stockard Channing, Sha-Na-Na. S/track includes: Frankie Valli, Cindy Bullens, Peter Frampton.

Great Balls of Fire!
Jim McBride, USA 1989. Cast: Dennis Quaid, Winona Ryder, John Doe, Joe Bob Briggs, Stephen Tobolowsky. Music: Jack Baran, Jim McBride. S/track includes: Jerry Lee Lewis, Valerie Wellington, Booker T. Laury, Bill Justis, Joe Nettles, Gene Autry, Les Paul, Mary Ford, Elvis Presley, Jackie Brenston, Bill Doggett, The Wailers, Perez Prado, Bill Boyd's Cowboy Ramblers, Dave 'Baby' Cortez, The Mar-Keys.

Great Rock 'n' Roll Swindle, The
Julien Temple, GB 1979. Cast: Malcolm McLaren, Sid Vicious, Johnny Rotten, Steve Jones, Paul Cook, Glen Matlock, Ronald Biggs, Eddie 'Tenpole' Tudor, Irene Handl. Music performed by: The Sex Pistols, Malcolm McLaren, The Black Arabs, Eddie 'Tenpole' Tudor, Jerzimy.

Gypsy
Mervyn LeRoy, USA 1962. Cast: Rosalind Russell, Natalie Wood, Karl Malden, Paul Wallace, Betty Bruce. Music: Julie Styne. Lyrics: Stephen Sondheim. S/track includes: Liza Kirk.

Hail! Hail! Rock n' Roll
Taylor Hackford, USA 1987. Music performed by: Chuck Berry, Linda Ronstadt, Robert Cray, Etta James, Julian Lennon, Eric Clapton, Keith Richards, Joey Spampinato, Steve Jordan, Johnnie Johnson, Chuck Leavell, Bobby Keys, Ingrid Berry, Cosmopolitan Hall Band. (aka **Chuck Berry Hail! Hail! Rock n' Roll**)

Hairspray

John Waters, USA 1988. Cast: Divine, Debbie Harry, Sonny Bono, Ricki Lake, Ruth Brown, Pia Zadora, Ric Ocasek. Music: Kenny Vance. S/track includes: Rachel Sweet, Barbara Lynn, Jan Bradley, Chubby Checker, Dee Dee Sharp, Bunker Hill, The Five Du-Tones, The Lafayettes, Little Peggy March, Lesey Gore, The Ikettes, The Ray Bryant Combo, Gene Pitney, The Champs, Toussaint McCall, The Bracelettes, Gene and Wendell, Jerry Dallman and the Knightcaps, The Two Dutones, The Dovells, Gene Chandler, The Flares.

Half a Sixpence

George Sidney, GB/USA 1967. Cast: Tommy Steele, Julia Foster, Cyril Ritchard, Penelope Horner, Elaine Taylor. Music: David Heneker. Songs performed by: Tommy Steele, Julia Foster.

1/2 Mensch (Halber Mensch)

Sogo Ishii, Japan 1985. Music performed by: Einstürzende Neubauten.

Halloween

John Carpenter, USA 1978. Cast: Donald Pleasence, Jamie Lee Curtis, Nancy Loomis, P.J. Soles, Charles Cyphers. Music: John Carpenter. S/track includes: The Bowling Green Philharmonic Orchestra.

Hammett

Wim Wenders, USA 1982. Cast: Frederic Forrest, Peter Boyle, Marilu Henner, Roy Kinnear, Lydia Lei. Music: John Barry.

Hard Day's Night, A

Richard Lester, GB 1964. Cast: John Lennon, Paul McCartney, George Harrison, Ringo Starr, Wilfrid Brambell. Songs performed by: The Beatles.

Harder They Come, The

Perry Henzell, Jamaica 1972. Cast: Jimmy Cliff, Carl Bradshaw, Basil Keane, Janet Bartley, Winston Stona. S/track includes: Jimmy Cliff, Scotty, The Melodians, The Maytals, The Slickers, Desmond Dekker.

Hardware

Richard Stanley, GB/USA 1990. Cast: Dylan McDermott, Stacey Travis, John Lynch, William Hootkins, Iggy Pop, Lemmy. Music: Simon Boswell. S/track includes: Iggy Pop, Motorhead, Ministry, Public Image Ltd.

Head

Bob Rafelson, USA 1968. Cast: The Monkees (Micky Dolenz, David Jones, Michael Nesmith, Peter Tork), Victor Mature, Timothy Carey, Annette Funicello, Frank Zappa. Music: Ken Thorne. Songs performed by: The Monkees.

Heartbreak Hotel

Chris Columbus, USA 1988. Cast: David Keith, Tuesday Weld, Charlie Schlatter, Angela Goethals, Jacque Lynn Colton. Music: Georges Delerue.

Hellraiser III: Hell On Earth

Anthony Hickox, USA 1992. Cast: Terry Farrell, Doug Bradley, Paula Marshall, Kevin Bernhardt, Ken Carpenter. Music: Randy Miller, Christopher Young. S/track includes: Soup Dragons, KMFDM, Armoured Saint, Material Issue, Ten Inch Men, Electric Love Hogs, House of Lords, Tin Machine, Chainsaw Kittens, Triumph, Motorhead.

Hell's Angels on Wheels

Richard Rush, USA 1967. Cast: Adam Roarke, Jack Nicholson, Sabrina Scharf, Jana Taylor, John Garwood. Music: Stu Phillips. S/track includes: The Poor.

Help!

Richard Lester, GB 1965. Cast: John Lennon, Paul McCartney, Ringo Starr, George Harrison, Leo McKern. Songs performed by: The Beatles.

High School Confidential

Jack Arnold, USA 1958. Cast: Russ Tamblyn, Jan Sterling, John Drew Barrymore, Diane Jergens, Jerry Lee Lewis. Music: Jerry Lee Lewis, Ron Hargraves. Songs performed by: Jerry Lee Lewis.

Hollywood Vice Squad

Penelope Spheeris, USA 1986. Cast: Ronny Cox, Frank Gorshin, Leon Isaac Kennedy, Trish Van DeVere, Carrie Fisher. Music: Keith Levine, Michael Convertino, Chris Spedding.

Hot Rods to Hell

John Brahm, USA 1967. Cast: Dana Andrews, Jeanne Crain, Mimsy Farmer, Laurie Mock, Paul Bertoya. Music: Fred Karger. Songs performed by: Mickey Rooney Jnr and his Combo.

Hot Spot, The

Dennis Hopper, USA 1990. Cast: Don Johnson, Virginia Madsen, Jennifer Connelly, Charles Martin Smith, William Sadler. Music: Jack Nitzsche. S/track includes: Bradford Ellis, Miles Davis, John Lee Hooker, Taj Mahal, Roy Rogers, Tim Drummond, Earl Palmer, Billy Squier, The New Hawaiian Band, '101 Strings' Orchestra, Terry de Rouen, Hank Williams Jnr., Scott Wilk, k.d. lang and the reclines, Roosevelt Williams, The Grey Ghost.

Hours and Times, The

Christopher Münch, USA 1991. Cast: David Angus, Ian Hart, Stephanie Pack, Robin McDonald, Sergio Morena. S/track includes: Carlos Calvo, David Loeb.

House Party

Reginald Hudlin, USA 1990. Cast: Kid 'n' Play (Christopher Martin, Christopher Reid), Robin Harris, Martin Lawrence, Tisha Campbell. Music: Marcus Miller.

Human Highway

Bernard Shakey (aka Neil Young), USA 1982. Cast: Neil Young, Devo, Russ Tamblyn, Dean Stockwell, Sally Kirkland, Dennis Hopper, Charlotte Stewart. Music: Neil Young; performed by: Neil Young, Devo.

I'll Cry Tomorrow

Daniel Mann, USA 1955. Cast: Susan Hayward, Richard Conte, Eddie Albert, Jo Van Fleet, Don Taylor. Music: Alex North.

I'm Gonna Git You Sucka

Keenen Ivory Wayans, USA 1988. Cast: Keenen Ivory Wayans, Bernie Casey, Antonio Fargas, Steve James, Isaac Hayes. Music: David Michael Frank. S/track includes: King Cotton, John Boudreaux, Jim Daniels, David Dyson, Bob Gibson, Fishbone, BDP featuring KRS-ONE, Ms. Melodie, D. Nice, Scotty Morris, The Gap Band, The Kids Next Door, Jennifer Holliday, Kim Wayans, The Four Tops, The Jackson Five, The Friends of Distinction, Isaac Hayes, Jermaine Jackson, Curtis Mayfield with Fishbone, Carl Douglas, Edwin Starr, Too Nice, K-9 Posse.

In Bed with Madonna (US title: **Truth or Dare**)

Alek Keshishian, USA 1991. Music: Jai Winding. Songs performed by: Madonna, Donna Delory, Niki Harris, Kevin Kendrick, Jonathan Moffett, David Williams, Luis Conte, Darryl Jones. S/track includes: Guy, Mix Masters.

Inferno
Dario Argento, Italy 1980. Cast: Leigh McCloskey, Irene Miracle, Eleonora Giorgi, Daria Nicolodi, Sacha Pitoeff. Music: Keith Emerson.

In the Name of the Father
Jim Sheridan, Eire/GB/USA 1993. Cast: Daniel Day Lewis, Emma Thompson, Pete Postlethwaite, John Lynch. Music: Trevor Jones. S/track includes: Bono, Gavin Friday, The Jimi Hendrix Experience, The Kinks, Bob Marley and the Wailers, Thin Lizzy, Sinead O'Connor.

In the Shadow of the Sun
Derek Jarman, GB 1972/80. Cast: Christopher Hobbs, Gerald Incandela, Andrew Logan, Kevin Whitney, Luciano Martinez. Music performed by: Throbbing Gristle.

Invocation of My Demon Brother (short)
Kenneth Anger, USA 1969. Cast: Speed Hacker, Lenore Kandel, William Kandel, Kenneth Anger, Van Leuven. Music: Mick Jagger.

It Couldn't Happen Here
Jack Bond, GB 1987. Cast: Neil Tennant, Chris Lowe, Joss Ackland, Dominique Barnes, Neil Dickson. S/track includes: Pet Shop Boys, Dusty Springfield.

It's Great To Be Young!
Cyril Frankel, GB 1956. Cast: John Mills, Cecil Parker, Jeremy Spenser, Dorothy Bromiley, Brian Smith. Music: Ray Martin, Lester Powell, John Addison. Songs performed by: Ruby Murray, Humphrey Lyttleton's Band, The Coronets, The London Schools Symphony Orchestra, Edna Savage.

It's Trad, Dad!
Dick Lester, GB 1962. Cast: Helen Shapiro, Craig Douglas, Felix Felton, Timothy Bateson, Frank Thornton. Music performed by: Helen Shapiro, Craig Douglas, John Leyton, Chubby Checker, Temperance Seven, Kenny Ball and His Jazzmen, Terry Lightfoot and His New Orleans Band, Chris Barber and His Band, Ottilie Patterson, Acker Bilk and His Paramount Jazz Band, Bob Wallis and His Storyville Jazz Men, Gene Vincent, Sounds Incorporated, Brook Brothers, Gary 'U.S.' Bonds, Del Shannon, Gene McDaniels, The Paris Sisters, The Dukes of Dixieland.

Jailhouse Rock
Richard Thorpe, USA 1957. Cast: Elvis Presley, Judy Tyler, Mickey Shaughnessy, Vaughn Taylor, Jennifer Holden. Songs performed by: Elvis Presley, The Jordanaires.

Jericho Mile, The
Michael Mann, USA 1979. Cast: Peter Strauss, Richard Lawson, Roger E. Mosley, Brian Dennehy, Geoffrey Lewis. Music: Jimmie Haskell, James Di Pasquale.

John and Yoko: A Love Story
Sandor Stern, USA 1985. Cast: Mark McGann, Kim Miyori, Kenneth Price, Peter Capaldi, Phillip Walsh.

Johnny Handsome
Walter Hill, USA 1989. Cast: Mickey Rourke, Ellen Barkin, Elizabeth McGovern, Morgan Freeman, Forest Whitaker. Music: Ry Cooder.

Johnny Suede
Tom DiCillo, USA/Switzerland/France 1991. Cast: Brad Pitt, Alison Moir, Catherine Keener, Calvin Levels, Nick Cave. Music: Jim Farmer, Link Wray. S/track includes: Ricky Nelson, Steve Flynn, Calvin Leeds, Christopher Faris, Steve Grandinetti, Nick Cave, Alert!.

Jubilee
Derek Jarman, GB 1977. Cast: Jenny Runacre, Little Nell, Toyah Willcox, Jordan, Hermine Demoriane, Wayne County, Adam Ant, The Slits. Music: Brian Eno. S/track includes: Chelsea, Wayne County and the Electric Chairs, Siouxsie and the Banshees, Suzi Pinns.

Juice
Ernest R. Dickerson, USA 1992. Cast: Omar Epps, Khalil Kain, Jermaine Hopkins, Tupac Shakur, Cindy Herron, Queen Latifah, Dr Dre, Fab 5 Freddie. Music: Hank Shocklee, Keith Shocklee, Carl Ryder, Gary G. Wiz. S/track includes: Naughty by Nature, Eric B. & Rakim, Teddy Riley, M.C. Pooh, Big Daddy Kane, Too Short, EPMD, Aaron Hall, Salt 'n Pepa, Cypress Hill Crew, Juvenile Committee, Son of Berzerk, Rahiem, The Brand New Heavies, N'Dea Davenport, Cameo, Bobby Torres, Fabulous Five.

Jungle Fever
Spike Lee, USA 1991. Cast: Wesley Snipes, Annabella Sciorra, Spike Lee, Ossie Davis, Ruby Dee. Music: Stevie Wonder, Terence Blanchard. S/track includes: The Boys Choir of Harlem and Orchestra, Mahalia Jackson, Public Enemy, Frank Sinatra, Wynton Marsalis, Kimberly Brewer.

Just Another Girl on the I.R.T.
Leslie Harris, USA 1992. Cast: Ariyan Johnson, Kevin Thigpen, Ebony Jerido, Chequita Jackson, William Badget. S/track includes: Nikki D, Cee Asia, Kimberly Davis, Paul Shabazz, Angela Stone, Ron Grant, Son of Bazerk, B.W.P., O'Jays.

Keep, The
Michael Mann, USA 1983. Cast: Scott Glenn, Alberta Watson, Jürgen Prochnow, Robert Prosky, Gabriel Byrne. Music: Tangerine Dream.

Kids Are Alright, The
Jeff Stein, USA 1979. Cast: The Who, Tom Smothers, Russell Harty, Melvyn Bragg, Ringo Starr. Music director: John Entwistle. Music performed by: The Who.

Killing Zoe
Roger Avary, USA 1993. Co-exec producer: Quentin Tarantino. Cast: Eric Stoltz, Julie Delpy, Jean-Hughes Anglade, Gary Kemp, Bruce Ramsay. Music: Tomandandy.

King Creole
Michael Curtiz, USA 1958. Cast: Elvis Presley, Carolyn Jones, Walter Matthau, Dolores Hart, Dean Jagger. Music: Walter Scharf. Songs by: Jerry Leiber and Mike Stoller et al. Various songs performed by Elvis Presley including songs written by: Leiber, Stoller; Tepper, Bennett; Wise, Weisman; Wayne; Kalmanoff; Schroeder, Frank.

King of Comedy, The
Martin Scorsese, USA 1982. Cast: Robert De Niro, Jerry Lewis, Diahnne Abbott, Sandra Bernhard, Ed Herlihy, Mick Jones, Joe Strummer, Paul Simonon, Ellen Foley. Music producer: Robbie Robertson. S/track includes: Bob James, Ray Charles, David Sanborn, The Pretenders, Frank Sinatra, Talking Heads, Ricki Lee Jones, Robbie Robertson, B.B. King, Ric Ocasek, Tom Petty, Van Morrison.

King of New York
Abel Ferrara, USA 1989. Cast: Christopher Walken, David Caruso, Larry Fishburne, Victor Argo, Wesley Snipes. Music: Joe Delia. S/track includes: Schooly D, Party Posse, Freddy Jackson, Haywood Gregory.

Kings of the Road (Im Lauf der Zeit)
Wim Wenders, West Germany 1976. Cast: Rüdiger Vogler, Hanns Zischler, Marquard Böhm, Rudolf Schündler, Lisa Kreuzer. Music: Axel Linstädt, Improved Sound Limited. S/track includes: Johnny Fikert, Harry Montez, Heinz, Roger Miller, Crispian St. Peters.

KISS Meets the Phantom of the Park
Gordon Hessler, USA 1978. Cast: KISS (Peter Criss, Ace Frehley, Gene Simmons, Paul Stanley), Anthony Zerbe, Deborah Ryan. Music: Hoyt Curtin, Fred Karlin. Songs performed by: KISS. British release title: **Attack of the Phantoms.**

Krays, The
Peter Medak, GB 1990. Cast: Billie Whitelaw, Tom Bell, Gary Kemp, Martin Kemp, Susan Fleetwood. Music: Michael Kamen. S/track includes: The Zombies, Matt Munro.

Krush Groove
Michael Schultz, USA 1985. Cast: Sheila E., Run-D.M.C. (Joseph Simmons, Daryl McDaniels, Jason Mizell), Kurtis Blow, The Fat Boys. Music performed by: Run-D.M.C., The Fat Boys, UTFO, LL Cool J, Nayobe, New Edition, The Beastie Boys, Chad Elliot. S/track includes: Deborah Harry, Force M.D.'s, The Gap Band, Autumn, Chaka Khan.

Kustom Kar Kommandos (short)
Kenneth Anger, USA 1965. Music: The Parris Sisters.

Labyrinth of Passions (Laberinto de Pasiones)
Pedro Almodóvar, Spain 1982. Cast: Cecilia Roth, Imanol Arias, Helga Liné, Marta Fernandez-Muro, Angel Alcazar. Music: Pedro Almodóvar, Bernardo Bonezzi, Fanny McNamara. Songs performed by: Pedro Almodóvar, Fanny McNamara.

Lady is a Square, The
Herbert Wilcox, GB 1958. Cast: Anna Neagle, Frankie Vaughan, Janette Scott, Anthony Newley, Wilfrid Hyde White. Music: Ray Noble.

Lady Sings the Blues
Sidney J. Furie, USA 1972. Cast: Diana Ross, Billy Dee Williams, Richard Pryor, James Callahan, Paul Hampton. Music: Michel Legrand. Songs performed by: Diana Ross.

Last Emperor, The
Bernardo Bertolucci, China/Italy 1987. Cast: John Lone, Joan Chen, Peter O'Toole, Ying Ruocheng, Victor Wong. Music: Ryuichi Sakamoto, David Byrne, Cong Su.

Last Movie, The
Dennis Hopper, USA 1971. Cast: Dennis Hopper, Stella Garcia, Julie Adams. Music: Kris Kristofferson, John Buck Wilkin, Chabuca Granda, Severn Darden. S/track includes: Poupée Bocar, Kris Kristofferson.

Last of the Mohicans, The
Michael Mann, USA 1992. Cast: Daniel Day Lewis, Madeleine Stowe, Russell Means, Eric Schweig, Jodhi May. Music: Trevor Jones, Randy Edelman, Daniel Lanois. S/track includes: Phil Cunningham, Clannad.

Last Temptation of Christ, The
Martin Scorsese, USA/Canada 1988. Cast: Willem Dafoe, Harvey Keitel, Paul Greco, Steven Shill, Verna Bloom, Barbara Hershey. Music: Peter Gabriel.

Last Waltz, The
Martin Scorsese, USA 1978. Songs performed by: The Band, Bob Dylan, Joni Mitchell, Neil Diamond, Emmylou Harris, Neil Young, Van Morrison, Ron Wood, Muddy Waters, Eric Clapton, The Staples, Ringo Starr, Dr. John, Ronnie Hawkins, Paul Butterfield, Charlie Keagle, Larry Parker.

Leadbelly
Gordon Parks, USA 1976. Cast: Roger E. Mosley, James E. Brodhead, John McDonald, Earnest L. Hudson, Dana Manno. Music: Fred Karlin. S/track includes: HiTide Harris.

Legend
Ridley Scott, USA 1985. Cast: Tom Cruise, Mia Sara, Tim Curry, David Bennent, Alice Playten. Music: Jerry Goldsmith (for Europe); Tangerine Dream (for US).

Let Him Have It
Peter Medak, GB 1991. Cast: Chris Eccleston, Paul Reynolds, Tom Courtenay, Tom Bell, Eileen Atkins. Music: Michael Kamen, Ed Shearmur.

Lisztomania
Ken Russell, GB 1975. Cast: Roger Daltrey, Sara Kestelman, Paul Nicholas, Fiona Lewis, Ringo Starr, Rick Wakeman. Music: Rick Wakeman, incorporating themes by Franz Liszt, Richard Wagner. Songs performed by: Roger Daltrey, Paul Nicholas. S/track includes: The English Rock Ensemble, Linda Lewis, Mandy Moore, David Wilde, William Davis, Jack Bruce.

Little Buddha
Bernardo Bertolucci, France/GB 1993. Cast: Keanu Reeves, Ying Ruocheng, Chris Isaak, Bridget Fonda, Alex Wiesendanger. Music: Ryuichi Sakamoto. S/track includes: Monks of the Dip Tse Chok Ling Monastery, Dharamsala; L. Subramaniam, Shiv Kumar Sharma, Zakir Hussain, Ustad Ali Akbar Khan, Iris DeMent, Shruti Sadolikar, Buckwheat Zydeco.

Live It Up
Lance Comfort, GB 1963. Cast: David Hemmings, Jennifer Moss, John Pike, Heinz Burt, Steve Marriott. Music: Joe Meek, Norrie Paramor, Kenny Ball. Songs performed by: Kenny Ball and his Jazzmen, Gene Vincent, Patsy Ann Noble, Kim Roberts, The Outlaws, Sounds Incorporated, Andy Cavell and the Saints.

Long Day Closes, The
Terence Davies, GB 1992. Cast: Marjorie Yates, Leigh McCormack, Anthony Watson, Nicholas Lamont, Ayse Owens. Music: Robert Lockhart. Music supervisor: Bob Last. S/track includes: Nat 'King' Cole, Doris Day, Kathleen Ferrier, Judy Garland, Debbie Reynolds.

Long Riders, The
Walter Hill, USA 1980. Cast: David Carradine, Keith Carradine, Robert Carradine, James Keach, Stacy Keach. Music: Ry Cooder.

Looking for Langston
Isaac Julien, GB 1989. Cast: Ben Ellison, Matthew Baidoo, Akim Mogaji, John Wilson, Dencil Williams. Music: Peter J. Spencer, Trevor Mathison, Wayson Jones. Music performed by: Blackberri, Joseph Bashorun, Gary Crosby, Tony Remy, Mark A. Mondesir, Jimmy Silver. S/track includes: Royal House.

Love at Large
Alan Rudolph, USA 1990. Cast: Tom Berenger, Elizabeth Perkins, Anne Archer, Kate Capshaw, Annette O'Toole. Music: Mark Isham, Steve Krause. S/track includes: Warren Zevon, Leonard Cohen, Grady Walker, Tarwater.

Love in Las Vegas; see **Viva Las Vegas**

Lucifer Rising (short)
Kenneth Anger, USA 1981. Cast: Myriam Gibril, Donald Cammell, Haydn Couts, Marianne Faithfull, Kenneth Anger. Music (in different versions of the film): Bobby Beausoleil and The Freedom Orchestra (Tracy Prison); Jimmy Page.

Mack, The
Michael Campus, USA 1973. Cast: Max Julien, Don Gordon, Richard Pryor, Carol Speed, Roger E. Mosley. Music: Willie Hutch. Songs performed by: The Sisters Love, The Ballads, The Uptights.

Made in Heaven
Alan Rudolph, USA 1987. Cast: Timothy Hutton, Kelly McGillis, Maureen Stapleton, Debra Winger, Ellen Barkin, Ric Ocasek, Neil Young, Tom Petty. Music: Mark Isham. S/track includes: Martha Davis, Luther Vandross, Ric Ocasek, R.E.M., Sly Stone, The Nylons, Buffalo Springfield, Alberta Hunter, Hank Williams, Ernest Tubbs, Red Foley, The Stank Band.

Magical Mystery Tour
The Beatles, GB 1967. Cast: Paul McCartney, John Lennon, George Harrison, Ringo Starr, Ivor Cutler. Music: The Beatles.

Manhunter
Michael Mann, USA 1986. Cast: William Peterson, Kim Greist, Joan Allen, Brian Cox, Dennis Farina. Music: Michael Rubini, The Reds. S/track includes: Kitaro, Klaus Schulze, Shriekback, The Prime Movers, Iron Butterfly, Red 7.

Mantrap (short)
Julien Temple, GB 1983. Cast: ABC (Martin Fry, David Palmer, Stephen Singleton), James Villiers, Lisa Vanderpump. Music: ABC.

Man Who Fell to Earth, The
Nicolas Roeg, GB 1976. Cast: David Bowie, Rip Torn, Candy Clark, Buck Henry, Bernie Casey. S/track includes: Stomu Yamashta, Louis Armstrong, Frank Glazer, Hank Snow, Jim Reeves, The Kingston Trio, Roy Orbison, Robert Farnon, Bing Crosby, Genevieve Waite, Artie Shaw.

Mean Streets
Martin Scorsese, USA 1973. Cast: Harvey Keitel, Robert De Niro, David Proval, Amy Robinson, Richard Romanus. S/track includes: The Rolling Stones, The Chantells, The Marvelettes, Eric Clapton, The Chants, The Chips, Johnny Ace, Ray Barretto, The Aquatones, Nutmegs, The Paragons, Little Caesar and the Romans, The Shirelles, The Miracles.

Menace II Society
The Hughes Brothers, USA 1993. Cast: Tyrin Turner, Jada Pinkett, Larenz Tate, Arnold Johnson, MC Eiht. Music: QD III. S/track includes: SPICE 1, MC Eiht, Ant Banks, R. Kelly and Public Announcement, Pete Rock, CL Smooth, DJ Quik, The Cutthroats, Mz. Kilo, Too Short, Hi-Five, Kenya Gruv, George Clinton, Al Green, Zapp, N.W.A., Marvin Gaye, the Isley Brothers, Xavier, Teddy Miller, Jerry Butler.

Merry Christmas Mr. Lawrence
Nagisa Oshima, GB 1982. Cast: David Bowie, Tom Conti, Ryuichi Sakamoto, Takeshi, Jack Thompson. Music: Ryuichi Sakamoto.

Mrs Parker and the Vicious Circle
Alan Rudolph, USA 1994. Cast: Jennifer Jason Leigh, Matthew Broderick, Campbell Scott, Peter Gallagher, Jennifer Beals. Music: Mark Isham.

Mi Vida Loca
Allison Anders, USA 1993. Cast: Angel Aviles, Seidy Lopez, Jacob Vargas, Marlo Marron, Nelida Lopez. Music: John Taylor. S/track includes: Proper Dos, Funkdoobiest, A Tribe Called Quest, Boss, Psycho Realm, Shootyz Groove, Lighter Shade of Brown, Tony! Toni! Toné!, 4 Corners, Honeycombs, War, Los Lobos *et al.*

Moderns, The
Alan Rudolph, USA 1988. Cast: Keith Carradine, Linda Fiorentino, Genevieve Bujold, Geraldine Chaplin, Wallace Shawn. Music: Mark Isham. S/track includes: Charlélie Couture, Lucienne Boyer, Sidney Bechet, Mistinguett, Josephine Baker.

Mo' Money
Peter Macdonald, USA 1992. Cast: Damon Wayans, Stacey Dash, Joe Santos, John Diehl, Harry J. Lennix. Music: Jay Gruska. S/track includes: Ralph Tresvant, Mo' Money Allstars, Damon Wayans, Johnny Gill, Krush, Lo-Key?, Public Enemy featuring Flavor Flav, MC Lyte, Luther Vandross, Janet Jackson, Bell Biv DeVoe, Big Daddy Kane, Mint Condition, Caron Wheeler, Sounds of Blackness, Jimmy Jam, Terry Lewis, Color Me Badd, Little Richard, The Harlem Yacht Club, Ali Baba.

Mortal Thoughts
Alan Rudolph, USA 1991. Cast: Demi Moore, Glenne Headly, Bruce Willis, John Pankow, Harvey Keitel. Music: Mark Isham.

Music Machine, The
Ian Sharp, GB 1979. Cast: Gerry Sundquist, Patti Boulaye, David Easter, Michael Feast, Ferdy Mayne. Music: Aaron Harry, Music Machine. Songs performed by: Patti Boulaye, Music Machine.

My Girl
Howard Zieff, USA 1991. Cast: Dan Aykroyd, Jamie Lee Curtis, Macaulay Culkin, Anna Chlumsky, Richard Masur. Music: James Newton Howard, Marty Paich. S/track includes: The Temptations, Creedence Clearwater Revival, The Rascals, Sly and the Family Stone, The Flamingos, Todd Rundgren, Albert Hammond, Ravi Shankar, Artie Shaw, Spiral Starecase, Chicago, The Fifth Dimension, Skylark.

Nashville
Robert Altman, USA 1975. Cast: Ned Beatty, Karen Black, Ronee Blakley, Keith Carradine, Geraldine Chaplin, Shelley Duvall, Allen Garfield, Lily Tomlin. Music performed by: Lily Tomlin, Smokey Mountain Laurel, Gwen Welles, James Dan Calvert, Donna Denton, Dave Peel, Karen Black, Henry Gibson, Ronee Blakley, Misty Mountain Boys, Keith Carradine, Barbara Harris.

Natural, The
Barry Levinson, USA 1984. Cast: Robert Redford, Robert Duvall, Glenn Close, Kim Basinger, Barbara Hershey. Music: Randy Newman.

Natural Born Killers
Oliver Stone, USA 1994. Story by: Quentin Tarantino. Cast: Woody Harrelson, Juliette Lewis, Robert Downey Jnr., Tommy Lee Jones, Tom Sizemore. Music: Budd Carr. S/track includes: Leonard Cohen, Chris McGregor, Robert Gordon, L7, tomandandy, Dan Zanes, Victor Young and his Singing Strings, The Shangri-Las, Duane Eddy, Patti Smith, Steven Jesse Bernstein, Cowboy Junkies, Scott Grusin, Brian Berdan, Bob Dylan, Richard Gibbs, Remmy Ongala and Orchestre Super Matimila, Patsy Cline, Peter Gabriel and Nusrat Fateh Ali Khan, Jane's Addiction, Diamanda Galas, A.O.S., Nine Inch Nails, Russell Means, The Hollywood Persuaders, Barry Adamson, Peter Gabriel, Brent Lewis and Richard Hardy, Peter Kater and R. Carlos Nakai, Dr Dre, The Specials, Sergio Cervetti, Juliette Lewis, Ramsey Lewis Trio, Melvins, Marilyn Manson, Rage Against the Machine, Spore, Nusrat Fateh Ali Khan Qawwal and Party, Kodo, Not Drowning, Waving.

New Jack City

Mario Van Peebles, USA 1991. Cast: Wesley Snipes, Ice-T, Allen Payne, Chris Rock, Mario Van Peebles. Music: Michel Colombier. S/track includes: Ice-T, Guy, Keith Sweat, Johnny Gill, Christopher Williams, Troop and Levert, Color Me Badd, 2 Live Crew, F.S. Effect, Grandmaster Flash, Danny Madden, Doug E. Fresh and the Get Fresh Crew, Redhead Kingpin and the FBI, N.W.A.

New York New York

Martin Scorsese, USA 1977. Cast: Liza Minnelli, Robert De Niro, Lionel Stander, Barry Primus, Mary Kay Place. Songs performed by: Liza Minnelli, Mary Kay Place, Diahnne Abbott. S/track includes: Hot Club of France Quintet, Georgie Auld.

New York Stories

Martin Scorsese, Woody Allen, Francis Coppola, USA 1989. Martin Scorsese episode ('Life Lessons'): Cast: Nick Nolte, Patrick O'Neal, Rosanna Arquette, Phil Harper, Peter Gabriel. S/track includes: Procol Harum, Cream, Ray Charles, Bob Dylan, Transvision Vamp, The Hot Club of France with Django Reinhardt, Stéphane Grappelli.

Nineteen Eighty-Four

Michael Radford, GB 1984. Cast: John Hurt, Richard Burton, Suzanna Hamilton, Cyril Cusack, Gregor Fisher. Music: Dominic Muldowney, Eurythmics.

Offenders, The

Scott B, Beth B, USA 1979. Cast: Adele Bertei, Bill Rice, John Lurie, Johnny O'Kane, Robin Winters, Lydia Lunch. Music: Bob Mason, Adele Bertei, Lydia Lunch, John Lurie, Scott B, Beth B, Terry Burns, Ed Steinberg, Alley.

Officer and a Gentleman, An

Taylor Hackford, USA 1981. Cast: Richard Gere, Debra Winger, David Keith, Robert Loggia, Lisa Blount. Music: Jack Nitzsche. S/track includes: Joe Cocker and Jennifer Warnes, Pat Benatar, Van Morrison, The Sir Douglas Quintet, ZZ Top, Dire Straits, Lee Ritenour, Gong Kebyar, Sebatu.

Once Upon a Time in America

Sergio Leone, USA 1983. Cast: Robert De Niro, James Woods, Elizabeth McGovern, Treat Williams, Tuesday Weld. Music: Ennio Morricone.

One by One (aka **Sympathy for the Devil**)

Jean-Luc Godard, GB 1968. Cast: The Rolling Stones, Anne Wiazemsky, Iain Quarrier, Frankie Dymon Jnr., Sean Lynch. Music by: The Rolling Stones.

One Flew Over the Cuckoo's Nest

Milos Forman, USA 1975. Cast: Jack Nicholson, Louise Fletcher, William Redfield, Will Sampson, Brad Dourif. Music: Jack Nitzsche. S/track includes: Stanley Turrentine.

One from the Heart

Francis Coppola, USA 1982. Cast: Frederic Forrest, Teri Garr, Raul Julia, Nastassja Kinski, Lainie Kazan. Music: Tom Waits. Songs performed by: Tom Waits, Crystal Gayle.

Order of Death

Roberto Faenza, Italy 1983. Cast: Harvey Keitel, John Lydon, Nicole Garcia, Sylvia Sidney. Music: Ennio Morricone.

Orlando

Sally Potter, GB/Russia/France/Italy/Netherlands 1992. Cast: Tilda Swinton, Billy Zane, John Wood, Lothaire Bluteau, Charlotte Valandrey. Music: David Motion, Sally Potter. Music producers: Bob Last (+ music supervisor), David Motion. S/track includes: Jimmy Somerville, Andrew Watts, Peter Hayward.

Out of the Blue

Dennis Hopper, Canada 1980. Cast: Linda Manz, Dennis Hopper, Sharon Farrell, Raymond Burr, Don Gordon. Music: Tom Lavin. S/track includes: Neil Young, Elvis Presley, The Pointed Sticks.

Paper, The

Ron Howard, USA 1994. Cast: Michael Keaton, Robert Duvall, Glenn Close, Marisa Tomei, Randy Quaid. Music: Randy Newman. S/track includes: Randy Newman, Mervyn Warren, Rose Stone, Marvin Gaye, Lester Lanin, Spectrum, Beth Hooker, Sweet Pea Atkinson, Tom Jones, Slave Raider.

Paris, Texas

Wim Wenders, West Germany/France 1984. Cast: Harry Dean Stanton, Dean Stockwell, Aurore Clément, Nastassja Kinski. Music: Ry Cooder.

Passion of Remembrance

Maureen Blackwood, Isaac Julien, GB 1986. Co-screenplay: Isaac Julien. Cast: Anni Domingo, Joseph Charles, Antonia Thomas, Carlton Chance, Jim Findley. Music: Tony Rémy for Surgery Management. S/track includes: Aleem, Roy Alton.

Pat Garrett & Billy the Kid

Sam Peckinpah, USA 1973. Cast: James Coburn, Kris Kristofferson, Bob Dylan, Richard Jaeckel, Katy Jurado. Music: Bob Dylan.

Peggy Sue Got Married

Francis Coppola, USA 1986. Cast: Kathleen Turner, Nicolas Cage, Barry Miller, Catherine Hicks, Joan Allen. Music: John Barry. S/track includes: Buddy Holly, Dion and the Belmonts, The Duprees, Little Anthony & the Imperials, The Champs, The Diamonds, Lloyd Price, Jimmy Clanton, Phil Upchurch Combo, The Olympics, Hank Ballard.

Performance

Donald Cammell, Nicolas Roeg, GB 1970. Cast: James Fox, Mick Jagger, Anita Pallenberg, Michèle Breton, Ann Sidney. Music: Jack Nitzsche. Music director: Randy Newman. S/track includes: Ry Cooder, Merry Clayton, Buffy Sainte-Marie, The Last Poets, Randy Newman, Mick Jagger.

Permanent Vacation

Jim Jarmusch, USA 1982. Cast: Chris Parker, Leila Gastil, Maria Duval, Ruth Bolton, Richard Boes, John Lurie. Music: Jim Jarmusch, John Lurie.

Philadelphia

Jonathan Demme, USA 1993. Cast: Tom Hanks, Denzel Washington, Jason Robards, Mary Steenburgen, Antonio Banderas. Music: Howard Shore. S/track includes: Bruce Springsteen, Neil Young, Sensible Shoes, Sade, Indigo Girls, The Neville Brothers, Pauletta Washington, REM, Gary Goetzman, Cyril Watters, Spin Doctors, Peter Gabriel, The Flirtations, Q. Lazzarus, Deborah Harry, Iggy Pop.

Pink Flamingos

John Waters, USA 1972. Cast: Divine, David Lochary, Mary Vivian Pearce, Mink Stole, Danny Mills.

Pink Floyd Live at Pompeii (Les Pink Floyd à Pompéi)
Adrian Maben, France/Belgium/West Germany 1971. Music performed by: Pink Floyd.

Platoon
Oliver Stone, USA 1986. Cast: Tom Berenger, Willem Dafoe, Charlie Sheen, Forest Whitaker, Francesco Quinn. Music: Georges Delerue. S/track includes: Jefferson Airplane, Merle Haggard, Smokey Robinson and the Miracles.

Pretty in Pink
Howard Deutch, USA 1986. Cast: Molly Ringwald, Harry Dean Stanton, Jon Cryer, Annie Potts, James Spader. Music: Michael Gore. S/track includes: The Psychedelic Furs, Orchestral Manoeuvres in the Dark, Danny Hutton Hitters, Maggie Lee, Belouis Some, The Rave-Ups, Barry Manilow, New Order, Code Blue, Echo and the Bunnymen, INXS, Otis Redding, The Association, The Smiths, Talk Back, Suzanne Vega, Jesse Johnson.

Pretty Woman
Garry Marshall, USA 1990. Cast: Richard Gere, Julia Roberts, Ralph Bellamy, Jason Alexander, Laura San Giacomo. Music: James Newton Howard. S/track includes: Karen Hernandez, Eugene Wright, Earl Palmer, Go West, Christopher Otcasek, Red Hot Chili Peppers, David Bowie, Robert Palmer, Jane Wiedlin, Natalie Cole, Richard Gere, Roy Orbison, Kenny G, Grand Dominion Jazz Band, Lauren Wood, Roxette, Peter Cetera.

Psych-Out
Richard Rush, USA 1968. Cast: Susan Strasberg, Dean Stockwell, Jack Nicholson, Bruce Dern, Adam Roarke. Music: Ronald Stein. Songs performed by: The Strawberry Alarm Clock, The Seeds. S/track includes: The Storybook, Boenze Cryque.

Pulp Fiction
Quentin Tarantino, USA 1994. Cast: Tim Roth, Amanda Plummer, John Travolta, Samuel L. Jackson, Uma Thurman. S/track includes: Dick Dale & his Del Tones, The Brothers Johnson, The Tornadoes, Dusty Springfield, Ricky Nelson, Link Wray & his Raymen, Kool & the Gang, Al Green, The Centurians, Gary Shorelle, The Rodins, Woody Thorne, Urge Overkill, The Statler Brothers, The Revels, Chuck Berry, Maria McKee, The Marketts, The Lively Ones.

Punk Rock Movie, The
Don Letts, GB 1978. Music performed by: The Sex Pistols, The Clash, The Slits, Siouxsie and The Banshees, X-Ray Spex, Slaughter and The Dogs, Generation X, Subway Sect, Shane, Wayne County, Eater, Johnny Thunders and The Heartbreakers.

Purple Rain
Albert Magnoli, USA 1984. Cast: Prince, Apollonia Kotero, Morris Day, Dez Dickerson. Music: Michel Colombier, Prince. Songs performed by: Prince and the Revolution, The Time, Dez Dickerson, Apollonia 6.

Quadrophenia
Franc Roddam, GB 1979. Cast: Phil Daniels, Leslie Ash, Philip Davis, Mark Wingett, Sting. Music directors: Roger Daltrey, John Entwistle, Pete Townshend. S/track includes: Cross Section, The Who, The High Numbers, The Merseybeats, Derrick Morgan, James Brown, The Ronettes, The Crystals, The Orlons, The Cascades, The Supremes, Marvin Gaye, The Chiffons, The Kingsmen, Manfred Mann, Booker T. & the MGs.

Radio On
Christopher Petit, GB/West Germany 1979. Associate producer: Wim Wenders. Cast: David Beames, Lisa Kreuzer, Sandy Ratcliff, Andrew Byatt, Sue Jones-Davies, Sting. S/track includes: David Bowie, Ian Dury, Devo, Robert Fripp, Kraftwerk, Wreckless Eric, The Rumour, Lene Lovich, Sting.

Rage in Harlem, A
Bill Duke, GB 1991. Cast: Forest Whitaker, Gregory Hines, Robin Givens, Zakes Mokae, 'Screamin' Jay' Hawkins. Music: Elmer Bernstein. S/track includes: Little Jimmy Scott and the Expressions, Clarence 'Frogman' Henry, Fats Domino, Bo Diddley, Chuck Berry, The Willows, Elmore James, Little Richard, Darryl Pandy, Jimmy Reed, Francine Taylor, Howlin' Wolf, 'Screamin' Jay' Hawkins, Little Walter, Lloyd Price, Shirley & Lee, Betty Boo, The Charles Ford Singers, James Brown, Johnny Ace, LaVern Baker, Robert & Johnny.

Raging Bull
Martin Scorsese, USA 1980. Cast: Robert De Niro, Cathy Moriarty, Joe Pesci, Frank Vincent, Nicholas Colasanto. Music: Robbie Robertson, Garth Hudson, Richard Manuel, Larry Klein, Dale Turner. S/track includes: Carlo Buti, Renato Carosone, Orazio Strano, Ella Fitzgerald, The Ink Spots, Louis Jordan, The Mills Brothers, Bob Crosby and the Bobcats, Ted Weems, Tony Bennett, Harry James, Gene Krupa, Benny Goodman, Nat King Cole, Louis Prima, Keely Smith, Patricio Teixeira, Perry Como, Russ Columbo, Artie Shaw, Larry Clinton and his Orchestra, Frankie Laine, Marilyn Monroe, The Hearts, Ray Charles.

Ragtime
Milos Forman, USA 1981. Cast: James Cagney, Brad Dourif, Moses Gunn. Music: Randy Newman. S/track includes: Jennifer Warnes.

Reality Bites
Ben Stiller, USA 1994. Cast: Winona Ryder, Ethan Hawke, Janeane Garofalo, Steve Zahn, Ben Stiller. Music: Karl Wallinger, Greg O'Connor. S/track includes: World Party, Gary Glitter, Crowded House, Squeeze, KMC, Dinosaur Jnr., The Knack, Peter Frampton, The Juliana Hatfield 3, The Trammps, Maldita Vecindad Y Los Hijos Del Quinto Patio, New Order, Arrested Development, Sepultura, Lenny Kravitz, Social Distortion, Alice Cooper, Salt-N-Pepa, Talking Heads, The Indians, U2, The Posies, Lisa Loeb and Nine Stories, Green Jelly, Me Phi Me.

Reeling with PJ Harvey (video)
Maria Mochnacz, Pinko, GB 1993. Music performed by: PJ Harvey.

Remember My Name
Alan Rudolph, USA 1978. Cast: Geraldine Chaplin, Anthony Perkins, Moses Gunn, Berry Berenson, Jeff Goldblum. Music: Alberta Hunter.

Renaldo & Clara
Bob Dylan, USA 1978. Cast: Bob Dylan, Sara Dylan, Joan Baez, Ronnie Hawkins, Ronee Blakley, Joni Mitchell, Mick Ronson, Arlo Guthrie, Roberta Flack. Music performed by: Bob Dylan, Roger McGuinn, Ronee Blakley, Mama Maria Frasca, Anne Waldman, Jack Elliott, Leonard Cohen, Thomas Mendez, Willie Nelson.

Repo Man
Alex Cox, USA 1984. Cast: Harry Dean Stanton, Emilio Estevez, Tracey Walter, Olivia Barash. Music: Tito Larriva, Steven Hufsteter. S/track includes: The Plugz, Tito Larriva, Steven Hufsteter, Charlie Quintana, Tony Marsico, Iggy Pop, Black Flag, Suicidal Tendencies, The Circle Jerks, Burning Sensations, Fear, Big Race.

Reservoir Dogs
Quentin Tarantino, USA 1991. Cast: Harvey Keitel, Tim Roth, Michael Madsen, Chris Penn, Steve Buscemi, Quentin Tarantino. S/track includes: George Baker Selection, Stealer's Wheel, Joe Tex, Sandy Rogers, Blue Suede, Harry Nilsson, Bedlam.

Resurrected
Paul Greengrass, USA 1989. Cast: David Thewlis, Tom Bell, Rita Tushingham, Michael Politt, Rudi Davies. Music: John Keane. S/track includes: Culture Club, Rod Stewart.

Return Engagement
Alan Rudolph, USA 1983. Cast: Dr Timothy Leary, G. Gordon Liddy, Carole Hemingway. Music: Adrian Belew.

Riot on Sunset Strip
Arthur Dreifuss, USA 1967. Cast: Aldo Ray, Mimsy Farmer, Michael Evans, Laurie Mock, Tim Rooney. Music: Fred Karger. Songs performed by: The Standells, The Chocolate Watch Band.

Roadie
Alan Rudolph, USA 1980. Cast: Meat Loaf, Kaki Hunter, Art Carney, Gailard Sartain, Don Cornelius. Music: Craig Hundley. S/track includes: Cheap Trick, Joe Ely Band, Alice Cooper, Hank Williams Jnr., Pat Benatar, Jerry Lee Lewis, Teddy Prendergrass, B-52's, Sue Saad and the Next, Jay Ferguson, Styx, Blondie, Asleep at the Wheel, Stephen Bishop, Yvonne Elliman, Alvin Crow, Roy Orbison, Emmylou Harris, Eddie Rabbitt, Adolph Hofner and his Texans.

Road to God Knows Where, The
Uli M. Schuppel, GB 1990. Music performed by: Nick Cave and the Bad Seeds (Mick Harvey, Blixa Bargeld, Martyn Casey, Conway Savage, Thomas Wydler).

Robin Hood: Prince of Thieves
Kevin Reynolds, USA 1991. Cast: Kevin Costner, Morgan Freeman, Mary Elizabeth Mastrantonio, Christian Slater, Alan Rickman. Music: Michael Kamen. S/track includes: Bryan Adams, Jeff Lynne.

Rock n' Roll High School
Allan Arkush, USA 1979. Cast: P.J. Soles, Vincent Van Patten, Clint Howard, The Ramones. Music: The Ramones. S/track includes: Paul McCartney and Wings, Fleetwood Mac, Alice Cooper, Chuck Berry, Todd Rundgren, MC5, Eddie and the Hot Rods, The Paley Brothers, Devo, Nick Lowe, Brian Eno, Velvet Underground.

Rock Around the Clock
Fred F. Sears, USA 1956. Cast: Johnny Johnston, Alix Talton, Lisa Gaye, John Archer, Henry Slate. Music: Fred Karger. Music performed by: Bill Haley and His Comets, The Platters, Tony Martinez and his Band, Freddie Bell and the Playboys.

Rocky Horror Picture Show, The
Jim Sharman, GB 1975. Cast: Tim Curry, Susan Sarandon, Barry Bostwick, Richard O'Brien, Jonathan Adams, Meat Loaf. Songs: Richard O'Brien. Music: Richard Hartley.

Rose, The
Mark Rydell, USA 1979. Cast: Bette Midler, Alan Bates, Frederic Forrest, Harry Dean Stanton, Barry Primus. Songs performed by: Bette Midler.

Rude Boy
Jack Hazan, David Mingay, GB 1980. Cast: Ray Gange, The Clash (Joe Strummer, Mick Jones, Paul Simonon, Nicky Headon), Jimmy Pursey. Music performed by: The Clash. S/track includes: Junior Murvin, The Slickers, Soul Sisters.

Rumble Fish
Francis Ford Coppola, USA 1983. Cast: Matt Dillon, Mickey Rourke, Diane Lane, Dennis Hopper, Diana Scarwid, Tom Waits. Music: Stewart Copeland.

Running Out of Luck
Julien Temple, GB 1985. Cast: Mick Jagger, Jerry Hall, Dennis Hopper, Rae Dawn Chong. Music: Mick Jagger.

St. Elmo's Fire
Joel Schumacher, USA 1985. Cast: Emilio Estevez, Rob Lowe, Andrew McCarthy, Demi Moore, Judd Nelson. Music: David Foster. S/track includes: John Parr, Billy Squier, Jon Anderson, Fee Waybill, Airplay, Elefante, Vikki Moss, Todd Smallwood, Aretha Franklin.

St. Louis Blues
Allen Reisner, USA 1958. Cast: Nat 'King' Cole, Eartha Kitt, Pearl Bailey, Cab Calloway, Mahalia Jackson, Ella Fitzgerald. Music arranged/conducted: Nelson Riddle, based on themes and songs by W.C. Handy.

Saturday Night Fever
John Badham, USA 1977. Cast: John Travolta, Karen Lynn Gorney, Barry Miller, Joseph Cali, Paul Pape. Music: The Bee Gees. S/track includes: The Bee Gees, Yvonne Elliman, Tavares, M.F.S.B., The Trammps, Kool and the Gang, Rick Dees, K.C. and the Sunshine Band.

Say Anything
Cameron Crowe, USA 1989. Cast: John Cusack, Ione Skye, John Mahoney, Lili Taylor, Amy Brooks. Music: Richard Gibbs, Anne Dudley. S/track includes: Peter Gabriel, Cheap Trick, Nancy Wilson, Living Colour, Joe Satriani, Red Hot Chili Peppers, Depeche Mode, Fishbone, The Replacements, Freiheit, Steely Dan, Mother Love Bone, Aerosmith, Soundgarden, Dave Brubeck Quartet, Looking Glass.

Scandal
Michael Caton-Jones, GB 1988. Cast: John Hurt, Joanne Whalley-Kilmer, Bridget Fonda, Ian McKellen, Leslie Phillips, Roland Gift. Music: Carl Davis. S/track includes: Dusty Springfield.

Scarface
Brian De Palma, USA 1983. Cast: Al Pacino, Steven Bauer, Michelle Pfeiffer. Music: Giorgio Moroder. S/track includes: Paul Engemann, Deborah Harry, Amy Holland, Maria Conchita, Elizabeth Daily, Beth Andersen, Giorgio Moroder.

Schauplätze (short)
Wim Wenders, West Germany 1966-67. Music: The Rolling Stones.

Scorpio Rising (short)
Kenneth Anger, USA 1963. Cast: Bruce Byron, Johnny Sapienza, Frank Carifi, Bill Dorfman, Steve Crandell. S/track includes: Little Peggy March, Elvis Presley, The Randells, The Angels, Bobby Vinton, Ray Charles, The Crystals, Kris Jensen, Claudine Clark, Gene McDaniels, The Surfaris.

Secret World Live (video)
François Girard, GB 1994. Music performed by: Peter Gabriel, Manu Katché, Tony Levin, Jean-Claude Naimro, Shankar, Levon Minassian, Paula Cole, Papa Wemba and Molokai.

Serious Charge
Terence Young, GB 1959. Cast: Anthony Quayle, Sarah Churchill, Andrew Ray, Irene Browne, Ciff Richard. Music: Leighton Lucas. S/track includes: Cliff Richard.

Shaft
Gordon Parks, USA 1971. Cast: Richard Roundtree, Moses Gunn, Charles Cioffi, Christopher St. John, Gwenn Mitchell. Music: Isaac Hayes. S/track includes: The Bar-Kays and Movement.

Shake, Rattle and Rock!
Edward L. Cahn, USA 1956. Cast: Lisa Gaye, Touch Connors, Sterling Holloway, Raymond Hatton, Douglass Dumbrille. Music: Alexander Courage. Songs performed by: Fats Domino, Joe Turner, Tommy Charles, Anita Ray.

Sheltering Sky, The
Bernardo Bertolucci, GB/Italy 1990. Cast: Debra Winger, John Malkovich, Campbell Scott, Jill Bennett, Timothy Spall. Music: Ryuichi Sakamoto, Richard Horowitz. S/track includes: Charles Trenet, Eric Lyle, Lionel Hampton, Om Kaldoum, Simon Shaheen, Mohamed Abdelwahab, the Akeulal Marrakesh, Brahim el Belkani and the Gnawa of Marrakesh, Ouled Nail Qusbah on Hauts-Plateaux d'Algérie, Moustapha Choki, Zarzis, Bashir Attar and the Master Musicians of Jajouka, Awash of Ouarzazate, Zayne and the Jillala de Tangier, Traditional Music of Burundi, Houria Aichi, Zahouania.

Shopping
Paul Anderson, GB 1993. Cast: Sadie Frost, Jude Law, Sean Pertwee, Fraser James, Sean Bean. Music: Barrington Phelong. S/track includes: Sabres of Paradise, One Dove, Elton John, Utah Saints, Perfecto, Wool, Jesus Jones, Orbital, Disposable Heroes of Hiphoprisy, Credit To the Nation, Kaliphz, Stereo MCs, Senser, James, Shakespears Sister, Smith & Mighty, EMF, Salt-N-Pepa, Rebecca van der Post, Clio Gould, Madeline Butcher, Monica Scott.

Short Cuts
Robert Altman, USA 1993. Cast: Andie MacDowell, Bruce Davison, Jack Lemmon, Zane Cassidy, Julianne Moore. Music: Mark Isham. Music producer: Hal Willner. Songs written by: Elvis Costello, Cait O'Riordan, Doc Pomus, Mac Rebennack, Bono, The Edge, et al. Songs performed by: Annie Ross and The Low Note Quintet.

Sid and Nancy
Alex Cox, GB 1986. Cast: Gary Oldman, Chloe Webb, David Hayman, Debby Bishop, Andrew Schofield, Iggy Pop. Music: Joe Strummer, The Pogues, Pray for Rain, Circle Jerks. S/track includes: Pray for Rain, The Pogues, Joe Strummer, John Cale, Althea and Donna, Black Sabbath, The Dynamiters, Link Wray, Pearl Harbour and the Palaminos, K.C. and the Sunshine Band.

Singles
Cameron Crowe, USA 1992. Cast: Bridget Fonda, Campbell Scott, Kyra Sedgwick, Sheila Kelley, Jim True. Music: Paul Westerberg, Chris Cornell, Richard Gibbs. S/track includes: Paul Westerberg, Soundgarden, Alice in Chains, Pearl Jam, Chris Cornell, Smashing Pumpkins, Mudhoney, The Lovemongers, Mother Love Bone, Jimi Hendrix, Screaming Trees, Citizen Dick, Jane's Addiction, Truly, Muddy Waters, The Pixies, John Coltrane, REM, Sly and the Family Stone, TAD, The Cult.

Slacker
Richard Linklater, USA 1991. Cast: Richard Linklater, Rudy Basquez, Jean Caffeine, Jack Hockey, Stephan Hockey. Music: Buffalo Gals, Triangle Mallet Apron, The Texas Instruments.

Some Kind of Wonderful
Howard Deutch, USA 1987. Cast: Eric Stoltz, Mary Stuart Masterson, Lea Thompson, Craig Sheffer. S/track includes: Pete Shelley, Furniture, Blue Room, Flesh For Lulu, Stephen Duffy, Jesus and Mary Chain, The Apartments, The March Violets, Lick the Tins.

Something Wild
Jonathan Demme, USA 1986. Cast: Jeff Daniels, Melanie Griffith, Ray Liotta, Margaret Colin, Tracey Walter. Music: John Cale, Laurie Anderson. S/track includes: David Byrne, Celia Cruz, Cheo Feliciano, The Mahotella Queens, Big Youth, Steve Jones, Sonny Okossun, The Fabulous Five, Natural Beauty, Big Audio Dynamite, The Troggs, Yellowman, New Order, Fine Young Cannibals, Lisa Chadwick, D.C. Stringer, The Feelies, Oingo Boingo, X, The Go-Betweens, G. Lazarus, Timbuk 3, The Motels, Bill Wharton, The Judy's, Electric Sheep, Jerry Harrison, The Crew, Tina Baker, Stanton-Miranda, Stephen Vitello, Jiggs & Co., Scott Rodness, The Community Holiness Church Choir, Danny Darst, The Knitters, UB40, Chuck Napier, Jasper Van't Hof, Jean-Michel Jarre, Jimmy Cliff, Sister Carol.

Songwriter
Alan Rudolph, USA 1984. Cast: Kris Kristofferson, Willie Nelson, Melinda Dillon, Rip Torn, Lesley Ann Warren. Songs by and performed by: Kris Kristofferson, Willie Nelson, Booker T. Jones.

Southern Comfort
Walter Hill, USA 1981. Cast: Keith Carradine, Powers Boothe, Fred Ward, Franklyn Seales. Music: Ry Cooder. S/track includes: Marc Savoy, Frank Savoy, Dewey Balfa, John Stelly.

Stand by Me
Rob Reiner, USA 1986. Cast: Wil Wheaton, River Phoenix, Corey Feldman, Jerry O'Connell, Kiefer Sutherland. Music: Jack Nitzsche, Brian Banks, Anthony Marinelli. S/track includes: Ben E. King, The Bobbettes, Bobby Day, Jerry Lee Lewis, Shirley and Lee, The Monotones, The Chordettes, Buddy Holly, The Del Vikings, The Fleetwoods, The Mystics, The Silhouettes, The Coasters.

Stardust
Michael Apted, GB 1974. Cast: David Essex, Adam Faith, Larry Hagman, Ines Des Longchamps, Rosalind Ayres, Marty Wilde, Keith Moon, Dave Edmunds. Music: Dave Edmunds.

State of Things, The
Wim Wenders, USA/Portugal 1982. Cast: Patrick Bauchau, Allen Goorwitz, Isabelle Weingarten, Samuel Fuller, Paul Getty III. Music: Jürgen Knieper. S/track includes: Joe Ely, David Blue, Allen Goorwitz, The Del Byzanteens, X.

Stop Making Sense
Jonathan Demme, USA 1984. Music performed by: Talking Heads, Tom Tom Club.

Straight to Hell
Alex Cox, GB 1986. Cast: Dick Rude, Sy Richardson, Joe Strummer, Courtney Love, Shane MacGowan, Elvis Costello. Music: The Pogues, Pray for Rain. S/track includes: The Coasters, Dick Rude, Joe Strummer, Sy Richardson, Bug Out Band, Fox Harris, The MacManus Gang, Pray for Rain, Zander Schloss, The Pogues.

Stranger than Paradise
Jim Jarmusch, USA/West Germany 1984. Cast: John Lurie, Eszter Balint, Richard Edson, Cecillia Stark, Danny Rosen. Music: John Lurie. S/track includes: The Paradise Quartet, 'Screamin' Jay' Hawkins.

Streets of Fire
Walter Hill, USA 1984. Cast: Michael Paré, Diane Lane, Rick Moranis, Amy Madigan, Willem Dafoe, Deborah van Valkenburgh. Music: Ry Cooder. S/track includes: Fire Inc., The Ry Cooder Band, Laurie Sargent, The Blasters, Winston Ford, The Fixx.

Suburbia: see **Wild Side, Th**e

Subway Riders
Amos Poe, USA 1981. Cast: Robbie Coltrane, Charlene Kaleina, Cookie Mueller, John Lurie, Amos Poe. S/track includes: Robert Fripp, Ivan Kral, Lounge Lizards.

Sugar Hill
Leon Ichaso, USA 1993. Cast: Wesley Snipes, Michael Wright, Theresa Randle, Clarence Williams III, Abe Vigoda. Music: Terence Blanchard. Music performed by: Duke Ellington and his Orchestra, Definition of Sound, Screechy Dan, Freestyle Fellowship, Dirt Nation, Simple E, Stefan Karlsson, After 7, Afro-Plane, Denetria Champ, Otis Redding, DBC, Snowman, Chaka Khan.

Summer Holiday
Peter Yates, GB 1962. Cast: Cliff Richard, Lauri Peters, Melvyn Hayes, Una Stubbs, Teddy Green, The Shadows. Music: Stanley Black. Songs performed by: Cliff Richard, The Shadows.

Summer in the City
Wim Wenders, West Germany 1971. Cast: Hanns Zischler, Gerd Stein, Muriel Werner, Helmut Färber, Edda Köchl. S/track includes: The Kinks, Lovin' Spoonful, Chuck Berry, The Troggs, Gene Vincent, Gustav Mahler.

Superfly
Gordon Parks Jnr., USA 1972. Cast: Ron O'Neal, Carl Lee, Sheila Frazer, Julius W. Harris, Charles MacGregor. Music: Curtis Mayfield.

Superstar: The Karen Carpenter Story (short)
Todd Haynes, USA 1987. S/track includes: The Carpenters.

Surviving the Game
Ernest Dickerson, USA 1994. Cast: Ice-T, Rutger Hauer, Charles S. Dutton, Gary Busey, F. Murray Abraham. Music: Stewart Copeland.

Sweet Dreams
Karel Reisz, USA 1985. Cast: Jessica Lange, Ed Harris, Ann Wedgeworth, David Clennon, James Staley. Music: Charles Gross. S/track includes: Patsy Cline, Benny Martin, Frank Sinatra, Ella Mae Morse, Freddie Slack and his Band, Gene Vincent, The Harptones, Sam Cooke, Acker Bilk, The Johnny Burnette Trio.

Sweet Sweetback's Baadasssss Song
Melvin Van Peebles, USA 1971. Cast: Melvin Van Peebles, Simon Chuckster, Hubert Scales, John Dullaghan, Rhetta Hughes. Music: Melvin Van Peebles, Earth Wind and Fire.

Take It or Leave It
Dave Robinson, GB 1981. Cast: Madness (Graham McPherson, Mark Bedford, Lee Thompson, Carl Smith, Dan Woodgate, Mike Barson, Christopher Foreman), Zoot Money. Music: Madness.

Taxi Driver
Martin Scorsese, USA 1976. Cast: Robert De Niro, Cybill Shepherd, Jodie Foster, Peter Boyle, Leonard Harris. Music: Bernard Herrmann.

Terminator 2: Judgment Day
James Cameron, USA 1991. Cast: Arnold Schwarzenegger, Linda Hamilton, Edward Furlong, Robert Patrick, Earl Boen. Music: Brad Fiedel. S/track includes: Guns N' Roses, George Thorogood and the Destroyers, Dwight Yoakam.

T.G.: Psychic Rally in Heaven (short)
Derek Jarman, GB 1981. Music performed by: Throbbing Gristle.

That'll Be the Day
Claude Whatham, GB 1973. Cast: David Essex, Ringo Starr, Rosemary Leach, James Booth, Billy Fury, Keith Moon. Music supervisors: Neil Aspinall, Keith Moon.

Thelma & Louise
Ridley Scott, USA 1991. Cast: Susan Sarandon, Geena Davis, Harvey Keitel, Michael Madsen, Christopher McDonald. Music: Hans Zimmer. S/track includes: Kelly Willis, Martha Reeves, Toni Childs, Charlie Sexton, Tammy Wynette, Glenn Frey, The Temptations, Chris Whitley, Grayson Hugh, Michael McDonald, Pam Tillis, Marianne Faithfull, Johnny Nash, B.B. King.

Thief
Michael Mann, USA 1981. Cast: James Caan, Tuesday Weld, Willie Nelson, James Belushi, Robert Prosky. Music: Tangerine Dream. (GB release title: **Violent Streets**)

Thirty Two Short Films About Glenn Gould
François Girard, Canada 1993. Cast: Colm Feore, Derek Keurvorst, Katya Ladan, Devon Anderson, Joshua Greenblatt. Music performed by: Glenn Gould, Bruno Monsaingeon, Gilles Apap, Jean-Marc Apap, Marc Coppey. Music: Bach, Beethoven, Wagner, Strauss, Sibelius, Prokofiev, Scriabin, Hindemith, Schoenberg.

This Is Spinal Tap
Rob Reiner, USA 1983. Cast: Christopher Guest, Michael McKean, Harry Shearer, R.J. Parnell, David Kaff. Music: Christopher Guest, Michael McKean, Harry Shearer, Rob Reiner.

3 American LPs (3 Amerikanische LPs) (short)
Wim Wenders, West Germany 1969. S/track includes: Van Morrison, Creedence Clearwater Revival, Harvey Mandel.

Three Tough Guys
Duccio Tessari, Italy 1974. Cast: Lino Ventura, Isaac Hayes, Fred Williamson, Paula Kelly, William Berger. Music: Isaac Hayes.

Tina: What's Love Got To Do With It? (US title: **What's Love Got To Do With It?**)
Brian Gibson, USA 1993. Cast: Angela Bassett, Laurence Fishburne, Vanessa Bell Calloway, Jenifer Lewis, Phyllis Yvonne Stickney. Music: Stanley Clarke. Songs performed by: Tina Turner, Laurence Fishburne. S/track includes: Big Joe Turner, Johnny 'Guitar' Watson, Dusty Springfield, Manfred Mann, Charles Martin Inouye, Ike Turner, Blue Cheer, Edgar Winter.

Tokyo-Ga
Wim Wenders, West Germany/USA 1985. Cast: Chishu Ryu, Yuharu Atsuta, Werner Herzog. Music: Laurent Petitgand, Meche Mamecier, Chico Rojo Ortega.

Tommy
Ken Russell, GB 1975. Cast: Ann-Margret, Oliver Reed, Roger Daltrey, Elton John, Eric Clapton, Keith Moon, Tina Turner, John Entwistle, Pete Townshend, Arthur Brown. Music: Pete Townshend and The Who. S/track includes: The Who, Elton John, Eric Clapton, Ronnie Wood, Kenny Jones, Nicky Hopkins, Chris Stainton, Fuzzy Samuels, Caleb Quayle, Mick Ralphs, Graham Deakin.

Tommy Steele Story, The
Gerard Bryant, GB 1957. Cast: Tommy Steele, Patrick Westwood, Hilda Fenemore, Charles Lamb, Peter Lewiston. Music performed by: Tommy Steele, The Steelmen, Humphrey Lyttelton and his Band, Charles McDevitt's Skiffle Group, Nancy Whiskey, Tommy Eytle Calypso Band, Chris O'Brien's Caribbeans.

Tommy the Toreador
John Paddy Carstairs, GB 1959. Cast: Tommy Steele, Janet Munro, Sidney James, Virgilio Texera, Pepe Nieto. Music: Stanley Black. Songs performed by: Tommy Steele.

Top Gun
Tony Scott, USA 1986. Cast: Tom Cruise, Kelly McGillis, Val Kilmer, Anthony Edwards, Tom Skerritt. Music: Harold Faltermeyer. S/track includes: Kenny Loggins, Teena Marie, Miami Sound Machine, Loverboy, Cheap Trick, Berlin, Marietta Waters, Larry Greene, Giorgio Moroder, Otis Redding, The Righteous Brothers.

Top Secret!
Jim Abrahams, David Zucker, Jerry Zucker, USA 1984. Cast: Val Kilmer, Lucy Gutteridge, Peter Cushing, Christopher Villiers, Jeremy Kemp. Music: Maurice Jarre.

Touch of Evil
Orson Welles, USA 1958. Cast: Charlton Heston, Janet Leigh, Orson Welles, Joseph Calleia, Akim Tamiroff. Music: Henry Mancini.

Tougher Than Leather
Rick Rubin, USA 1988. Cast: Run-D.M.C. (Joseph Simmons, Darryl McDaniels, Jason Mizell), Richard Edson, Jenny Lumet. Music performed by: Run-D.M.C., The Beastie Boys, Slick Rick, Junkyard Band.

Towers Open Fire (short)
Antony Balch, GB 1963. Cast: William Burroughs, Brion Gysin, Ian Sommerville, David Jacobs, Bachoo Sen.

Toys
Barry Levinson, USA 1992. Cast: Robin Williams, Michael Gambon, Joan Cusack, Robin Wright, LL Cool J. Music: Hans Zimmer, Trevor Horn. S/track includes: Jeff Rona, Nico and Tha Gang.

Trespass
Walter Hill, USA 1992. Cast: Bill Paxton, Ice-T, William Sadler, Ice Cube, Art Evans. Music: Ry Cooder. S/track includes: Junior Brown, Ice-T featuring Daddy Nitro, W.C. and The Maad Circle, Lord Finesse, Public Enemy, Donald D, AMG, Sir Mix-A-Lot, Gang Starr, Black Sheep.

Trip, The
Roger Corman, USA 1967. Cast: Peter Fonda, Susan Strasberg, Bruce Dern, Dennis Hopper, Salli Sachse. Music: The Electric Flag.

Triple Bogey on a Par Five Hole
Amos Poe, USA 1991. Cast: Eric Mitchell, Daisy Hall, Angela Goethals, Jesse McBride, Alba Clemente. Music: Anna Domino, Michel Delory, Mader, Chic Streetman.

Trouble in Mind
Alan Rudolph, USA 1985. Cast: Kris Kristofferson, Keith Carradine, Lori Singer, Genevieve Bujold, Joe Morton. Music performed by: Mark Isham, The Rain City Industrial Art Ensemble. S/track includes: Marianne Faithfull, Louis Jordan, Joanne Klein, Jimmy Witherspoon.

Trouble Man
Ivan Dixon, USA 1972. Cast: Robert Hooks, Paul Winfield, Ralph Waite, William Smithers, Paula Kelly. Music: Marvin Gaye.

Truck Turner
Jonathan Kaplan, USA 1974. Cast: Isaac Hayes, Yaphet Kotto, Alan Weeks, Nichelle Nichols, Sam Laws. Music: Isaac Hayes.

True Romance
Tony Scott, USA 1993. Cast: Christian Slater, Patricia Arquette, Dennis Hopper, Val Kilmer, Gary Oldman. Music: Hans Zimmer. S/track includes: Charlie Sexton, John Waite, Charles & Eddie, Billy Idol, The Skinny Boys, Nymphomania, Shelby Lynne, Big Bopper, Aerosmith, Clem Alfor, Robert Palmer, Soundgarden, Jerry Delmonico, Chris Isaak.

True Stories
David Byrne, USA 1986. Cast: David Byrne, John Goodman, Annie McEnroe, Jo Harvey Allen, Spalding Gray. Music: David Byrne. S/track includes: Talking Heads, Capucine DeWulf, Terry Allen and the Panhandle Mystery Band, Carl Finch, Steve Jordan y Rio Jordan, Banda Eclipse.

Tucker: The Man and His Dream
Francis Ford Coppola, USA 1988. Cast: Jeff Bridges, Joan Allen, Martin Landau, Frederic Forrest, Mako. Music: Joe Jackson, Carmine Coppola. S/track includes: The Mills Brothers.

Two Lane Blacktop
Monte Hellman, USA 1971. Cast: James Taylor, Warren Oates, Laurie Bird, Dennis Wilson, David Drake.

Undercover (short)
Julien Temple, GB 1983. Cast: Mick Jagger, Keith Richards, Elpidia Carrillo, The Rolling Stones. Music performed by: The Rolling Stones.

Underground U.S.A.
Eric Mitchell, USA 1980. Cast: Patti Astor, Eric Mitchell, Rene Ricard. Music: James White and the Blacks, Walter Stedding, Lounge Lizards, Seth Tillet. S/track includes: James White and the Blacks, Walter Stedding; additional music: The Supremes, The Four Tops, Stevie Wonder, Bob Dylan, Lou Reed, Diana Ross.

Under the Cherry Moon
Prince, USA 1986. Cast: Prince, Jerome Benton, Kristin Scott Thomas, Steven Berkoff, Emmanuelle Sallet. Music performed by: Prince and the Revolution.

Union City
Mark Reichert, USA 1979. Cast: Dennis Lipscomb, Deborah Harry, Irina Maleeva, Everett McGill. Music: Chris Stein.

Unmade Beds
Amos Poe, USA 1977. Cast: Duncan Hannah, Eric Mitchell, Patty Astor, Debbie Harry.

Until the End of the World (Bis ans Ende der Welt)
Wim Wenders, Germany/France/Australia 1991. Cast: Solveig Dommartin, William Hurt, Sam Neill, Jeanne Moreau, Max von Sydow. Music: Graeme Revell. S/track includes: Talking Heads, Elvis Presley, Julee Cruise, Neneh Cherry, Fred Smith, Patti Smith, Can, U2, Elvis Costello, Laurent Petitgand, Jane Siberry, k.d. lang, Daniel Lanois, Lou Reed, Crime and the City Solution, Nick Cave and the Bad Seeds, Boulevard of Broken Dreams Orchestra, Chubby Checker, T. Bone Burnett, R.E.M., Peter Gabriel, Depeche Mode, Gondwanaland, Robbie Robertson.

Untamed Youth
Howard W. Koch, USA 1957. Cast: Mamie Van Doren, Lori Nelson, John Russell, Don Burnett, Eddie Cochran. Music: Les Baxter. Songs performed by: Eddie Cochran, Mamie Van Doren.

U2 Rattle and Hum
Phil Joanou, USA 1988. Music performed by: U2, Brian Eno, Benmont Tench, B.B. King and his Band, New Voices of Freedom, George Pendergrass, Dorothy Terrel, The Memphis Horns. S/track includes: Jimi Hendrix.

Vallée, La
Barbet Schroeder, France 1972. Cast: Jean-Pierre Kalfon, Bulle Ogier, Michael Gothard, Valerie Lagrange. Music: Pink Floyd.

Velvet Underground and Nico, The
Andy Warhol, USA 1966. Cast: The Velvet Underground (Lou Reed, John Cale, Sterling Morrison, Maureen Tucker), Nico, Ari Boulogne. Music: The Velvet Underground.

Violent Playground
Basil Dearden, GB 1958. Cast: Stanley Baker, Anne Heywood, David McCallum, Peter Cushing, John Slater. Music: Philip Green.

Violent Streets: see Thief

Viva Las Vegas
George Sidney, USA 1963. Cast: Elvis Presley, Ann-Margret, Cesare Danova, William Demarest. Music: George Stoll. Songs by: Doc Pomus and Mort Shuman, *et al.* Various songs performed by Elvis Presley including songs written by: West, Cooper; Pomus, Shuman; Byers; Giant, Baum, Kaye. (GB release title: **Love in Las Vegas**)

Wanderers, The
Philip Kaufman, USA/Netherlands 1979. Cast: Ken Wahl, John Friedrich, Karen Allen, Toni Kalem. S/track includes: Four Seasons, Lee Dorsey, The Angels, The Shirelles, Chantays, Smokey Robinson and The Miracles, The Surfaris, Ben E. King, the Isley Brothers, The Contours, Dion, Bob Dylan.

Warriors, The
Walter Hill, USA 1979. Cast: Michael Beck, James Remar, Thomas Waites, Dorsey Wright, Brian Tyler. Music: Barry De Vorzon. S/track includes: Joe Walsh, Arnold McCuller, Frederick LaPlano, Mandrill, Genya Ravan, Johnny Vastano, Desmond Child, Rouge, The Mersh Brothers.

Wayne's World
Penelope Spheeris, USA 1992. Cast: Mike Myers, Dana Carvey, Rob Lowe, Tia Carrere, Brian Doyle-Murray, Meat Loaf, Alice Cooper. Music: J. Peter Robinson. S/track includes: Queen, Ugly Kid Joe, Gary Wright, Soundgarden, BulletBoys, Eric Clapton, Cinderella, Red Hot Chili Peppers, Kix, Jimi Hendrix, Temple of the Dog, Rhino Bucket, Alice Cooper, Black Sabbath.

Wayne's World 2
Stephen Surjik, USA 1993. Cast: Mike Myers, Dana Carvey, Tia Carrere, Christopher Walken, Ralph Brown. Music: Carter Burwell. S/track includes: Edgar Winter, Gary Wright, Golden Earring, Aerosmith, 4 Non Blondes, Robert Plant, Badfinger, Joan Jett and the Blackhearts, Bad Company, The Ventures, Stereo MCs, Village People, Superfan, Norman Greenbaum, Stan Getz, Astrud Gilberto, Antonio Carlos Jobim, Gin Blossoms, Dinosaur Jnr., Peter Frampton, The Jimi Hendrix Experience, Simon & Garfunkel, Lemonheads.

Welcome to LA
Alan Rudolph, USA 1976. Cast: Keith Carradine, Sally Kellerman, Geraldine Chaplin, Harvey Keitel, Lauren Hutton. Songs by and performed by: Richard Baskin.

What About Me?
Rachel Amodeo, USA 1993. Cast: Rachel Amodeo, Richard Edson, Richard Hell, Nick Zedd, Judy Carne, Gregory Corso, Dee Dee Ramone, Rockets Redglare, Johnny Thunders. Music: Johnny Thunders, Marc Ribot, Robert Quine.

What a Crazy World
Michael Carreras, GB 1963. Cast: Joe Brown, Susan Maughan, Marty Wilde, Harry H. Corbett, Avis Bunnage. Music: Alan Klein, Stanley Black. Songs performed by: Joe Brown.

What's Love Got To Do With It?: see Tina: What's Love Got To Do With It?

Who's That Knocking at My Door?
Martin Scorsese, USA 1968. Cast: Harvey Keitel, Zina Bethune, Lennard Kuras, Ann Collette, Michael Scala.

Wild Angels, The
Roger Corman, USA 1966. Cast: Peter Fonda, Nancy Sinatra, Bruce Dern, Lou Procopio, Coby Denton. Music: Mike Curb. S/track includes: The Arrows.

Wild at Heart
David Lynch, USA 1990. Cast: Nicolas Cage, Laura Dern, Diane Ladd, Willem Dafoe, Isabella Rossellini. Music: Angelo Badalamenti. S/track includes: Jessye Norman, Powermad, Glenn Miller, Nicolas Cage, Duke Ellington, Ray Brown, John Ewing and the Allstars, Shony Alex Braun, Koko Taylor, Billy Swan, African Headcharge, Them, Les Baxter, Gene Vincent and the Blue Caps, Chris Isaak, The Big Three Trio.

Wild in the Streets
Barry Shear, USA 1968. Cast: Shelley Winters, Christopher Jones, Diane Varsi, Hal Holbrook, Millie Perkins. Music: Les Baxter. Music performed by: Christopher Jones, Paul Weiler, The Thirteenth Power.

Wild Side, The
Penelope Spheeris, USA 1983. Cast: Chris Pederson, Bill Coyne, Jennifer Clay, Andrew Pece, Wade Walston. Music: Alex Gibson. S/track includes: DI, T.S.O.L., Steve Berlin, Del Hopkins, The Germs, The Vandals. (GB release title: **Suburbia**)

Wings of Desire (Der Himmel über Berlin)
Wim Wenders, West Germany/France 1987. Cast: Bruno Ganz, Solveig Dommartin, Otto Sander, Curt Bois, Peter Falk. Music: Jürgen Knieper, Laurent Petitgand. Songs performed by: Crime and the City Solution, Nick Cave and the Bad Seeds.

Withnail & I
Bruce Robinson, GB 1986. Cast: Richard E. Grant, Paul McGann, Richard Griffiths, Ralph Brown, Michael Elphick. Music: David Dundas, Rick Wentworth. S/track includes: King Curtis, Jimi Hendrix, Al Bowlly, Charlie Kunz, The Beatles.

Woodstock: 3 days of peace & music
Michael Wadleigh, USA 1970. Supervising editors: Thelma Schoonmaker, Martin Scorsese. Music performed by: Crosby, Stills and Nash, Richie Havens, The Who, Joan Baez, Sha-Na-Na, Joe Cocker, Country Joe and The Fish, Arlo Guthrie, Ten Years After, John Sebastian, Santana, Sly and the Family Stone, Jimi Hendrix with Noel Redding and Mitch Mitchell. (see also below)

Woodstock: 3 Days of peace & music: The Director's Cut
Michael Wadleigh, USA 1994. Music performed by (in addition to the above): Canned Heat, Jefferson Airplane, Janis Joplin.

Young Americans, The
Danny Cannon, GB 1993. Cast: Harvey Keitel, Iain Glen, John Wood, Terence Rigby, Keith Allen. Music: David Arnold. S/track includes: Padraig Gilhooly & The Rattling Bog Cutters, Sheep On Drugs, Nine Inch Nails, Keith Le Blanc, Tim Simenon, Disposable Heroes of Hiphoprisy, Stereo MCs, Björk, David Arnold.

Young Man With a Horn
Michael Curtiz, USA 1949. Cast: Kirk Douglas, Lauren Bacall, Doris Day, Hoagy Carmichael, Juano Hernandez. S/track includes: Harry James, Buddy Cole, Jimmy Zito.

Young Soul Rebels
Isaac Julien, GB 1991. Cast: Valentine Nonyela, Mo Sesay, Dorian Healy, Frances Barber, Sophie Okonedo. S/track includes: Parliament, The Blackbyrds, The Players Association, El Coco, Eddie Henderson, Funkadelic, Dr Buzzard's Original Savannah Band, Sylvester, Charles Earland, X-Ray Spex, Roy Ayers, The Heptones, Sly and the Revolutionaries, War, Junior Murvin, The O'Jays, Mica Paris.

You Only Live Twice
Lewis Gilbert, GB 1967. Cast: Sean Connery, Akiko Wakabayashi, Tetsuro Tamba, Mie Hama. Music: John Barry. S/track includes: Nancy Sinatra.

Your Cheatin' Heart
Gene Nelson, USA 1964. Cast: George Hamilton, Susan Oliver, Red Buttons, Arthur O'Connell, Shary Marshall. Music: Fred Karger, Hank Williams. S/track includes: Hank Williams Jnr.

Zabriskie Point
Michelangelo Antonioni, USA 1969. Cast: Mark Frechette, Daria Halprin, Rod Taylor, Paul Fix, G.D. Spradlin. Music: The Pink Floyd. S/track includes: Kaleidoscope, The Grateful Dead, Jerry Garcia, The Rolling Stones, The Youngbloods, John Fahey, Roscoe Holcomb, Patti Page.

select bibliography

Bennett, Tony; Frith, Simon; Grossberg, Lawrence; Shepherd, John; Turner, Graham (eds.),
Rock & Popular Music: Politics, Policies, Institutions (London: Routledge, 1993)

Crenshaw, Marshall, *Hollywood Rock: A Guide to Rock 'n' Roll in the Movies* (London: Plexus, 1994)

Dellar, Fred, *NME Guide to Rock Cinema* (London: Hamlyn, 1981)

Frith, Simon, *Sound Effects, Youth Leisure and the Politics of Rock 'n' Roll* (London: Constable, 1983)

Gillett, Charlie, *Sound of the City* (London: Souvenir Press, 1971; revised ed. 1984)

Goodwin, Andrew and Grossberg, Lawrence; ed. Frith, Simon, *Sound & Vision: The Music Video Reader* (London: Routledge, 1993)

Guralnick, Peter, *Lost Highway – Journeys & Arrivals of American Musicians* (Harmondsworth: Penguin, 1992)

Guralnick, Peter, *Feel Like Going Home* (Harmondsworth: Penguin, 1992)

Guralnick, Peter, *Last Train to Memphis: The Rise of Elvis Presley* (London: Little, Brown & Co., 1994)

Guralnick, Peter, *Portraits in Blues & Rock 'n' Roll* (Harmondsworth: Penguin, 1992)

Guralnick, Peter, *Sweet Soul Music* (Harmondsworth: Penguin, 1991)

Hardy, Phil and Laing, Dave, *Faber Companion to 20th Century Popular Music* (London: Faber & Faber, 1990)

Hershey, Gerri, *Nowhere To Run; The Story of Soul Music* (London: Pan, 1984)

Heylin, Clinton (ed.), *Penguin Anthology of Rock 'n' Roll Writing* (Harmondsworth: Penguin, 1992)

Hugh, Gregory, *Who's Who in Country Music* (London: Weidenfeld & Nicholson, 1993)

Marcus, Greil, *Mystery Train* (London: Omnibus Press, 1971)

Marcus, Greil, *Dead Elvis: A Chronicle of Cultural Obsession* (Harmondsworth: Penguin, 1992)

Marcus, Greil, *In the Fascist Bathroom: Writings on Punk* (Harmondsworth: Penguin, 1993)

Milne, Tom (ed.), *The Time Out Film Guide: Third Edition* (Harmondsworth: Penguin, 1993)

Murray, Charles Shaar, *Crosstown Traffic. Jimi Hendrix and the Story of Post-War Pop* (London: Faber & Faber, 1989)

Savage, Jon, *England's Dreaming: Sex Pistols and Punk Rock* (London: Faber & Faber, 1991)

Tee, Ralph, *Who's Who in Soul Music* (London: Weidenfeld & Nicholson, 1991)